Cannonball!
World's Greatest Outlaw Road Race

Cannonball!
World's Greatest Outlaw Road Race

Brock Yates

MBI Publishing Company

First published in 2002 by MBI Publishing Company, Galtier Plaza, Suite 200, 380 Jackson Street, St. Paul, MN 55101-3885 USA

MBI Publishing Company books are also available at discounts in bulk quantity for industrial or sales-promotional use. For details write to Special Sales Manager at Motorbooks International Wholesalers & Distributors, Galtier Plaza, Suite 200, 380 Jackson Street, St. Paul, MN 55101-3885 USA.

Library of Congress Cataloging-in-Publication Data Available

ISBN 0-7603-1090-4

Cover: The Yates/Stanner/Brown Challenger ready to start from the Red Ball Garage. **Cover, top:** Yates driving west in *Moon Trash II.*

Back cover: Gurney and Yates with the winning Ferrari Daytona, Portofino Inn, November 17, 1971.

Edited by Darwin Holmstrom
Cover designed by Tom Heffron

Printed in China

The publishers gratefully acknowledge Hachette Filipacchi Magazines for the use of materials previously published in *Car and Driver*. All materials used by permission.

To my beloved grandchildren,
Sarah and Scott Lilly,
who have brought magic to my life.

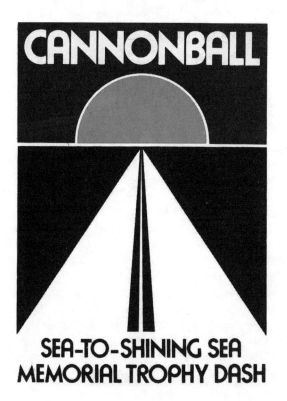

SEA-TO-SHINING SEA
MEMORIAL TROPHY DASH

Erwin G. "Cannon Ball" Baker

No one has ever equaled the exploits of Cannon Ball Baker in the realm of cross-country endurance driving. His legend began in 1914 when he rode coast-to-coast on an Indian motorcycle in 11 days, running only on rutted trails and dusty dirt roads. His 143 record-setting exploits came on motorcycles and at the wheel of a variety of automobiles, racing from city to city, and valley to mountaintop with the guarantee, "No record, no money." A gifted motorcycle and automobile racer, Cannon Ball finished 11th in the 1922 Indianapolis 500 at the wheel of a Frontenac. His greatest feat came at age 51, when he drove a Graham-Paige Bluestreak 8 from New York to Los Angeles on two-lanes *solo* in just over 53 hours, having grabbed only a half-hour's sleep midcountry. This drive, one of the most prodigious in history, was the inspiration for the Cannonball races organized in the 1970s. After retiring from competition, Cannon Ball Baker became the first commissioner of NASCAR and actively supported that fledgling series in the early 1950s. He died, at age 78, at his home in Indianapolis, Indiana, in May 1960.

Contents

Introduction

WHEN MOTORBOOKS INTERNATIONAL editor Darwin Holmstrom first suggested that I write a history of the Cannonball Sea-to-Shining-Sea Memorial Trophy Dash, I hesitated. It seemed ancient history, long forgotten and perhaps a bit musty. Then a young man from a small eastern university called and asked for an interview. He was writing a senior thesis on the Cannonball races and their impact on society. "Their impact on society?" I asked. "You've got to be kidding." "Believe me, sir. Every kid I know has heard about the Cannonballs. We watch the movie over and over. It's a kind of cult thing. You can't believe how it's become legend."

A legend? Perhaps. I began to ruminate over how the Cannonball had clung to me, refusing to go away, for over 20 years. It had been almost preordained that when my wife, Pamela, and I opened a restaurant in our village of Wyoming in upstate New York that the pub would be called the "Cannonball." Had not the One Lap of America events run since 1984 retained a certain Cannonball flavor, despite my early attempts to separate the two contests? Was I not in discussion with investors about writing yet another Cannonball movie—the *seventh* based on the old event? Had I not recently teamed up with Hachette Filippachi, the parent company of *Car and Driver,* to defend the Cannonball trademark and prevent its use by a California production company doing a "survivor-style series for the USA Network?"

Perhaps there was something to this legend thing. Perhaps a book ought to be written.

"Do it for your grandchildren," suggested my wife, Pamela, who had played such a major role in the 1979 race. "It will mean a great deal to them."

My two beloved grandchildren, Sarah and Scott Lilly, living in far-away Colorado with my daughter Claire and husband Bob, were aged five and seven and surely had never heard of the madness engaged in by their grandfather—the old geezer who read them bedtime stories. Perhaps one day the tales of the Cannonball would amuse them. That alone would be sufficient justification to write the book.

But the stories would not be written exclusively by me. I was but one of many who played the mad game. Others deserved a personal voice. Some had already written their reports and had them published. Others offered to write their recollections and in turn provide the rich and varied voices printed within. I thank them all for providing the range and depth this story deserves.

I also owe debts of gratitude to the guys at *Car and Driver*—editor Csaba Csere, art director Jeff Dworin, and his compatriots Tom Cosgrove and Dan Winter—for permission to reprint material from the magazine and for preparation of old photos. I also owe thanks to Jim Williams, a longtime friend and participant in the first Cannonball, for his help in preparing other photos, and to Jim Hunt of Montreal, a 1979 runner, for his detailed compilation of the participants and their finishing times that is at the end of the book.

The source of the photographs, which have moldered in my files and in those of *Car and Driver*, produced a knotty problem. Credit is given when it is identifiable, but many of the shots included here are of obscure origin. Numerous photographers recorded the races over the decade when the Cannonball was run, and many have either left the business or dropped out of sight. I have attempted to give proper credit but openly apologize to those who took pictures yet remain anonymous. Twenty-three years have passed since the last shots were taken, in 1979, while better than 30 years have gone by since the first Cannonball was run. That is an eternity for negatives of a then-obscure series of races to survive. It is a miracle that any did, no matter who took them.

Sadly, time has also taken its toll of participants. While it has been impossible to keep track of all those who ran, it is a sad reality that some have passed to their reward. We know that the last cowinner, David Heinz, is gone, as is former offshore Powerboat Champion Sandy Satullo. Loyal Truesdale's riding buddy on their epic BMW motorcycle ride in 1979, Keith Patchett, has also died, as has Wes Dawn, one of only a handful of men who ran all four of the full-tilt Cannonballs. Terry Ehaich, the respected owner of *Hemmings,* who ran in 1979, died in early 2002.

The memory of the Cannonball lives on, despite the losses of those veterans. Many have attempted to put it all into words. Many have denounced it as antisocial pathology. Others have refused to believe that it really happened or have given it grudging praise, while still others have celebrated it as the last great open road race. Perhaps the English prose stylist and motor racing historian L.J.K. Setright came close to nailing it, when in 1981 he wrote about the races in his *Pirelli History of Motorsport*.

> Brainwashed and cowed as he may be by government agencies galore and social pressure groups operating at all levels of hypocrisy, the American motorist can still occasionally show a cloven hoof; and when he goes, it appears he really goes, the law and profits notwithstanding. Every so often and not more than once a year, a bunch of renegade lead foots set off in commemoration of the great transcontinental driver, Cannon Ball Baker. Their object is to simply repeat his run from "sea to shining sea" as quickly as possible and quicker than everybody else, facing every imaginable hazard of roads, traffic and police. Despite a nationwide speed limit of 55 miles per hour, those who are able to do so maintain cruising speeds of 140 miles per hour or more. Organized informally and unofficially by well-known motor journalist Brock Yates, the race offers little or nothing in the way of prizes but a good deal in the way of penalties, and he is a fine fellow who wins it. A few years ago Brock traveled as codriver with the celebrated all-arounder, All-American Racer Dan Gurney in a Ferrari, and they only finished second, which gives an idea of how hectic the pace can be. The 1979 commemorative run was won by a Jaguar XJS from a 6.9-liter Mercedes-Benz, and some of the vehicles with which they were competing were almost beyond belief. If these be the last of the great road races, there is hope for the sport after all—but then, as it was said in the beginning, "man cannot help being an idealist."

Setright missed the mark on some details, but his take on the Cannonball pinpointed the rationale about as well as anyone. Over two decades and a new century later, the races have in fact lapsed into legend.

But they did happen. And what follows is, in the words of those crazy enough to try it, the real story.

The plot is hatched. It was during sessions like this—testing an Autodynamics Formula Vee at Lime Rock in March 1965—that Car and Driver *editors Steve Smith (standing, right) and Brock Yates (in car) began early discussions about high speed cross-country runs .*

1971: The Madness Begins

PEG THE START OF THE ENTIRE cockamamie affair at noon on a win-
try day in New York, early 1971. I was on my way to lunch at Brew's Pub
on 34th Street with *Car and Driver* editor Bob Brown and fellow
senior editor Leon Mandel. Walking near the magazine's One Park
Avenue offices, it came to me, "Why the hell not run a race across the
United States? A balls-out, shoot-the-moon, fuck-the-establishment
rumble from New York to Los Angeles to prove what we had been
harping about for years, for example, that good drivers in good automobiles could employ the American interstate system the same way
the Germans were using their Autobahns? Yes, make high-speed travel by car a reality! Truth and justice affirmed by an overtly illegal act."

The early 1970s were a time when illegal acts were in style. Everybody was going nuts with causes, most of them against the law. The
Vietnam War was at its crazed peak and everybody was protesting
something. We were smoking dope. College guys were burning their
draft cards and blowing up ROTC buildings. Blacks were marching in
the South. Redneck Klanners were wrecking churches. They were riot-
ing at Attica. George Wallace was yelling defiance at the Feds, as was
Daniel Ellsberg, who gave the secret Pentagon Papers to the *New York
Times* and was charged with espionage. Even the Army was in the act,
destroying Vietnamese villages "in order to save them," massacring
civilians at My Lai and drilling hapless students at Kent State. The
entire system was unraveling. Peace and love was the cry in San Francisco's Haight-Ashbury and New York's Greenwich Village, where vile
hatred of the "pigs," "the establishment," the government, and everybody over 30 was a life force.

Everybody was paranoid about everything. At *Car and Driver* we
were convinced that the automobile as we knew and loved it was as
dead as the passenger pigeon. Ralph Nader was at full cry, drumming
his tocsin of automobile doom into the brains of the public, convincing

them that that lump of chrome and iron in the driveway was as lethal as a dose of Strontium 90 or a blast from a Viet Cong AK-47. A few months before my idea for a race, Congress had passed a mass of legislation that was sure to transform our muscle cars and sporty machines into pallid, padded prams with all the visceral passions of a pint of yogurt. The Clean Air Act gave the automobile industry six years to cleanse its products of 90 percent of all toxic exhaust emissions. Worse yet, we were sure the new Environmental Protection Agency and the Occupational Safety and Health Agency—OSHA—were bound to unleash legions of nanny state bureaucrats on us with the sole mission of herding us into a mass of spineless, subservient humanity obedient to the will of Big Brother.

Such was the unhinged fear and loathing that pervaded the land in early 1971. Therefore, what better time to add to the national psychosis? We trekked along 34th Street with me preaching about the grand scheme of a race, to be named for Erwin G. "Cannon Ball" Baker, the greatest cross-country record-breaker of them all. It had been Cannon Ball who set all kinds of point-to-point records in the early half of the century, driving everything from motorcycles to lumpy, low-powered sedans, to supercharged sports cars, to dump trucks and army tanks, all run with his simple guarantee, "No record, no pay."

Baker, a craggy Hoosier with a big nose, a defiant smile, and a pugnacious jaw, broke into the business on motorcycles after gaining a ride with the Indian motorcycle factory team. He began to set open records, first between small cities, then across the nation, which was still unconnected, coast-to-coast, by anything that could be described as decent highways. In 1915 he drove a Stutz Bearcat from Los Angeles to New York in 11 days and seven hours, an amazing time, considering that most of eastern California, Arizona, and New Mexico offered little in the way of roads besides cattle trails and open range. On his way to setting 143 distance records before his death in 1960, Baker raced against the New York Central 20th Century Limited from New York to Chicago in 1928, beating the elite passenger train into the Windy City. His greatest drive came in 1933, when he drove *solo* across the nation in 53½ hours, sleeping for a half-hour behind the wheel of his Graham-Paige Model 57 Blue Streak 8. Even today, with the two coasts linked by interstates, a one-man nonstop drive in that time frame would be a prodigious feat. But to do it on 1933-vintage two-lanes, many of them unpaved, borders on the miraculous. Therefore, what better man to celebrate in a madcap intercoastal adventure than Cannon Ball Baker?

Existential, high-speed drives across the nation were in style, at least in Hollywood. The most famous of them was the 1969 hit, *Easy Rider*, the drug-fogged chronicle of Peter Fonda, Dennis Hopper, and Jack Nicholson's motorcycle ride to doom at the Mardi Gras. In 1971 two low-budget pictures hit the screen, both of which became cult favorites, and one of which no doubt influenced my decision to run the first Cannonball. Barry Newman starred in *Vanishing Point*, in which he attempted, for no apparent reason, to drive a Dodge Challenger from Denver to San Francisco in 15 hours. The second film, *Two Lane Blacktop*, was trumpeted by *Esquire* (at the time at the height of its powers as an avant-garde literary journal) as "the movie of the year." It starred two rock stars, James Taylor and Beach Boys stalwart Dennis Wilson, as a pair of racers driving their beat-up, primer-painted 1955 Chevrolet hardtop around the country, making money from impromptu drag races. They hooked up with fabled character actor Warren Oates, driving a flashy new Pontiac GTO, and dueled him in a mad dash on back roads to—in classic existential themes—nowhere for no real reason.

Erwin George "Cannon Ball" Baker (1882–1960), legendary cross-country record-setter for whom the Cannonball Run was named. He's pictured here astride an Indian motorcycle during a North American crossing along the U.S.-Mexico border.

While *Vanishing Point* wasn't released until after the first Cannon-ball had been run, the *Esquire* hype surrounding *Two Lane Blacktop* was a factor in my conception of the Cannonball.

Bob Brown was nervous about the idea. Mandel, always the dys-peptic contrarian, denounced it as childish and ridiculous. But Steve Smith loved it. Smith, my longtime friend and former fellow-staffer on *Car and Driver* during the glory years of the 1960s, and I had long been intrigued with the notion of long-distance open road drives as the ultimate test of automobiles. What better environment in which to evaluate cars? After holding the editorship of *Car and Driver*, Smith had drifted to Los Angeles, then back to New York and a copywriting job with the giant J. Walter Thompson advertising agency. When visit-ing Manhattan from my upstate New York home in the village of Castile, I always bunked with Smith, who, like the rest of us, was con-sumed with the fevers of antiestablishmentarianism.

We convinced ourselves that all manner of crazies, race drivers, hot car wackos, fellow journalists, etc., would immediately throw in their lot if a coast-to-coast Cannonball was announced. Aside from Baker's known records, legend had it that basketball superstar Wilt Chamberlain had driven a Lamborghini from New York to Los Angeles solo in 36 hours and 10 minutes. But Wilt had also claimed to have boffed women equaling the entire population of southern California, and there was no way of confirming his time on the road or in the sack. John Christie, a former editor of *Car and Driver* who had defected to the Petersen Publishing empire in L.A., bragged about driving an Austin-Healey from Los Angeles to Washington, D.C., in 48 hours, which sounded impressive until it was acknowledged that he had counted only the time on the road and not his overnight stops. Any number of other so-called records floated around, but now it was time to lay down some legitimate times against a real clock. The concept would be exquisitely simple: Contestants would clock out of the Red Ball Parking Garage on 32nd Street (where the magazine housed its tiny test fleet) in midtown Manhattan and drive, ad hoc, to the Por-tofino Inn in Redondo Beach, (a noted racers' hangout) where they would clock in again. The lowest elapsed time point-to-point would determine the winner. This would be the Cannonball Baker Sea-to-Shining-Sea Memorial Trophy Dash. Here with an anomaly: While Baker called himself "Cannon Ball," I, for reasons I cannot recall, contracted the name to "CannonBall," thereby separating the late, great driver from the event, if only in name, but not in deed.

Who among serious car nuts could resist such a challenge? Every-body, it turned out.

Smith had read a story in *Rolling Stone* titled "Roaring Around with Robert Redford," in which the author recounted some high-speed driving by the actor. This prompted a letter from Smith to Redford. A surrogate responded indicating interest, then silence. Others in the car business expressed initial enthusiasm then began to fret about speeding tickets, punishment from employers, angry wives, etc., and steadily dropped out. We faced the prospect of a nonevent.

Our vehicle would be a 1971 Dodge Custom Sportsman van pow-ered by a 360-cubic-inch, 225-horsepower V-8 that had been featured in *Car and Driver* as *Boss Wagon III*—the most recent of a series of vehicles that had been mildly customized by the staff. *Boss Wagon III* became *Moon Trash II*, a paean to the well-liked, Manhattan-based Chrysler Corporation Dodge Division public relations expert, B.F. "Moon" Mullins. He was a good friend of the magazine and had arranged for the Dodge van to be loaned, after which it had been equipped with Scheel bucket seats, Cragar S/S mag wheels mounted with Firestone, 60-series Wide Oval tires, and other goodies, including a small Norcold refrigerator.

Two other drivers were recruited. I had met Jim Williams at a clothesline art show in Rochester, New York, in the fall of 1970 and had purchased a painting of a sprint car he had done while finishing up his studies at the Rochester Institute of Technology. A fine artist and fledgling writer, Williams was on the verge of being hired by Bob Brown as an associate editor at *Car and Driver* and was an enthusias-tic recruit for the Cannonball. A fourth, expert mechanic and club racer Chuck Kneugen, with whom I had campaigned in a Sadler Formula Junior and a Dodge Trans-Am car, was also set to run, but had to defer to a house-building project at the last hour. Kneugen's main contribu-tion was to tune up *Moon Trash* and to install a small rooftop wing at my request—a disastrous accoutrement that would not only slow us down but would butcher our fuel mileage in the name of high style.

With three drivers, there suddenly became room for my 14-year-old son, Brock Jr., who, while too young to drive the vehicle, would serve as an observer for cops—a sort of human adjunct to our secret weapon, a crude "Radar Sentry" radar detector that was at the time a state-of-the-art device against the rising employment of X-band radar by the highway patrols. The Radar Sentry was but one of a handful of radar detectors on the market at the time. All of them were essentially useless, although the police were limited to using stationary, hand-held radar guns. Antispeed technologies like Instant-on, K-and Ka-band, laser, etc., were unknown. VASCAR was beginning to be employed, but on a limited basis. The notion of using citizen band radio was unthought of and would not come into vogue until the middle of the decade.

Smith and I devised several high-speed cross-country strategies, including one ill-fated idea to run a straight-line Mercator-style route from upstate New York to Manhattan that dead-ended in a gravel pit somewhere in Bath, New York. After much planning, it was decided to take the classic route westward on the Pennsylvania Turnpike, across the Midwest to St. Louis, then angling southwest, utilizing as much as possible of the still-incomplete interstate system to Los Angeles. The symbolism appealed: The westward movement. To the Golden State! Hollywood! The streets paved with gold! Go west, young man! Look out, Horace Greeley, here comes *Moon Trash!*

Then came word from Redford. His secretary, a woman named Becky, called to say that he would like to go—Los Angeles to New York, if possible—but had a heavy film schedule and wondered if the run could be postponed until August. A second call from a Redford surrogate named Ed Jones confirmed that the actor was not available, although Kirk F. White, a Philadelphia exotic car dealer, told us he

Moon Trash II *stops in Flagstaff, Arizona. Young Brock Yates Jr. (right) examines limited supply of snacks.* Jim Williams

would provide a Ferrari Daytona for Redford, if he were prepared to participate. No dice. Redford was out. Other phone calls to friends in the business initially produced an agreement to race, but slowly each fell off the wagon. Kim Chapin, the *Sports Illustrated* writer, dropped out after he lost a codriver. Jean Shepard, the New York-based humorist and fellow *C/D* columnist, demurred because of a heavy television schedule. Russ Goebel, the publisher of *Autoweek/Competition Press* claimed scheduling problems, as did Ford public relations man Monty Roberts, West Coast magazine writer Ocee Rich and hotshot advertising director/cinematographer Joe Pytka.

Worse yet, *Car and Driver* editor Bob Brown was getting nervous. He fretted over reader reaction to an overtly illegal race and began to waffle over coverage, although he finally agreed that I could write an extended column covering the event. As the proposed May 3, 1971, start edged closer, the race appeared to be devolving into nothing more than a solo run across the nation in an attempt to set a coast-to-coast record, if such a thing existed.

Once we decided to actually make the run, I wrote my monthly *Car and Driver* column for the July issue (two months early due to printing and distribution deadlines) just prior to leaving. It was there

Yates driving west. Note useless Radar Sentry detector on visor and the American flag installed on the windshield by Smith to ward off redneck cops. Jim Williams

that the announcement was made for what would forever after be known as *Cannonball Baker Sea-to-Shining-Sea Memorial Trophy Dash.* A "trophy dash" was a short race, generally five laps, for the four fastest qualifiers in sprint car and midget competition and seemed an appropriately absurd play on words for a race several thousand times longer. "Memorial" was included in the title as a veiled lament to what we considered at the time to be the impending doom to high-performance cars and fast driving, at the hands of the government and the Nader forces.

In the summary paragraph of the column I made reference to some of the inspiration for the race: "Those fey sweethearts over at *Esquire* gave you the entire script of *Two Lane Blacktop* in a recent issue. Keep your eyes glued on this spot for the real thing. Maybe we'll call ours *Four Lane Cement.*"

After installing several additional performance items to *Moon Trash II* in a shop near my upstate home, including a small racing-style wheel, Cibie driving lights, Fiamm air horn, a map-reading light and the above-mentioned rear wing, we made for Manhattan and a midnight start in front of Smith's apartment at 35 East and 35th Street. My log recorded the following inventory:

Five-gallon jerry can	Assorted soft drinks and fruit
Tool kit	beverages
One roll of super tape	27 Macintosh apples
Police receiver (nonworking)	36 Mounds bars
8 quarts of Shell oil	4 large Hershey bars
Trouble light	32 garbage bags
2½-gallon water tank	12 packets Vivarin
Sleeping bag/foam mattress	12 packets Dentyne
Spare Cibie headlight bulbs	10-ounce Pepto-Bismol bottle
Folding chair	1 roll of paper towels
Fire extinguisher	2 pounds Jarlsberg cheese round

EXCERPTS FROM THE LOG OF

Moon Trash II

Midnight, May 3, 1971

Departed Smith's apartment. Odometer reading 1,312.4 miles. Smith driving through Lincoln Tunnel, south on Jersey turnpike to Route 22 and interstate 78. Light rain and fog.

Smith wearing a construction worker's hard hat bearing an American flag decal. He is convinced this will endear him to the Bull Connor-style traffic cops that he claims infest the roads of rural America, i.e., all the territory between Manhattan and metro L.A.

2:55 A.M.: Enter Pennsylvania Turnpike. Yates takes over during gas stop at 4:40 A.M. 22.9 gallons.

6:42 A.M.: Williams drives. 24.1 gallons taken on. Poor MPG.

Noon: U.S. 40 westbound. Average 70 miles per hour.

Ran out of fuel trying to pass a truck on a two-lane section. Barely make it to the roadside. Hairy situation. Fill from auxiliary can and limp into Casey, Illinois.

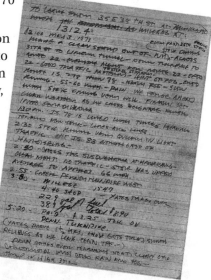

2:15 P.M.: Cross the Mississippi. Quick calculations indicate a 40-hour trip will take a miracle. Getting less than 9 miles per gallon.

4:00 P.M.: Crossing Oklahoma at steady 90 miles per hour. Brock Jr. sleeping in the back. Yates and Williams eating constantly.

Midnight May 4

24 hours on the road. 40 miles east of Amarillo, Texas. 1,695 miles covered, averaging 70.6 miles per hour. 10 stops for gas cost us at least an extra half an hour.

4:00 A.M.: Vibration in right front wheel limits speed to 80 miles per hour.

6:30 A.M.: Wheeze into Flagstaff, Arizona, on an empty tank.

We cross the border into California. Hope rises, although L.A. is 500 miles away. Big state. We jettison what's left of our apples prior to the fruit inspection station a few miles west of Needles.

We try what we call the Amboy cutoff south and west, which offers clear running until we hit 29 Palms, a suburban sprawl in the middle of the high desert that bogs us down for half an hour.

Heavy winds in the San Bernardino Freeway toss *Moon Trash* around in alarming fashion.

We jump off the San Diego Freeway and hit 3 miles of heavy traffic on 190th Street headed for Redondo Beach.

Finally, desperately, we roll into the Portofino Inn, a wondrous little hotel on the Pacific Ocean owned by ex-racer and California Sports Car Club stalwart Mary Davis. Luminaries like Peter Revson and Vasek Polak have apartments in the complex and with Ascot and numerous race shops nearby, the Portfino bar is a racer's hangout.

We made the trip in a disappointing 40 hours and 51 minutes. The total distance, 2,858 miles, at an average speed of 70.0 miles per hour. We had consumed a prodigious 314.5 gallons of high-test, averaging a dismal 9.1 miles per gallon.

Moon Trash II *on the edge of the Pacific Ocean after a rather disappointing 40-hour, 51-minute transcontinental trip. Note the rear spoiler, which, while looking racey, ate up inordinate amounts of gasoline and chewed perhaps 10 miles per hour off the van's top speed.* Jim Williams

CONCLUSIONS: Trip could be much quicker. Fuel stops were a disaster. A range of 400–500 miles a necessity. A better route, fewer, quicker stops, no more than two minutes in length, are the keys to a really fast cross-country trip.

Once home I wrote an extended version of my *Car and Driver* column for the August 1971 issue. Other than a brief column in the *Boston Globe* by motorsports writer Ron Mead, it would serve as the only published acknowledgment of the event that, unbeknownst to us, would ultimately trigger a global reaction.

In a summary to my column, I wrote:

> We are ready for the Cannonball Baker. In fact, Smith says we've got the pole. Anyway, this kind of an event opens up an entire new area of motorsport. Oh, God, the anarchistic barbarity of it all! Out there Uncle Sam's own 31,000 miles of superhighways driving at speeds sometimes beyond the legal limits, in actual conscious violation of our traffic laws. That's the way it's going to be, car freaks, in the first demonstration that some people are aware enough to handle their own destinies behind the wheel of an automobile. Of course the whole thing is going to raise hell, and the day might come when guys are busting across the nation in disguised ambulances (note: an accidental act of prescience on my part), official limousines, Greyhound buses, you name it, in some sort of nutball protest that people who like cars, who understand cars, and who know how to keep cars under control, are not going to collapse in the self-energizing lunacy of government bureaucracy. The other guys in the automotive press can sit around and recommend letter writing to your congressman, but I've had it. From here on in I am going to use the road according my own skills and capabilities and not in conformity with a 49-year-old, cradle-to-grave, squarehead bureaucrat who wouldn't know a good automobile if it ran over him.
>
> I hate to take another swipe at the swaying props that are holding this society. Everywhere somebody is protesting about something, defying the laws of the land while the establishment seems to burrow deeper into its bunkers in defense. But it appears to be the only course. If the movements of automobiles can be monitored and controlled (as with goodies like VASCAR and ORBIS) we are a long way down the road to 1984. Therefore, this mindless government urge to make us safe from ourselves, can, in the long haul, lead to an electronic nightmare whereby you couldn't buy five gallons of gas or run a half-mile over the speed limit without ringing a gong in the Big Mutha computer in Washington. Remember this, you can write off the Cannon Ball Baker and all the weirdos who might take part in such

an event, but let me leave you with a quote from the greatest American observer of them all in regard to the ancient battle we must rage against authoritarianism. The words were written nearly 150 years ago, by Alexis de Tocqueville in his epic work, *Democracy in America*:

> The dread of disturbance and the love of well-being insensibly lead democratic nations to increase the functions of central government as the only power which appears to be . . . sufficiently strong, enlightened, and secure to protect them from anarchy . . . All particular circumstances which tend to make a state a democratic community agitated and precarious enhance the general prosperity and lead private persons more and more to sacrifice their rights to their tranquility. This sacrificing of rights becomes an indiscriminate passion and the members of the community are apt to conceive a most inordinate devotion to order.

LONG LIVE CANNON BALL BAKER.

And so the call to arms was made in the summer of 1971. But was it more polemical yammering from a columnist in a relatively small automobile enthusiast magazine, soon to be forgotten, or would it radiate outward into something larger and more outrageous? It would be only a matter of weeks before we learned the answer.

Steve Smith
FIRST CANNONBALL, 1971

Brock Yates didn't invent the Cannonball Baker Sea-to-Shining-Sea Memorial Trophy Dash. I did. Sort of. I've been a dedicated point-to-point racer since I was in boarding school, when I and the only other kid on campus who was allowed to have a car (he had a Porsche America 1300 Super coupe; I had a surplus World War II Navy Jeep) were given to making outrageous claims about how fast we could make it from the school, in Lenox, Massachusetts, to New York City. Nobody believed our speeds, so we dragooned two hapless under-classmen into riding shotgun as observers to certify the times. They returned blubbering about how we'd made them wet their pants, yada-yada. But to give you an indication of how "liberal" this school was, our antics inspired the headmaster (who drove a fire-engine red '51 Chevy convertible) to try his hand at beating our record claims. We had to let him win: he was also the soccer coach.

Later, I organized (or, more fancifully, conjured) the Preppie Grand Prix, from P. J. Clarke's bar at 55th and 3rd in New York City to Dick

Ridgeley's celebrated gin mill in Southampton, on Long Island, the twin poles of the protoyuppies' world, precisely 100 miles apart as the crow flies. Friday night, all the would-be Masters of the Universe would foregather at Clarke's (made famous as the watering hole in *Come Back, Little Sheba*), get well oiled, and then tackle traffic on the dreaded Long Island Expressway—a.k.a. "The World's Longest Parking Lot"—which did not then have a four-lane connection with the Sunrise Highway, the main thoroughfare of the Hamptons. The trick was to find the best shortcut between the LIE and the Sunrise. My theory then was to find the shortest stretch of two-lane, no matter how tortuous its path, that joined the main roads. It seemed to work . . . at least in my addled state.

In my early days at *Car and Driver*, I continued to expound the efficacy of the shortest distance between two points, and eventually inveigled Brock into attempting a new record between his house (then in upstate Castile, New York) and *Car and Driver* (then at One Park Avenue in the city) by laying a steel ruler between the two points on a topo map, tracing a straight line, and connecting a blue-veined network of obscure secondary roads that deviated the least from the theoretical mean. (Subsequently, this route proved to add no less than a couple of hours and probably 50 miles to the journey . . . duh!)

The genesis of a coast-to-coast contest was the number-crunchers' (Pat Bedard had replaced my choice, Pete Hutchinson, as tech editor of the magazine) insistence that the answer to the age-old question, "What's the Best Car in the World?" could be divined by reading the tea-leaves of acceleration, braking, and skid-pad figures. Yates and I, the Luddites, argued that a car geared for 110 miles per hour at the drag strip would be desperately noisy at normal cruising speeds; that tires capable of generating 1G cornering forces would dislodge your fillings traversing ordinary expansion strips; that racing-style brakes were treacherous unless you kept them up to operating temperature by dragging your foot on the brake pedal, etc. The Mercedes-Benzes of the era generated ho-hum numbers at the test track, we pointed out, but were clearly superior in over-the-road performance to, say, a Camaro Z-28. Moreover, I insisted, we could prove it.

The question was, over what road? And at what distance? I proposed that the techies race their choice (presumably a souped-up muscle car) against our choice (probably a Mercedes SL or a Porsche 911) from Brock's humble abode upstate to the infamous Red Ball Garage on 30th Street and publish the results. This idea faltered when it was pointed out that none of our readers would have the faintest idea of the road conditions between obscure Castile, New York, and the Big Apple. My next choice of a venue was New York to Florida, a route well publicized by *The Tonight Show's* bandleader, Skitch Henderson, who had regaled America with lurid takes of outrunning the cops (or, sometimes, not) in speed-trap-infested Georgia in his 300SL gullwing. The New York-to-Miami bogie was 24 hours or so.

Then I remembered that John Christie, a former editor of *Car and Driver,* had once claimed to have set a coast-to-coast record of 48 hours in an Austin-Healey 3000. Subsequently it was revealed that he had only counted the time he'd actually spent on the road, not the time occupied by the long-distance driver's essential "three esses" (sleeping, supping, and . . . well, you get the idea), and moreover, he had not driven from Los Angeles to New York, but had only got as far as Washington, D.C., before packing it in. No matter, the die had been cast. Coast-to-coast it would be, although I held out for interstate 80, from New York to San Francisco, then the only cross-county route without a stoplight.

Once New York to L.A. had been chosen as a better benchmark (I had to concur: Southern California was the epicenter of car culture in the United States), I then, as the self-anointed navigator, fell yet again into the trap of the shortest-distance algorithm. Hence, the disastrous Amboy "shortcut." Looking at a map, it was obvious that interstate 40, the most direct route across the country from Oklahoma City westward, takes an unconscionable loop to the north after crossing the California border at Needles. Moreover, Yates had designated the Portofino Inn *south* of L.A. as the western terminus (he had a friendship with Mary Davis, then the Portofino's owner), and nobody wanted to brave L.A.'s murderous traffic on the infamous 405 Freeway.

Once again wielding my trusty straightedge, I reckoned that it would be best to start winding our way southward once we drew abeam of the famous meteorite crater at Amboy, and head across the high desert to connect with interstate 10, which runs straight as an arrow into L.A. Only the peaceful hamlet of Twenty-nine Palms stood astride our path. Wrong! Twenty-nine Palms turned out to be a major Marine base, and we got mired in ADL (Anti-Destination League) traffic behind endless columns of six-bys, Mutts, DUKWs, M-113A1s, and Pattons on flatbeds, thus ruining the spectacular average speeds we'd established up till then. At that point my mind went blank, and the journey became a bad acid trip.

About all I could remember from the previous 30 hours was setting the trip's fastest average speed during my first stint (through Ohio, of all places), and realizing as we approached the California border that the powers that be took a dim view of bringing suspect produce into the Golden State. Having loaded the intrepid *Moon Trash* with baskets of apples and oranges (few of which were consumed on the way; we were too wired, and subsisted mainly on caffeine-laced chocolate bars), I desperately tried to jettison the excess as we approached the state line. I dimly remember motorists in our wake swerving to avoid the apples bouncing down the road behind us (I was squeezing them out the vent windows one at a time). And I remember Brock's wicked grin when the inspector leaned in and asked if we had any fruits or vegetables on board. "Only Smith," answered Yates.

That said, I have to admit Edison was wrong. Sometimes genius is 99 percent inspiration and only 1 percent perspiration. I did all the work inventing the Cannonball Baker Sea-to-Shining-Sea Memorial Trophy Dash, but *naming* it was pure Yates . . . and pure genius. I probably would have called it "The Cross-Country Race to Determine the Best Car in the World" and the event never would have been heard of again.

Longtime friend Steve Smith was a fellow editor during the glory days of Car and Driver *in the 1960s before going on to high achievements in advertising and automotive journalism.*

Jim Williams
1971

Here's to you, Mrs. Robinson . . . On the eve of the first Cannonball in the spring of 1971, I was 22, going on 23—mere weeks away from graduating from college. Today, when I encounter young men and women in similar circumstances, I'm amazed at how focused or at least practical they seem about their futures. I, on the other hand, was not unlike young Benjamin in *The Graduate*. I was unconstructively "concerned."

It wasn't a matter of not knowing what I liked. I liked cars. However, unlike the "like" that then as now is not uncommon among adolescent or postadolescent males, my interest was, in a word, pervasive. Years later, when asked by an employer (a large New York ad agency) to write something about myself as part of a pitch for a new car account, I started by saying, "Cars are the monocle through which I have always viewed the world . . ." And unlike other occasional utterances in the ad business, this one was sincere.

I first met Brock Yates in the fall of 1970. I had been exhibiting in an outdoor art show and sale that received coverage on the local Saturday evening news. The next day Brock decided to take his Ferrari Lusso for a ride and, having noted the event on the news, ended up at the art show, where he found me. He bought one of my sprint car paintings and invited me to visit him sometime at his house.

Beyond being honored and delighted to be invited, I had no expectations when I visited Brock for the first time. He was an established authority. I regarded myself as a kid. Brock turned out not only to be a kind host, but actually indulged me with conversation on all manners of automotive stuff, including his opinion that Americans were losing their enthusiasm for cars. What was worse, we'd arrived at a point where cars had become safe and reliable. We'd built a highway system to allow for high-speed individual travel over great distances, yet we were less inclined to use and enjoy these fruits than those of the pioneer automotive era when cars were primitive conveyances and roads were virtually nonexistent. In fact, no one had really made a point of celebrating and seeing how fast the continent could be crossed since E.G. "Cannon Ball" Baker.

It made perfect sense to me. Besides, it was coming from a grownup with a house, a family, a barn full of cars, and a dog named Fred. It never occurred to me to question the necessity of a Cannonball Baker Sea-to-Shining-Sea Memorial Trophy Dash. And as Brock's plan for the event developed, I never seriously considered that I might be asked to participate. However, as the weeks passed, and as people began to wimp out, Brock eventually inquired if I would be willing to sign on as a reserve driver. "Absolutely!"

My family was a bit more circumspect. To allay their concerns, I paraphrased what I'd overheard Brock say to one or another nay-sayer on the phone, "If this was dangerous, or irresponsible, would Brock be taking his first-born son?" It worked on just about everyone. But as I got out of the car at Brock's house on the morning the first Cannonball was supposed to launch, I was reminded of young Ben, who ended up in bed with Mrs. Robinson merely because events had placed him there. Had I, too, been seduced by chance or inertia . . . or was this a bad dream come true?

The story of the first Cannonball Run has been well chronicled elsewhere. For my part, I can say that I didn't do anything really stupid, and I don't think I said anything really dumb in the course of the actual run or on the return crossing. After all, Brock has continued to tolerate me as a friend for more than 30 years. Steve Smith still talks to me, as does Brock Junior, whenever our paths have crossed. Within a month of the Cannonball, I went to work at *Car and Driver*, not as an art guy, but as an editor. I would eventually serve as art director, but parted company with the magazine when it moved to Michigan. While with the magazine, I'd go with Brock on other driving expeditions—a banzai blast to Alaska in a Corvette, and a lap of America with him and another *Car and Driver* staffer, John Eberhart, in a 450SEL.

Was the Cannonball a good thing? I'm convinced the general automotive landscape of the last 30 years would have been a lot drearier without it. As for me, without it I, too, might have grown up to be a lot drearier. There was no sequel to the *Graduate*, so we don't know what might have happened to young Ben. But over the last 30-odd years, I've managed to eke out a living doing things with cars. And a couple of ex-wives notwithstanding, it's been a pretty good ride.

Thanks, Brock.

Jim Williams is a former staff member at Car and Driver *and a successful author and copywriter in the automotive field.*

Brock Yates Jr.
1971

The years removed most of the memories of this trip, though as a 14-year-old, wandering through the endless years of self-doubt and uneasiness that puberty and growing up provided, a few things are permanently etched in my mind. Lost are the recollections of the panic of looking for gas along the lonely, empty stretches of nighttime highways, the scrolling of an ever-changing America through the windshield, and the concern of my mother as we embarked. But I do remember it as a grand adventure, one I am profoundly proud to have participated in.

One of the more vivid memories was of an early radar detector, the Radar Sentry. Purchased by mail order from the back pages of some magazine, it was the first one claiming to alert a motorist to the expense and inconvenience of a speeding ticket. I think everyone was optimistic about the budding technology. Clipped onto the visor, this little square box of strange electronics, instead of finding police lurking behind the overpasses, found every power line in the country. It was irritating and ineffective, and the consensus was to pull it from the windshield and discard it. Little did anyone guess at the time, it predates a whole industry of detection and countermeasures. I never leave my driveway without one now.

One of the biggest disappointments of the era of the Cannonball has to do with the 1979 running. Riding on the first one, unable to drive, caused me to look for a ride for a future run. By the time of the last one, I had found a codriver with a Corvette willing to go. Of course, the timing was a secret, and having moved out of the house, I waited like everyone else for the announcement. This came as a surprise one afternoon while I was working. The phone call from my father was not what I hoped to hear. Knowing that I was six hours away from the city, he said the Cannonball was starting in two hours, and that he'd see me in a couple of weeks. I suppose this was my father's way of keeping me out of harm's way, but I do remember not being happy about it.

Perhaps I was too young, didn't have enough money to bail myself out of jail, or was otherwise just not ready for a banzai cross-country assault, but I do remember that conversation vividly. In the subsequent years, on each of my many trips across country, I think about the Cannonball experience, the effect it had on my driving and the lessons we learned, at somewhat over the posted limit.

Brock Yates Jr. is the manager of the annual Cannonball One Lap of America and is a former class winner in that event and the Silver State Classic.

CHAPTER
TWO

1971: The Race That Shook the World

RETURNING FROM THE FIRST CANNONBALL, I plunged into a summer of racing. I was working on a book titled *Sunday Driver* that
chronicled my experience in various sports cars as well as a pair of
Trans-Am races in a factory-supported Camaro entered by the Warren
Agor/Hoselton Chevrolet team of Rochester, New York. My life
changed directions away from the Cannonball for a while, at least
until my column appeared in the August 1971 issue of *Car and Driver.*

It brought a flood of mail, letters by the hundreds, some critical of
such an insane gesture, but a vast majority were favorable, and dozens
of correspondents wanted to participate in the next race—an event I
had assured them would take place at some hazy point in the future.
But once the initial burst of excitement about the run subsided, the
Cannonball began to give way to other distractions. Trans-Ams' racing
season was beginning to move ahead at full speed, and I was preparing
for the Watkins Glen Trans-Am when a telegram brought the Cannonball back to the forefront of my thinking. It was from the Polish Racing
Drivers of America, a tongue-in-cheek collection of car freaks that had
been formed by Brad Niemcek, a New York public relations man, and
Oscar Kovaleski, a well-known amateur sports-car racer and auto-
accessory seller. The telegram read

THIS CONSTITUTES FORMAL ENTRY BY THE POLISH RACING
DRIVERS OF AMERICA IN THE NEXT OFFICIAL
CANNONBALL BAKER SEA-TO-SHINING-SEA MEMORIAL TROPHY DASH.
THE DRIVERS ARE OSCAR KOVALESKI, BRAD NIEMCEK, AND
TONY ADAMOWICZ. IF WE CAN FIND CALIFORNIA,
WE'LL BEAT YOU FAIR AND SQUARE.

That was it. We had a challenge. And a race. While they refused to
take anything with complete seriousness, the PRDA weren't fooling

about the Cannonball. Their third driver, Tony Adamowicz, was one of the best young professional prospects in the nation and, with Mario Andretti, the only American to be graded by the FIA. (Thanks to a high finish at LeMans, Tony had qualified for such an obscure, complicated international rating.) What's more, a follow-up phone call by Niemcek indicated that they were building a specially modified Chevy van with enough auxiliary gas tanks to make the trip nonstop!

We decided to go on November 15, after the racing season had ended and the roads had cleared of vacation traffic. After returning from Riverside, I began to prepare for the Cannonball in earnest. The first order seemed to involve getting a faster car. While *Moon Trash* was a fine machine, its limited top speed—perhaps 105 miles per hour—and stock fuel tank presented severe handicaps in the face of the PRDA challenge. Kirk White offered a solution. Within his stable was a 4.4-liter Ferrari 365GTB/4 Daytona, a slippery, ground-hugging coupe with a V-12, four-cam engine and five forward speeds, considered to be the fastest road automobile built. Its top speed was in the neighborhood of 175 miles per hour and with a large gasoline tank, cruising ranges of 300–350 miles could be expected. It was handicapped in that only two men could fit into its small cockpit, which

A confident Oscar Kovaleski and Brad Niemcek (in van) of the Polish Racing Drivers Team prior to the New York City start.

meant greater fatigue, but I accepted Kirk's deal anyway. Now my only problem was finding a codriver. Why not get a real, honest-to-God racer, someone suggested. The idea made sense. I called Dan Gurney. He loved the plan. I could hear him chuckling on the other end of the transcontinental connection as I explained the Cannonball to him. He accepted. Jubilation. Then he called back a day later and declined. He mumbled about pressures from sponsors and how a man in his position shouldn't be out roaring around on the public highways. I understood. I called Phil Hill. A perfect choice, I thought. After all, Phil was America's only World Champion, a title he had won at the wheel of a Ferrari, and I had heard that he was an excellent endurance driver with three wins at Le Mans. What's more, Phil was a terribly bright and engaging man whose company would not wear thin after a day and a half of steady association. Phil said it sounded like fun, but he was simply too busy to go.

"What are you going to do about the cops?" he asked.

"What about the cops? I figure we'll have to treat them just like other road hazards: like ice, rain, snow," I said.

"Yeah, but if we get caught . . . "

"You know, Phil, your reaction is typical. Every guy I talk to about Cannonball asks right away, 'What about the cops?' like they're the most fearsome thing on earth. Look at yourself. You spent half your life risking your ass in a race car, and the thought of getting a traffic ticket sounds worse than a 200-mile-per-hour crash at LeMans."

"That's madness, isn't it?" he said reflectively. "I suppose we've been so preconditioned that it's a reflex action. Good God, I'm terrified about losing my driver's license. How screwed up can our priorities get?"

With Phil and Dan unavailable, I decided to call Don "Big Daddy" Garlits, the drag-racing champion. He was a good friend, a fine highway driver, and was possessed of the kind of iconoclastic, problem-solving mind that would be fascinated with the challenge of racing nonstop across the United States. Like Gurney, Garlits accepted, then had to refuse a day later when several critical business appointments could not be rescheduled. With less than a week to go, I was without a driving partner, although Mo Campbell, an associate of Kirk's, was prepared to run if I was unable to find a serious pro.

As the word of the Cannonball spread through the underground of the sport, more and more entries began to surface. Unlike the first time, these appeared to be serious competitors. Suddenly one afternoon, a pair of bearded young men and a young woman appeared at the offices of *Car and Driver*. They announced themselves as Tom Marbut and Randy Water, plus Marbut's girlfriend, Becky Poston, and said that they had driven from their home in Little Rock, Arkansas, nonstop to test their new van for the Cannonball. Finding their story hard to believe, Jim Williams followed them down to the curbside of Park Avenue, where he found a brightly painted Dodge van, similar to *Moon Trash II* but rigged with a special, 190-gallon fueling system. They planned to run across the country with one stop, they said. The co-owners of the Sound 'n' Sirloin restaurant in Little Rock, Waters and Marbut had customized their new Dodge after reading my August column about the initial run. In addition to the special paint and fuel system, the van carried a 2.94 final drive, outside exhaust system, and a thickly carpeted interior, presumably to muffle the rumble of the 360-cubic-inch engine, which was equipped with a larger Holley CFM four-barrel carburetor. Marbut and Waters had named their machine *Snoopy II*. However, based on its large fuel supply and its southern origins, we immediately dubbed the team the "Little Rock Tankers."

My phone began to jangle constantly. As the originator, or Dr. Frankenstein, of the Cannonball, I was the recipient of unending calls from people who wanted to enter; who had entered and were dropping out; who would enter if I could find them a suitable car; who thought the whole thing was childish madness. Bill Broderick, the racing public relations director for Union 76 Oil Company, called to say that he and a crew of four friends were entering the event in a rented Travco motor home. The chief pilot would be Joe Frasson, a NASCAR Grand National stock-car driver. "We don't expect to beat all you fast guys, but we'll set a record for motor homes, I'll guaranteed that," announced Bill. Joining Broderick and Frasson in the tired, 38,000-mile Travco, which had been rented from Lou Klug's Motor Home Rentals in Cincinnati, Ohio, were Phil Pash, a columnist for *Chicago Today*; Pal Parker, a photographer; and Bob Carey, editor of a small stock car racing magazine.

Larry Opert, a Cambridge, Massachusetts lawyer and sometime SCCA club racer, entered with a pair of friends, but said, "Unfortunately, we don't have a satisfactory car, but we'll have that problem solved by race time." He wouldn't elaborate on his plan.

Robert Perlow, a rotund graduate student from Hofstra University on Long Island, said he was prepared to compete with his MGB GT coupe, but was having trouble finding a riding partner. Perlow had originally planned to enter his Volvo P1800 coupe, but it had been stolen a month earlier at the U.S. Grand Prix at Watkins Glen, and he had replaced it with the used MG, displaying 10,000 miles on the clock. Aside from the addition of driver lights, the neat little wire-wheeled coupe was box-stock. Acting as a matchmaker, I rooted through the lists of interested people who had called and teamed Perlow up with Wes Dawn, a California television technician and club racer who wanted to use the Cannonball as a high-speed hitchhike to the West Coast.

Moon Trash II was back in the program, minus the gas-sucking spoiler, despite some misadventures. Poor Williams had crunched the front end (including those expensive quartz-iodine driving lights) in a chain collision on Manhattan's East River Drive, and Jim Stickford, Chrysler's area public-relations director, had worked long and hard to arrange for a quick repair. Its crew would be Kim Chapin, a regular contributor to *Sports Illustrated* who had tried to run in May, and Steve Behr, a competent young race driver, who among other accomplishments, shared the distinction of being the highest-placed (12th) American finisher in the history of the famed Monte Carlo Rally. In phoning to announce that *Moon Trash II* would also carry Holly Morin, a particularly game TWA stewardess as a nondriving member of the crew, Behr commented, "In the Cannonball, we'll be sneaking along, trying to avoid the police. In the Monte Carlo, they stand on the side of the road and flag you through the tough spots. That says something about our philosophy of law and order, I think."

The eighth and last team to enter the Cannonball roared across the country just in time to make the start. Ed Bruerton, a supermarket manager in Oakland, California, and his younger brother, Tom, a pharmacy student at Cal-Tech, left their home a few days before the Cannonball, drove south to the Portofino, and ran across the country in the reverse direction as a sort of reconnaissance. The car was a tired AMX sport coupe with 90,000 miles on the odometer. They had already made numerous endurance trips with the old car, including a rocky ride the entire length of the Baja Peninsula.

Everybody was riding except me. While I knew and liked Mo Campbell, I had virtually no knowledge of his skill as a driver, and it seemed a shame that the lofty performance of the Ferrari might not be used to its full potential. That might be possible with Mo, but I knew it would have been assured if an experienced veteran like Gurney or Hill could have been persuaded to go. The evening before we were to gather in Manhattan for the start of the race, I was having dinner with friends when the telephone rang. It was Gurney. We exchanged a few niceties, then I asked him why he had called. After all, we had known each other for years and had liked each other, but our friendship was not so strong that we exchanged phone calls to engage in innocent chatter. He paused for a moment, then said, "I'm ready to go on the Cannonball."

"Are you drunk, or have you lost your mind?" I asked.

"I don't know, maybe a little of both," he said, laughing. "But I've had a change of mind about the whole thing. Something I read. I'll tell you about it when I get there. I've decided we just can't sit on our asses anymore. Everybody's terrified of offending somebody, and I almost got caught in that trap. Anyway, we'll talk about it later. I'm jumping on the red-eye out of Los Angeles right now. I'll meet you just before the start."

Beautiful. I hung up the phone knowing that the Ferrari would be used the way ol' Enzo had intended it to be.

Steve Smith's apartment on 35th Street was to be the rendezvous point for the racers. The actual start was to be at the Red Ball Garage, a typically grubby Manhattan commercial parking establishment on 31st Street, between Third Avenue and Lexington. It had been chosen because it was near midtown and because, since it was the regular

The Bruerton Brothers, Ed and Tom, outside the Red Ball Garage. One of the parking lot attendants asks why two guys would want to drive a clapped-out, 90,000 mile AMX in a cross-country race.

parking area for *Car and Driver*, its staff would be calm in the face of almost any lunacy involving automobiles. Since everybody had intended to start about midnight, we had scheduled a driver's meeting at Smith's place for 10:30 P.M. Slowly the apartment began to fill up, not only with entrants, but with a vast collection of friends, *Car and Driver* staff members, photographers, etc., all milling around in the relatively cramped confines of Smith's one-bedroom lodgings. The Bruerton brothers staggered in, unshaved and exhausted. They had just completed a 44-hour nonstop run from California and announced that they were going to sleep for eight hours before restarting.

Larry Opert burst in smiling. With him were his two friends, Ron Herisko, a law partner, and Nate Pritzker, an engineer. They had a car, they announced, thanks to *The New York Times* and the unconscious generosity of a wealthy Long Island man. It seemed that the trio, determined to find a car to race in the Cannonball, had looked in the "*Times*" classifieds in search of a "drive-away" deal—an arrangement where one would drive another's car to a destination for nominal expenses. This is a common tactic used to transport personal cars by people who don't like to drive long distances. The Long Island gentleman wanted his new Cadillac Sedan DeVille driven to California. Opert

November 15, 1971: Pre-race meeting at Steve Smith's 35th Street apartment in Manhattan. Left to right: Jim Williams (in background), Bob Brown, Charles Fox, Bruce McCall, Dan Gurney, Steve Smith. Kim Chapin of Sports Illustrated *is seated in the foreground.*

and company obliged, nodding hazily at his firm orders that his prized machine not be driven after eight o'clock at night, and not before nine o'clock in the morning, and not run faster than 75 miles an hour. All the regulations would be violated before they left Manhattan!

The Polish Racing Drivers arrived, decked out in full Nomex driving suits. Niemcek, always the PR man, had arranged for one of the team's sponsors, a Pennsylvania Polish Kishkie manufacturer, to sponsor an afternoon prerace reception at the Auto Pub, a chromy, car-oriented saloon situated, appropriately enough, in the basement of the General Motors building. "They'll need more than fireproof uniforms if those goddamn gas tanks in that thing explode," mused Smith. "If those 300 gallons let go, it'll make Hiroshima look like a wet match!" The room was full of good-natured banter, as if nobody was thinking of the 3,000 miles that spread out before us. I kidded Niemcek about their spectacular uniforms and how they must have mystified the Sunday-afternoon pedestrians along Fifth Avenue. "That was a lot of fun, but now we get serious." Brad said, still smiling.

"Yeah, like they say, 'When the green flag drops, the bullshit stops,'" added Tony Adamowicz, who was standing nearby.

"The Detroit street racers—the guys who drag-raced up and down Woodward Avenue for money—have a saying: 'Money talks and bullshit

Brad Neimcek in his PRDA driver's suit works the crowd at a pre-event party held at the Auto Pub, a saloon located at the lower level of Fifth Avenue's General Motor Building.

walks,'" I added. "The only trouble is, we haven't got a cent riding on this thing. Goddamn, when was the last time guys like Adamowicz and Gurney raced for nothing?"

"And 3,000 miles yet," said Tony. "Good God, I must be crazy."

The doorbell rang over the din and there was Gurney. It was that familiar chiseled face, revealing half the age of its 40 years, with its firm mouth set in a crooked, little boy grin. Dan Gurney is a big man—6 feet 2 and perhaps 200 pounds—so big, in fact, that he spent much of his career on the Grand Prix circuit wedged into tiny cockpits that had been intended for smaller men, racing sort of sideways, with one buttock perched on the seat. He was wearing a tweed sport coat, a navy blue LaCoste pullover, and a pair of khaki pants. He carried only a shaving kit. Dan obviously intended to get the trip over with in a hurry.

The drivers' meeting was brief. I outlined the Rule once again, noting that we would start from the Red Ball in one-minute intervals, with the PRDA going first. They had, after all, requested the "pole" position. The team arriving at the Portofino Inn in Redondo Beach in the briefest elapsed time—to be documented by the electronic time clocks at the Red Ball and at the Portofino's registration desk—would be the winner. Beyond that, everybody was on his own.

The cars had been parked on the main floor of the Red Ball, lined up under the light of the bare ceiling bulbs. There was the Little Rock

Well-known automotive cartoonist Deal celebrated the PRDA second-place finish with this drawing shortly after the event.

van, with its spectacular red, white, and blue paint work; the red and white PRDA van, with its flanks covered with sponsors' decals and large type proclaiming: "THE POLISH RACING DRIVERS OF AMERICA GO COAST-TO-COAST NONSTOP!" By contrast, *Moon Trash II* had been painted, bumper to bumper, in a murky coat of flat black. Crouching beside it was our Ferrari Daytona, its mirror-polished, Sunoco blue paint glinting in the raw light, its elegant finish highlighted by a masterful network of yellow pinstriping, and its fenders amply covered with decals from sponsors that Kirk White's staff had attracted to help defray expenses. Gurney's and my names were displayed in neat lettering under the windows. It had been the first time I'd seen the car up close. "It's been cunningly disguised as a racing car!" I gasped.

Wind was kicking up litter on 31st Street as the midnight starting time approached. While the first four cars departed, Gurney and I went off to gather up some provisions at an all-night delicatessen. We bought a few large blocks of Swiss cheese, a batch of gum, some chocolate bars, peanuts, and some cans of soft drink and Gatorade. Smith provided us with a large thermos bottle of hot coffee and a jar of chewable Vitamin C tablets, a most useful remedy for the dryness in your mouth and nasal passages that seems to trouble long-distance travelers.

No good-housekeeping awards were forthcoming for the Gurney/Yates team. Hershey and Mounds bars attest to the healthy diet employed on the trip.

We rolled the Ferrari out of the Red Ball and into the dark street. As a cluster of friends stood by, Gurney and I fitted our gear around the seats; the food, maps, flashlight, watches, average-speed computer, etc., and wound ourselves into the elaborate seat belts and shoulder harnesses. We were set. Already the PRDA, the Cadillac, the MG, and the Little Rock van were on the road. *Moon Trash II* would leave half an hour after us, while Broderick's motor home and the Bruerton brothers would depart later in the day.

Dan would drive the first leg. He cranked the engine over and a potent, whirring rumble rose out of the Ferrari's long hood. He flipped on the headlights, and the black leather cockpit glowed with the soft green luster of the large instrument panel. A friend stamped out tickets on the Red Ball time clock—our official record of departure—and amid a tiny chorus of windswept cheers, we accelerated away, roaring down 31st Street toward the Lincoln Tunnel and California. We went about 200 feet. The stoplight at the corner of 31st and Lexington winked red as we approached, and we sat there through its full cycle. Every cross-town light then conspired to stop us, and we were immobilized at seven intersections before reaching the tunnel.

Our route was to be different from the others'. While most planned to cut directly westward to the Pennsylvania Turnpike, I'd decided that a more northern route across interstate 80, with a subsequent cut south to Columbus, Ohio, was fastest. It was a trifle longer, but I-80 had less traffic and fewer patrols than the Turnpike and appeared to permit higher cruising speeds. It had to be reached via a series of two-lane roads in the daytime. However, in the deep of night, and with Dan driving with relish, we traversed the slow section with an average speed that approached 60 miles per hour.

In the process of trying to reach various road maps, lights, and other paraphernalia, I found my movements restricted by the safety harness. I unsnapped the latch and let the belts fall free. "That's better—at least I can move around," I said.

"These damn things," complained Gurney. "I'm taking mine off, too. They drive me nuts." So off we went on a headlong rush to California, with our live-saving seat belts crumpled on the floor of the Ferrari. We knew about the benefits of seat belts and had both advocated their use from various public platforms, but somehow, cocooned inside that uncanny car, which purred along with the precision and control of a big cat, they seemed superfluous. At first I felt like a naughty boy smoking corn silk behind the barn, but within a few miles the belts were forgotten.

Gurney began to hit his stride as we reached the broad expanses of interstate 80. He was cruising the Ferrari at 95 miles per hour—a virtual canter. At that speed, it was so positively in contact with the road that Gurney complained it was boring to drive. To understand the excellence of a machine like the Ferrari, one had to have driven a thoroughbred sports car. There is no other way. Otherwise, the statement that such a car is cantering at 95 miles per hour seems ludicrous. But the fact remains that some machines—such as the Ferrari, Maserati, Porsche, BMW, Mercedes-Benz, Jaguar—have a poise and élan at high speeds that is virtually beyond the realm of comprehension for the average American driver. The absence of speed limits in Europe had helped to stimulate advances in suspensions, brakes, and steering that were simply unavailable on domestic cars in 1971.

Lights appeared behind us. Thinking it might be the highway patrol, we backed off slightly and let the car overtake us. It was a Camaro with a man in his early 20s at the wheel. He was cruising at about 100 miles per hour. Gurney watched him sail past, then accelerated to keep pace. I knew he wouldn't let the Camaro stay ahead. He

The winners. Yates (left) ruminates as Gurney is congratulated by Portofino Inn owner Mary Davis and Miss Redondo Beach.

opened the throttle plates on the Ferrari's 12 carburetor throats, and the big car clawed ahead, gobbling up the distance between it and the Camaro. We rocketed past. The engine noise increased slightly, but hardly to objectionable levels. The Camaro's headlights dwindled in the distance. "That's 150, just as steady as you please," said Gurney. Then he laughed.

Dan eased back to an indicated 120 miles per hour, and we cruised down the deserted road, cutting over the humpbacked Allegheny Mountains of central Pennsylvania without effort. Gurney was driving with one hand and drinking coffee with the other when he sighted a dim pair of taillights far ahead. Again, it could be the police, so he slowed to about 100 and approached cautiously. I had 20–20 vision. I saw well at night, yet I was still trying to get some rough identification of the vehicle ahead when Gurney announced, "It's OK, it's only a Volkswagen," and got back on the throttle. Sure enough, it was a Volkswagen lumping along there in the dark, and I silently pondered the power of Gurney's eyesight. It is said that most great drivers possess uncanny eyes, but I had never taken that seriously. Now I was a believer.

I napped sporadically while Dan sailed onward, running for an hour in excess of 100 miles per hour and increasing our trip average to 81 miles per hour. That was exceptional time, but neither of us expected it to hold up across the country. Three hundred miles from Manhattan, we stopped for gas, I had leaped out and stuffed the pump nozzle into the tank before the sleepy attendant had gotten out of his chair. Dan, in the meantime, had lifted the hood and was making a routine check of the oil. This pit stop procedure would be repeated for most of the trip, with me concluding the stop by stuffing a wad of dollar bills (brought specifically for that purpose) into the startled attendant's hand, leaping into the Ferrari, and spurting back onto the highway. In this manner we were able to keep most of our stops under five minutes.

It started to rain in western Pennsylvania, and the windshield wipers wouldn't work. Dan drove on for a while, letting the air stream blow the glass clear, but finally cut into a rest area to make repairs. We jumped out into the cold, predawn air and raised the hood. We checked the fuses, the switches, the linkage. Everything seemed in order. With time ticking away, I angrily gave the wipers a jerk, which freed them from their mysterious obstruction and caused them to begin cycling routinely across the windshield. Back on the road, Dan asked, "You have any idea what was wrong?"

"Hell, no, I just jerked on them, and they started working. Typical Italian car. They all have personalities of their own. I suppose this one is reminding us that it's in command and we're just along for the ride."

Again Gurney's miraculous eyes identified another pair of tail lights. This time it was a Pennsylvania Highway Patrol Plymouth, and we slowed accordingly, falling obediently into his wake at 65 miles per hour. It felt like we were walking. We reached Columbus in six and a half hours. We were one hour ahead of the time I'd run with *Moon Trash II* and averaging 81 miles per hour. We presumed we were far ahead of the rest of the entrants. The sun was bringing a bright, warm morning to the Midwest, and we felt great. Purring along interstate 70 in western Ohio, Dan began honking the powerful air horns at the herds of cows and porkers that lined the fences. Not one animal even raised his nose at the sight and sound of the blue Ferrari Daytona whistling past at 100 miles per hour.

Dan had been at the wheel nearly 12 hours when we reached St. Louis. He claimed he felt fine, and I believed him. After years of being around automobiles, one can sense a change in the reactions and movements of a driver—his very cadence with the car alters—when he becomes fatigued. Gurney was in excellent shape. As the traffic got slightly heavier west of St. Louis, we backed off our speed to about 85 miles per hour, keeping a steady eye open for the law. We passed three pimply youths in a GTO, and they tried to race us. Gurney, racer to the end, responded. The Ferrari shot ahead and, witnessing that awesome burst of acceleration, the boys gave up.

Slouching back in his seat, driving with his left hand and nibbling a hunk of Swiss cheese with his right, Dan began to chat. It was our first steady communication since leaving. The deep concentration necessary to drive quickly on the highway required the full attention of us both—Gurney driving and me navigating, computing fuel stops, average speed, etc. (For example, the radio was never turned on the entire trip. Too distracting.) But now the big cat was merely loafing, and we began to talk—inevitably about racing. We discussed the separation of Swede Savage from Gurney's team. A simple cutback in finances was forcing Gurney to campaign a single Indianapolis car next season. It would be for Bobby Unser, an established star. Swede, the junior of the team, was released. It was not something Gurney had done with enthusiasm; he had after all brought Swede into the big-time and had wanted very badly for him, as his protégé, to become a champion. But reality intervened.

Money was tight, and one driver would have to go. That would have to be Swede.

"You told me you were going to explain why you changed your mind and came on this nutball trip," I said, shifting the subject.

Gurney paused for a second, gathering his thoughts. He was inclined to do that, to fall silent, his jaw set, his eyes glazed in a far-away look, while he carefully composed a reply. He was a complicated man—infinitely deeper than his public image as an affable, all-American nice guy. While he was engaging and easy to reach in public, he was essentially a private person. Most experts believed him to be among the very best race drivers who have ever lived. I remember his manager, Max Muhleman, telling me of an incident at the funeral of the great Jim Clark, a man usually mentioned with Tazio Nuvolari and Juan Manuel Fangio as perhaps the best ever. As Dan and Max were leaving the Clark family home near Duns, Scotland, Jim's father escorted them to the door. The old gentleman, still stunned at the loss of his son, took Gurney's hand and said, "You know, Dan, Jim often told me that of all the men he ever raced against, he felt that you were his strongest competitor." At that, Dan Gurney broke into tears. It was the only time Muhleman had ever seen him lose his composure. For the most part, he used his good looks and easy smile as a shield, letting them serve as representatives of the real Dan Gurney. Even at that, there was a powerful aura of decency and integrity about the man that transcended the perpetual smile and the airy chatter that inevitably rose out of his public interviews. Of the elite of world-ranked drivers, probably none is better liked, and less understood, than Dan Gurney.

"This race, it was kind of a turning point for me," he said thoughtfully. "When you first called, it sounded like a great idea, a real lark. Then I began to think about my sponsors, about their reaction to my doing such a thing. I was letting concern for myself get in the way of my real feelings. What in the bleeding hell is that worth? Anyway, somebody had given me an essay by Ayn Rand. I'll show it to you when we get to California. It's called *Moratorium on Brains*, and it deals with the rising power of the federal government and the loss of individual freedoms. Now I'm no great Ayn Rand nut, but this particular thing hit home. There I was, sitting around worrying about my image, when I thought the Cannonball could be an act of protest, a kind of personal adventure that could prove that we still know how to handle ourselves without a cop stationed every 50 feet on the highway. So I said, to hell with it, and I decided to come.

When was the last time Ayn Rand sent somebody on a cross-country motor race? I asked myself. Dan's reaction to her protests about a mindless, shapeless system overwhelming individuals and stifling any desire on behalf of any self-fulfillment made a certain amount of sense. In any case, he hadn't embarked on the enterprise with a simpleton "hunger for thrills" and a "lust for speed," which are rote reasons given by the hacks of the world for driving quickly. I wondered if Miss Rand would consider driving down a superhighway at 100 miles per hour as a healthy objectivist outlet.

I took the wheel for the first time in mid-Missouri. Dan had driven 14 hours and 35 minutes. A long time, to be sure, but with the near-mystical ease with which a Ferrari gobbles distance, the time becomes less amazing. "This thing is a whole new dimension in driving," I said as I accelerated onto the deserted interstate. "If you told some Joe Doak who'd spent his life lumping around in a Pontiac or something that a guy could drive a car at speeds over 80 miles per hour for 14 hours straight in utter safety, he'd probably call you a lying Commie weirdo. And the beautiful part about the whole thing is that if the bureaucrats have their way, thoroughbred machines like this will be illegal, run off the road by herds of dumb Detroit iron."

Racing drivers make notoriously bad passengers. They generally trust no one but themselves, and some refuse to ride with anyone at all. Therefore, I tried my very best to put Gurney at ease. With the Ferrari on my side, the chore was simplified. After an hour of watching me like a mother hen, I saw his body relax and slide back in the form-fitting leather passenger's seat. "You drive well. Very smooth. Most people make me nervous. You don't. I think I'll catch some rest." He slouched in the corner of the car, resting his head against the window. I drove on, as proud as if I'd taken the checkered flag at Indianapolis.

The sun dropped behind a thick bank of clouds in the west, luring us into our first full night on the road. I drove for eight hours before Dan took over. We were maintaining our average speed at 83.5 miles per hour. As we reached the New Mexico border, a nasty thunderstorm lit the sky with orange fireballs and sent sheets of rain pelting against the windshield. It turned to sleet, and thickets of fog lurked in the dips of the highway. But I slept. With a man like Dan Gurney at the wheel, I think I could have rested if we'd been traversing the South Col of Mt. Everest.

We reached Albuquerque in the 24th hour of our trip, convinced that not one of our competitors was within three states of us. As we stopped at Gallup, New Mexico, we spotted several approaching cars with their grillwork smudged with snow. We had just crested the Continental Divide and were heading for the high country of eastern Arizona. If we were to encounter ice, it would be in this dark and desolate stretch. I called the Highway Patrol from a gas station, while the attendant leisurely filled the tank and Gurney sipped a can of hot soup from a vending machine. We were getting cocky, and the urgency of our earlier gas stops had given way to a kind of relaxed elegance reserved for big winners. The phone operator at the Highway Patrol was vague: some snow squalls, some fog, perhaps a little ice, but nothing alarming. With the temperature sitting somewhere in the low 30s, I took the wheel and headed for the mountains, knowing that conditions were perfect for hellish weather.

I might as well have talked to the Highway Patrol in Honolulu. The lights of Gallup still winked in the valley below when the highway became sheathed in a thick layer of slush, punctuated by long stretches of hard ice. First came the fog, then fat lumps of wet snow that flung themselves into our headlights, cutting visibility to zero. The Ferrari was slewing all over the road. It was nearly uncontrollable, and we couldn't understand why our wonderful machine had become so inept in the face of this nasty but hardly unusual squall. Dan figured it out. He recalled that the Kirk White crew had increased the tire pressure to 40 pounds for added safety and efficiency in the high-speed dry stretches. Surely they hadn't anticipated snow. The tires, of course! As we were debating whether or not to stop and cut the pressure to perhaps to 26 pounds—which would mean a double penalty with more time lost when we hit the desert reinflate—a quartet of headlights blazed in my mirrors. A car was overtaking us at a high speed, seemingly navigating the ice without difficulty. It disappeared in a patch of fog, then surged alongside and swept past. It was a cream-colored Cadillac. Gurney and I paid it little attention, still engrossing in strategy talk about what to do with our slipping tires.

"Jesus Christ, wait a minute!" I yelled as Dan was in midsentence. "That Cadillac. That thing had New York plates! That couldn't be the those three guys from Boston!" Or could it? Stunned, even horrified that any other competitor could be that close, we pressed on, trying to narrow the distance between us and the fleeting Sedan DeVille. "If those guys are with us, where are the PRDA and some of the others that left earlier?" Gurney wondered. "In the lead, hell, we may be dead last!" I said bitterly.

The lights of the agricultural inspection station on the New Mexico-Arizona border loomed out of the fog and snow. A car was stopped under the canopy. Its trunk was up. A smiling man with a heavy shock of black hair was standing beside the machine—a cream-colored Cadillac with New York plates—while a uniformed official probed through the luggage.

"Oh, shit, that's Larry Opert," I moaned. "Those are the guys, and they're blowing our doors off!" They squirted away into the night as we stopped for our inspection. Realizing there was precious little room for any dangerous quantities of wormy peaches or infected chickens to be stowed on board the Ferrari, the officer let us pass after a few routine questions. Our cockiness of a few miles back had given way to shocked despair. Our only comfort lay in the knowledge that the Caddy had started about 20 minutes earlier and was, therefore, still behind us on elapsed time. But what about the others? Surely *somebody* was in front of the Caddy. "Us cruising across half the damn country figuring we were hundreds of miles ahead, what a bad joke that was," I mumbled as I rushed through the black, fog-shrouded night. Fortunately, the roads were improving, and while they remained wet, the ice was disappearing. The fog lifted for a minute, and we saw their taillights, perhaps a mile in front. As the road and visibility cleared, we began to gnaw at their advantage, although the Cadillac seemed to be running in the neighborhood of 100 miles per hour on the straight stretches. Mile after mile we traveled, losing them for long periods in the gloom, then catching tantalizing glints of red up ahead. We had them in sight by the time the outskirts of Winslow, Arizona, were breached. They pulled into a gas station. As they leaped out under the bright lit canopy, I gave them a blast of the Ferrari's air horns. They waved wildly as we accelerated past, no doubt figuring we would have to stop soon ourselves. We had chased them for over 100 miles in a frantic period that seemed to have been condensed into minutes. Most of the road between Winslow and Flagstaff, 58 miles away, was deserted, dry interstate, and I kept the Ferrari humming along at a steady 125 miles per hour—a speed that could not be exceeded without overrunning the range of our headlights.

We were fully awake now, vibrating with the idea of the newfound competition. We had not sought it out; in fact, we would have been perfectly contented to putter on toward California at a leisurely pace. But now that the Cadillac was surely thundering down the road behind us, its gas tank topped off and set to run for hours, we readied ourselves to play our trump cards. That meant Dan would take over at Flagstaff, in preparation for a run down our secret shortcut—a pair of moves that might put us back into the lead. My earlier run with *Moon Trash II* had revealed that by taking Arizona Route 89 south to Prescott, then cutting toward the desert and interstate 10, we could trim at least half an hour off the trip. To our knowledge, everyone else would take the conventional old Route 66-interstate 40 network that was slightly shorter but more congested. Admittedly, our route was more dangerous. It involved negotiating the endless switchbacks on the 15-mile stretch of Route 89 through the Prescott National Forest and the murderous plunge down a mountainside south of Yarnell, where the road featured minimal guard rails and 1,000-foot drop-offs.

Our stop for gas in Flagstaff was slow, simply because the pumps of that particular station moved fuel into our tank at a rather slow rate. By the time we got under way again, with Dan driving, the Cadillac had caught up. We immediately passed it after returning to the interstate. Opert and Co. were running the big crock at its maximum, perhaps 115 miles per hour, and it was easy to see how they had not lost any time with their stop. Their tank was smaller, and therefore more quickly filled, and their top speed at night was only a few miles per hour less than ours. They were back in contention.

Gurney was opening gobs of distance on the Caddy as we rushed down the winding, pine-bordered four-lane. It was a lovely stretch of road, made even more beautiful by the thick layer of snow that had fallen on the trees earlier in the night. But the highway surface seemed clear, and Dan was running 125 miles per hour when we sailed onto the bridge that was part of a long, downhill bend to the left. It was covered with a glaze of ice. Suddenly Gurney was jabbering and his hands began a series of blinding twists of the wheel. "This is glare ice! Glare ice! This is BLEEDING GLARE ICE!" he repeated with increasing volume as he slashed at the steering wheel. I had been in the middle of a statement about something (I cannot recall the exact subject), and I remember that I kept on blathering throughout the trip across the bridge, as if my brain had decided that if I did not acknowledge Gurney's alarm, perhaps the ice would go away. Thanks to the talents of Gurney, we traversed the bridge with merely a slight twitch of the Ferrari's tail. Because he so skillfully maintained control of the car, only he will ever know how far beyond the ragged edges we had traveled.

"That's enough of the shit," said Gurney firmly as he slowed down. "Race or no race, we aren't going to wipe ourselves out on ice like that. Man, that was scary, and I don't mind telling you I didn't like it one bit!"

"God, I wonder about the Cadillac. I sure hope those guys get across the stretch all right," I said. We cruised onward, our speed reduced to a modest 70 miles per hour. I was relieved to see the Caddy's lights pop up behind us. They had slowed, indicating they, too, had encountered a few thrills on the bridge.

"That would have been a helluva crash," I mused. "And just think, not a soul within miles to see it. Most of your crashes take place in front of thousands of people. What a switch this would have been." I was talking rather aimlessly, trying to get our minds off the recent adventure. "That crash business. I get so tired of telling people who don't understand motor racing that fans don't go to races to see smashups."

"That's crap," Dan said edgily.

"Huh?"

"That's crap about people not wanting to see crashes. *Of course* they want to see crashes. They want to be where the action is. That's a natural thing. If you were in a rowboat in the middle of the ocean, which would you rather see sail past, the *Queen Mary* or the *Titanic*?"

"I get your point. But I still don't think people actually *like* to see death and destruction," I said.

"I agree. Very few people at races want to see anybody get killed. Wild crashes are all right, but they don't ask for blood. But I'll tell you this: *if* it was going to happen anyway, you'd be surprised how many of them would rather see it than not," said Dan.

"I guess I'm double happy that we didn't crash on that bridge," I said.

"Why?"

"Because if you're right, think of all the folks we'd have deprived of a little healthy entertainment."

A tactical problem was arising. With the Cadillac cruising behind us, it was possible that they would trail after us on our shortcut. The turn to Route 89 was only a few miles ahead at Ash Fork, and we somehow had to get the Caddy out of sight before then. Outrunning them was impossible, considering the treacherous roads. Our only choice was to let them pass, then drop back and make our turn as they sped ahead.

"Hey, slow down and pull over on the shoulder," I told Dan. "Maybe they'll just drive past and we'll let 'em get out of sight before restarting."

Gurney stopped the Ferrari on the roadside. The Cadillac pulled over, too, drawing alongside as it came to a halt. We switched off our engines and sat there in the still, clear mountain night. The three men in the Cadillac looked haggard and hollow-eyed, obviously fatigued from the run.

"How'd you guys like that icy bridge?" Dan asked through his open window.

"Bad shit. We thought we'd had it," said a voice from inside the Caddy.

We chattered for a few minutes about the various adventures we had encountered. They reported that so far they'd been stopped by the police four times. Gurney started the Ferrari's engine, preparing to leave. The Cadillac hesitated, as if to follow us onto the road in the original order. "Go ahead. You guys go first," said Dan casually. "After all, we've got a 20-minute lead on you." Taking the bait, the Cadillac scurried away and rushed down the road. We followed at a discreet distance, letting them get a half-mile ahead. By the time we reached the Route 89 turnoff, they were out of sight.

Thanks to the lower altitude, the road to Prescott was bare, clear of ice or any evidence of precipitation. It was a wide, level stretch of two-lane, virtually deserted, and Gurney ran the entire 51 miles with the speedometer needle glued to 130 miles per hour. Whisking through Prescott and not seeing a soul on its streets, we plunged into the National Forest. Mile after mile of tight mountainside switchbacks whispered underneath us. The masterful timing and discipline of Gurney became apparent with each passing yard. I sat there in admiration, watching him run quickly and easily though the nasty turns, never squealing a tire, never wasting a motion on the steering wheel. Each corner was negotiated with a precision of line that seemed to place the car in perfect position for the next, until we hurried onto the open road again with me wondering why I had thought Prescott National Forest was so difficult in the first place. I had witnessed a virtuoso playing with a fine instrument, and it came to me that this had to be the peak of excellence that every driver must aspire to. Surely all men cannot be Gurneys, nor all cars Ferraris, but such lofty goals still must remain, as opposed to the current egalitarianism that presumed all drivers helpless dolts who must be packaged in mediocre, crash-proof capsules, lest they hurt themselves. The same mentality would determine that because a Van Cliburn appeared only in every few million piano students, all piano lessons must be restricted to the teachings of "Chopsticks."

The nasty cut beyond Yarnell was traveled with similar ease, and suddenly we were on the desert floor. Flat, open road lay between us and Los Angeles. Dawn lit the way, and Gurney upped the pace to 140 miles per hour across the desolation. Not even a stray jackrabbit or a tumbleweed was moving in the morning stillness; only the rounded, bullet-shaped Ferrari shrieking southward toward interstate 10 and possible victory.

He caught us on a back street in Quartzite, Arizona. I'd spotted his car, a mud-brown Dodge Highway Patrol sedan, parked in front of a run-down café at the roadside. The car had been empty, indicating that he'd been having his morning coffee when we'd ripped past, doubtlessly rattling the windows in the little place. I'd told Gurney about the car, then kept my eyes focused on the café, watching for movement. I saw headlights flick on. "He's coming. He's chasing us."

"He'll never catch us," Dan said firmly.

"He's gaining. He must be running 140 miles an hour!" I reported.

We sat there, speeding along in limbo, trying to figure out what to do. There was no sense trying to elude him on the side road. There were no side roads; outrunning him was out of the question. A short distance ahead was the Arizona-California border on the Colorado River. He could easily radio ahead and stop us at the agricultural inspection station. We drove onward, as if in a trance, letting him close the gap.

"We'll turn off in Quartzite and get some gas. Maybe he'll miss us," said Gurney. He sailed onto an off-ramp and scuttled down a back street. Sighting an empty self-service gas station, he braked the Ferrari to a stop. Perhaps our pursuer in the mud-brown Dodge hadn't seen us get off the interstate.

Perhaps he had. In fact, we had barely shut off the Ferrari's engine when the boxy form of the Dodge, its twin gumball roof lights flashing crazily, skidded to a halt in the gravel beside us. A tall patrolman in a starched khaki uniform leaped out. He was wearing a crash helmet. His glands still pulsing from the pursuit, his feathers ruffled in a kind of cock-rooster triumph, he marched over to Gurney and curtly demanded his license and registration. Little more was said as he strode back to his car and removed a pad and pencil. We stood there, the silence broken only by the furry, electronic jabbering from his radio and the hushed background rumble of an occasional passing truck. He obviously recognized Gurney, and for a few minutes hope rose in us that he might issue a stern warning and send us on our way. But he kept on writing. A summons was being issued and a hardness crept across Dan's face.

Ripping the ticket off the pad and handing it to Gurney, the highway patrolman, as if to signal the end of official business, turned to regard the Ferrari for a moment, then asked rather affably, "Just how fast *will* that thing go?"

"C'mon out on the highway, and we'll let you find out," Gurney snapped.

Fortunately, the officer chose to take Dan's crack as an attempt at humor and let us go. Although he had spared us the agony of being dragged off to a justice of the peace, which would have consumed perhaps an hour, the incident had used up at least 10 minutes. "That does it, we've probably lost for sure," I said dejectedly as we pulled back on the interstate. "What really kills me about a deal like that is the whole absurd logic of high-speed pursuit. If we are being unsafe at 120 miles per hour, isn't he at least *doubling* the hazard by driving faster to catch us?"

"It's simple enough," said Gurney. "Those guys are just like you and me—they like to drive fast. Imagine having a license to go flat-out anytime you wanted. Just look at this bleeding highway, for example." Ahead lay a black asphalt expanse of four-lane that stretched to the horizon. It was deserted. "And the speed limit is 65 miles per hour. No wonder people crash out here. They die of boredom."

The ticket issued to Dan Gurney east of Quartzite, Arizona, on November 17, 1971. It cost him $90.

An evil smile spread across Gurney's face. "He was wondering how fast this thing will go. Let's find out." The Ferrari began to gain speed, whisking easily at 150 miles per hour. The car felt smooth and steady. There was not much wind noise, considering the velocity. "There's 170!" said Gurney. The needle pushed its way around the big dial, then stabilized at 172 miles per hour. Gurney laughed. "This son of a bitch *really* runs," he said in amazement. "And it's rock steady." He took his left hand off the wheel, and we powered along toward Los Angeles, the Ferrari rushing through the desert morning at 172 miles per hour.

"You think we ought to turn back and answer the cop's question?" I asked. But our amusement from the 172-miles-per-hour run was only temporary. As we slipped back to a more normal cruising speed, we both decided that the delay from the arrest had ended our chances of winning the Cannonball. "Those other guys have to be miles ahead by now," I grumbled. We stopped for gasoline in Indio, California, where our general discouragement led to more torpor and lost time. Once on the road again, with the end in sight, we managed to perk up, drawing on our final reservoirs of energy. "Listen, at least we ought to try to make the trip in under 36 hours," said Gurney. "If we can do that, we can't shame ourselves too badly."

We were back in it again, running hard. To reach our goal, we had a little over two hours to run about 130 miles—practically all of it over heavily patrolled Los Angeles freeways. "You watch out the back for the Highway Patrol, and I'll run as fast as I can," said Dan. I turned in my seat, scanning the off-ramps and the passing traffic for the familiar black-and-white California Highway Patrol cruisers. Gurney drove through the building traffic with incredible smoothness, seldom braking and never making severe lane changes. We took Riverside Freeway to the Newport, up the Garden Grove to the San Diego. Traffic was heavy, but we still had a chance. We turned off at the Western Avenue exit and bustled through 3 miles of heavy urban congestion, heading for Redondo Beach and the Portofino Inn. The masts and spars of the yachts moored in the Redondo Beach marina appeared, and Dan accelerated the Ferrari the last few yards into the Inn's parking lot. I was out of the car before it stopped moving and sprinting into the lobby, where a pair of mildly shocked bellhops looked up to see an unshaven, grubby form rush up to the desk. The clerk punched our ticket.

Our elapsed time was 35 hours and 54 minutes. What's more, no one else had arrived. We were the first car to finish. Unless *Moon Trash II* or the Bruerton brothers bettered our time, we were the winners. A couple of photographers appeared, a reporter from the Torrance *Daily Breeze* showed up, and a representative of the local Chamber of Commerce brought along the bikini-clad "Miss Redondo Beach" to peck our cheeks for the cameras. Groggy and filthy, we staggered upstairs to a room to shower and shave. Suddenly we felt great. The tiredness drained out of our bones as the impact of what we'd managed became clear. We'd crossed the nation, a matter of nearly 2,900 miles, in less than a day and a half.

Gurney (left) and Yates with the winning Ferrari Daytona, Portofino Inn, November 17, 1971.

With the Pacific Ocean puffing a soft breeze into the balcony window, Dan ran a comb through his hair and turned serious. "You know," he said, "the best thing about this whole deal is the fact that we came the entire bleeding distance without bothering *anybody.* Nobody else even knew we were on the road."

"Except that cop," I mused.

"I don't count him. I'm talking about the average guys out there with their families. We did it all without them having the slightest idea of what was going on. As long as you can do something without endangering anybody or inconveniencing them, how can you say something like the Cannonball Baker is wrong?"

Leaving the question unanswered, we went back to the lobby to find that the PRDA had arrived. As I had expected, they had been forced to make a fuel stop in Albuquerque. They had also engaged in a 200-mile duel with the *Moon Trash II,* running with them from Needles, California, to a point where they had snuck away on a shortcut in Los Angeles. Their time was 36 hours and 47 minutes, and they hadn't been bothered by the police.

Rear view of the Gurney/Yates Ferrari.

Then came the Bruerton brothers' AMX, Little Rock Tankers, and *Moon Trash II*, all of which had encountered minor mechanical problems and tickets that slowed their pace. We received word that the MG had blown its clutch in Columbus, Ohio, and had limped back to New York. As the hours passed, it became obvious that no one was going to beat our time. The Travco team arrived last, over 20 hours late, but relaxed and well fed. For whatever it meant, we had won the Cannonball Baker Sea-to-Shining-Sea Memorial Trophy Dash. The *Los Angeles Times* mentioned the race briefly, noting our time and quoting Dan as testifying that we never exceeded 175 mph. They had no doubt thought he was kidding.

I slept a night on the edge of the Pacific and headed home, alone. Dan was back at work at his race shop, preparing a new Eagle that he was convinced would be the fastest Indianapolis racing car in history. It was the Ferrari and I. Sympatico. I took a southern route, heading for Texas, to avoid the mountain squalls. It was warm and sunny, and the big car was as strong and supple as ever. I felt great. I felt like a winner. I stopped in a music store and bought some eight-track stereo

Randy Waters and Tom Marbut arrived unannounced from Arkansas with their van. They became known to their fellow competitors as the "Little Rock Tankers."

tapes for the car's tape deck. We hadn't used it on the trip, but at a more leisurely pace on the way home, they would provide pleasant company. Country-and-Western seemed appropriate.

I was cruising across New Mexico, with the guys high in the cabs of the giant Kenworth and Peterbilt semitractors tossing friendly waves, when a yellow 4-4-2 Oldsmobile Cutlass appeared in the rearview mirror. It was running fast, coming up on me at an impressive rate. Two guys were on board, and I sensed that they were looking for a race. They drew even, and we ran along for a way nose-to-nose. I looked over to catch eager grins on their faces. I smiled back and slipped the Ferrari from the fifth to fourth gear. We were running a steady 100 miles per hour when the Olds leaped ahead. I let him have a car-length lead before opening the Ferrari's tap. The big cat burst forward, its pipes whooping that lovely siren song, and shot past the startled pair in the Oldsmobile. I glanced over at them to see their faces covered with amazement. Like most of the populace, they had no comprehension of an automobile that would accelerate from 100 miles per hour that quickly. The Ferrari yowled up to 150 miles per hour without effort, leaving the Olds a minuscule speck of yellow in the mirror.

I slowed and turned up the volume on the stereo. Buck Owens and his Buckaroos were singing "I've Got a Tiger by the Tail."

"Yates, you are a silly son of a bitch," I said out loud. And I laughed all the way to Las Cruces.

The event received considerable coverage, including a full-page story in *Autoweek*. The British publication *Motoring News* notified the racing community before the complete story was published in the March 1972 issue of *Car and Driver* with the cover blurb: "Coast to Coasting in 36 Hours." By then it was clear that another Cannonball would be run the following November with the same format. It appeared that dozens of teams were lining up to take a shot at winning the record.

The *Car and Driver* story ended with a summary and results—plus a disclaimer insisted on by the magazine's publisher, Orison B. Curpeir. This only stirred the pot for the next time. Our insane version of a race had outraged and energized the world of automobiles. The story reads as follows:

> While the justification (or lack of it) for the Cannonball Baker will be debated for some time, a number of tangible conclusions were forthcoming regarding routes, types of vehicles, tactics, etc.

While the Ferrari won, it was not driven fastest. The Cadillac's over-the-road average (excluding stops) was faster and *Moon Trash's* was equal to the winner (see following chart). There is little question that the Ferrari won for other reasons, such as excellent mileage—the highest of the eight competitors was 12.2 miles per gallon—combined with a 29-gallon gas tank that provided a range of 300–350 miles. This, coupled with its extraordinary high-performance capabilities in acceleration, braking, comfort, cornering, and cruising speed (plus Gurney), made the difference.

The Ferrari made nine stops for gas, consuming approximately 50 minutes. The PRDA van made one 7-minute stop. The Ferrari consumed 240 gallons of fuel, averaging 80 miles per hour; the PRDA van used 356 gallons while traveling a slightly shorter route averaging about 3 miles per hour less. On the other end of the scale, the Cadillac and *Moon Trash*, both with stock tanks, made 15 and 19 stops, respectively, but were in the thick of competition, other factors like police and mechanical troubles discounted. In sum, the extra weight, lower mileage, poorer handling, and general hazard of massive fuel loads produce strong limitations.

Big car or little car, vans or Ferraris, sedan or sports car, economy car or monster machine—there is no clear-cut solution. When it is remembered that the first five finishers were separated by less than two hours, the difficulty of deciding on the perfect long-distance vehicle came into focus.

The problem of tactics provides a clearer answer. To run flat-out or to cool it, that is the question, and the "cool it" school seems to be the way in any long-distance journey. Speeds in excess of 100 miles per hour, regardless of how safe they might be on modern interstates, simply attract too many lawmen. The Cadillac, with five apprehensions that cost them several hours, is a perfect example of the limitations of this mode of travel. By contrast, the two fastest cars, the Ferrari and the PRDA, collected but one ticket between them and both made the trip at carefully paced, ever-watchful speeds in the 90–100 mph range. (The Ferrari was stopped during the period that rule was violated.) Sustained speed is the key to the Cannonball, and any time lost to the police is a disaster. Therefore a happy medium must be found without attracting attention, around 70 to 80 miles per hour. Sounds simple, what?

Seven of the eight competitors used essentially the same route—the Pennsylvania Turnpike, interstate 70, interstate 40 network running through Columbus, St. Louis, Oklahoma City, Flagstaff, etc. Only the Ferrari took a different route. Rather than run interstate 78 from northern New Jersey to the intersection of the Pennsy Turnpike at Harrisburg, its crew cut northward across New Jersey's Route 46, through Netcong and Hackettstown, to interstate 80 due west across Pennsylvania. From there they cut southwest across Ohio for Akron to Columbus, intersecting with the conventional route. This is a good choice if one leaves in the middle of the night. Otherwise Route 46 is clogged with traffic over much of its two-lane distance. It is unusable during the daylight hours.

The Ferrari also used the Ash Fork cutoff west of Flagstaff, Arizona, heading south on Routes 89, 71 and 60 to reach interstate 10. While good roads, there are several mountainous sections on Route 89 that are extremely dangerous and should not be attempted except by expert drivers in excellent cars.

The Ferrari traveled approximately 35 miles farther than its rivals, but the higher speeds attained over that extra distance helped to win. Yet the perfect route, especially with the constant addition of new interstate highways, is still unknown. (Nearly six hours was lopped off *Moon Trash*'s original record, set last May, primarily because of better route knowledge and the new four-lane sections that were opened this summer. If this trend continues, a 32-hour trip may be possible.)

There has been lengthy discussion of the so-called Iowa, Nebraska, Wyoming, and Utah northern route, then cutting southwest across Nevada to take advantage of the absences of speed limits in that state. However it is 200 miles longer and winter comes early in Wyoming, making the trip in November extremely risky. The southern route, using interstate 81 to Knoxville, Tennessee, then cutting west across the deep south, and Texas, has been studied, but it is again 200 miles farther. But then, if there were bad weather in the central states. . . .

One conclusion is clear, better roads in the west and central the United States permit faster average speeds than in the far west. The slowest running comes in New Mexico and Arizona, mainly because many towns have to be safely traversed. And don't forget, five of the 10 traffic tickets came near the Arizona-California border. It is ironic that here, in the vastness of the West, there is the heaviest concentration of police. Why? Because, given one-on-one situations in the desert, it is easier to make arrests. No competitor was even looked at in the heavy traffic of New York, St. Louis, Oklahoma City or Los Angeles, where the accident probability is highest.

That was the Cannonball Baker Sea-to-Shining-Sea Memorial Trophy Dash. No one who ran, not Gurney, not Adamowicz, not anybody, got a dime for the race, making it some kind of milestone in modern automotive annals.

	Elapsed Time	Average Speed	Miles Run (Approx.)	Fuel Stops	Miles Per Gallon	Stops By Police	Total Time Stopped	Avg. Speed Without Stops (est.)
Ferrari	35:54	80.0	2,876	9	12.2	1	1:05	82.5
PRDA Van	36:47	77.2	2,840	1	8.5	0	0:07	77.5
Cadillac	36:56	77.2	2,855	15	8.9	5	3:15	84.6
Little Rock Tankers	37:45	75.4	2,845	1	9.0	3	2:15*	80.1
AMX	37:48	76.7	2,897	14	11.5	0	1:31	79.8
Moon Trash II	39:03	74.0	2,890	19	8.0	1	4:00*	82.5
Union 76 Travco	57:25	50.8	2,915	12	6.9	0	1:30	52.2
MGB GT	DNF (Slipping clutch, Columbus, Ohio. Ran 560 miles in 7:45, averaged 74 Mph)							

*Lost additional time running extended periods at reduced speed

OFFICIAL RESULTS
1971 Cannonball Sea-to-Shining-Sea Memorial Trophy Dash
November 15–17, 1971

Finish	Car	Driver	Elapsed Time	Avg.mph
1	Ferrari Daytona	Dan Gurney/Brock Yates	35:54	80.8
2	PRDA Chevy Van	Oscar Kovaleski/Tony Adamowicz/Brad Niemcek	36:47	79.5
3	Cadillac Sedan DeVille (drive-away)	Larry Opert/Ron Herisko Nate Pritzker	36:56	79.3
4	Dodge Van	Randy Waters/Tom Marbut/ Becky Poston	37:45	77.4
5	1969 AMX	Ed Bruerton/Tom Bruerton	37:48	77.3
6	Dodge Van (*Moon Trash II*)	Steve Behr/Kim Chapin/ Holly Morin	39:03	74.3
7	Travco Motor Home	Bill Broderick/Phil Pash/ Bob Carey/Pal Parker/ Joe Frasson	57:25	50.6
8	MGB GT	Bob Perlow/Wes Dawn	DNF—Columbus, Ohio	

The following is from Brock Yates' column
in the March 1972 issue of *Car and Driver* magazine

I suppose half the fun of the Cannonball Baker was anticipating the indignant hen-clucking that would arise in its wake. That the expected denouncement of the affair by responsible, clear-headed citizens, properly outraged by the idea of motorized Visigoths ripping over the highways of America, was going to be a by-product of the event that would offer us a rebuttal wherein the more serious motives of the Cannonball might be articulated. That wave of indignation never came. Aside from a pubescent West Coast motorsports writer whining that it was a "crime" and *Sports Illustrated* grumbling that certain aspects of the race were "deplorable," very little flack came our way. In fact, praise arrived from utterly shocking sources. One highly prestigious member of the FIA called Kirk White *twice* to express his enthusiasm for the Cannonball Baker concept. Both Radio Free Europe and the Voice of America gave the race coverage in an effort, one producer told me, to inform the world that far from being a police state, America was still the scene of enterprising individual adventure.

Nevertheless, I think the Cannonball Baker does demand justification, mainly because we feel it symbolizes something far deeper than a simple-minded dash from coast to coast. To begin with, it was not a flat-out race. Surely the idea of running across this nation in under 36 hours conjures up visions of hammering along for hours on end at 150 mph. Dan Gurney's whimsical, rather ironic statement to the press that "we never exceeded 175 mph" only reinforced that idea. We did in fact briefly run the Ferrari to an indicated 172 mph on an empty stretch of interstate 10 in California, merely to determine the limits of the machine, but a majority of the trip was run at 90-95 mph—a mere saunter for the Ferrari. The quickness of the journey was hardly attributable to outright speed, but rather to good routes, rapid stops and assiduously staying clear of traffic. When Dan and I got to the Portofino, we agreed that the part of the Cannonball about which we were proudest was the fact that we had bothered no one—we hadn't jeopardized the safety of anyone, including ourselves. We had driven very fast, but we had driven cleanly, efficiently and safely.

What exactly was the Cannonball Baker trying to prove? In a purely simplistic sense, it was an adventure, a challenge to be met. On a more serious level, it was a gesture. New York City to Los Angeles is the most storied overland route in the United States ("Get Your Kicks on Route

66") and it seemed worthwhile to find out just how fast the trip could be made. But what about the cops? This question probably arose more often than any other in relation to the event. OK, what *about* the cops? This, if anything, was a central intent of the Cannonball: to prove the hypocrisy and futility of the speed laws in the nation today. Hopefully we added some testimony to the case that they are farcically unworkable; that they are designed to catch the wrong people and not only have no positive effect on traffic safety but may be a contributory factor to accidents, as indicated during the period of merciless enforcement in Connecticut (which has recently been quietly suspended).

Gurney and I were arrested once. We passed a highway patrolman who was having a dawn cup of coffee in a roadside café. He never saw the Ferrari, but the rush of sound triggered his pursuit. He overtook us when we stopped for gas—having run his Dodge patrol car up to 140 mph in order to make the arrest. Now then, why did he arrest us? Standard answer: We broke the law. Why are there speed laws? Standard answer: To promote safety. If we were being unsafe at 120 miles per hour—in a machine that is so eminently safe that I cannot express it to anyone who has not driven a Ferrari Daytona, then what about the patrolman careening along at 140 mph, in his gussied-up four-door? Was he not compounding the hazard, *if* we accept the argument that our speed was automatically unsafe?

But is this not elitism at its worst? Here we are seeking justification for one of the world's greatest drivers running probably the best passenger car ever built at 120 mph on a public road. But not everyone is Dan Gurney behind the wheel of a Ferrari Daytona, the rebuttal goes. Of course that is true, but should we not aspire to those heights of excellence, both in car and driver, rather than settling back to accept a level of mediocrity whereby everyone is assumed to be incompetent? This is the basic objection that I have to the mentality of the so-called "safety" crusade of today. We are being led to standardize at a shockingly mundane level—a level that will ultimately drive the Dan Gurneys and the Ferrari Daytonas off the road. This is akin to eliminating French cuisine because it is too "rich" for the masses, or suspending basic scientific research because it doesn't have any immediate, practical applications. If we do not seek perfection in any given field, regardless of cost or risk, we will inevitably be cursed with the ordinary. Although I risk damnation by every liberated thinker to so state, all men are not created equal, and I resent the egalitarian balderdash that modern culture must somehow grovel toward the lowest common denominator to attain stability.

We are inclined to blame the government ("they") and its sleazy politicos and faceless civil servants. But we are the government. "We" are "they." In this sense, to quaver at the idea of seeking the outer limits of accomplishment—even in so minuscule an enterprise as driving coast to coast in the shortest possible time—because "they" might disapprove, is a hopeless cop-out. Gandhi once said, "It is a superstition and an ungodly thing to believe that an act of the majority binds a minority."

I believe sincerely in the vast capabilities of individual men, especially when they are challenged. But these instincts for challenge can easily be blanketed in an over-protective environment, where the comforts of the status-quo overwhelm any urges for change. We are becoming a nation of spectators, content to face our risks vicariously, watching other men bashing heads on a football field or pumping bullets at each other on that haunted fish-bowl known as television. DeGaulle, shortly before his death, looked scornfully at those around him and grumbled that he was doomed to die in "an age of midgets."

To imply that the Cannonball Baker in any way advanced the human spirit would be fatuous in the extreme, but its symbolism remains. Its participants were willing to embark on an adventure, risking formal and informal censure, in order to reach a goal, no matter how limited. In a broader sense, others—Gurney and myself included—were eager to make a point about individual options and enterprise, coupled with striking a blow for automotive excellence. Is it so foolish to dream of a time when all good men, driving graceful, efficient machines like the Ferrari (only costing perhaps a fifth as much) can drive between New York and Los Angeles in 36 hours legally and safely? We are not advocating highway anarchy, only highway good sense and intelligence and a natural state that rewards skill and intelligence and punishes blunders. Until that day arrives, we are lawbreakers. But before we are condemned, remember the warning of Louis Brandeis, who seemed to be talking about our highways when he said, "If we desire respect for the law, we must first make the law respectable."

Let Nader and his ilk maunder inside their air bags. The question arising from the Cannonball Baker and other "deplorable crimes" is not whether we are willing to drive for speed, but whether we are willing to drive for excellence.

The following letters appeared in the
June 1972 issue of *Car and Driver* magazine

I have to say that Yates' piece and his accompanying column on the Cannonball Baker Sea-to-Shining-Sea Memorial Trophy Dash in the March issue of *C/D* was great. He captured the true essence of one of the great motorsports events of our time. In years to come, when others are rehashing their memories of great moments in motorsports history, I will have my recollections of the Cannonball Baker: a motor home chugging up a steep grade, a lasagna-stained rug, and the incredible Cadillac.

> Phil Pash
> *Chicago Today*
> Chicago, Ill.

Yates' column on the Cannonball Baker should be reprinted as an open letter in newspapers across the land. He has shown that all men are not created equal, the only things equal are their rights.

> Mike Kenyon
> Juppa, Md.

By Yates' participation in, and coverage of the Cannonball Baker, he has assumed heights few others will ever see. As a blow struck for free men everywhere, it was inspiring. As a race, it must have been fun as hell. And as a towering question as to the validity of present laws and the government's moronic preoccupation with the passive protection of all its little sheep, it was downright superb.

> Lawrence Guthrie
> South Norwalk, Conn.

One way to try to reduce the response an editorial might normally generate is to put your potential critics in the class of "indignant hen-cluckers" before they can put pen to paper. It's just not possible to ignore such a stupendous compilation of naiveté and plain tripe as you spread before your readers. Every block-headed, lead-footed, ego-crazed moron with four wheels available to him is now preparing to show Yates that he can beat his time. How many will die trying? How many innocent non-participants will be killed or maimed? Your asinine effort to "prove the hypocrisy and futility of the speed laws" will give great encouragement to the kids who are as determined to demonstrate this fact to anyone in authority now as they have been for the past fifty years.

Donald Sondel

Oakland, Cal.

Those 50-year-olds will do it to you.—Ed.

My husband and I both hold valid SCCA National Competition Licenses. We have maintained for a long time that a competent driver, in a good handling and braking car, is safer at 100 mph than an ill-handling, ill-braking hulk with a petrified driver at 50.

Dee Garfinkle

Gettysburg, Pa.

Admittedly, Yates and Gurney are less of a threat to society cruising along at 120 mph in their Ferrari Daytona, than say, Joe Bloe in his GTO Pontiac at the same speed, trying to impress the girl around his neck. The next problem is how to differentiate between Dan Gurney and Joe Bloe.

Gene Cote

Providence R.I.

Ask the girl.—Ed

Perhaps the real problem is not trying to justify race drivers, such as Gurney and Yates, driving a Ferrari 120 mph on public roads. There are only a few real race drivers around, and even fewer Ferraris. Perhaps the greater danger is produced by practically every virile male thinking that he is among the top 10 percent in driving skill, and that his car is among those capable of safe, high speed operation.

James Michaels

Durham, N.C.

No law on the books can convince my 28-year-old mind that I am a danger when doing 90 on the freeway in my Porsche 911, when Mrs. Broadbottom, aged 50 plus, doing 70 mph in her five-year-old station wagon, is within the law's blessing.

Paul Donkin

Lebanon, Ore.

Racing across the country on public roads is reprehensible enough in its own right without publicizing it. Congratulations on confirming what every insurance company and legislator has already suspected—that every automobile enthusiast is an overgrown adolescent who views every strip of asphalt as a personal race track. With friends like Yates, the sport deserves enemies.

    Louis Ryan
    Charlottesville, Va.
    And you're volunteering?—Ed.

The Cannonball Baker is the editorial coup of the century. It is the realization of the secret dream of anyone who ever drove a good car on an empty interstate.

    Richard Stewart
    Costa Mesa, Cal.

Yates is a righteous dude. The whole concept of the Cannonball Baker—the implications, results, and conclusions—was great. It is about time somebody *did* something.

    Bill Barnes
    Carrollton, Ga.
    Righteousness, like somebody almost once said, had very little to do with it. —Ed.

Having put his money and his license where his mouth is, I offer Yates my gratitude for having expressed the philosophy of a lot of us. He has done it far more dramatically and eloquently than anyone of us could have done singularly.

    Bruce Fisher
    Wichita Falls, Texas

I hope Yates and the rest of the drivers who took part in the Cannonball Baker will help to open a few eyes in Washington. This little race has restored my faith in the true American spirit of adventure.

    Rusty Sinclair
    Tulsa, Okla.

This venture showed that there is still some spirit of adventure left in America. What surprised me, however, was that the Ferrari, by far the wildest looking contestant, got only one ticket, while the normal looking Cadillac got five.

    Eric Seaberg
    Severna Park, Md.

How does Yates justify the ethics of the Opert/Pritzker/Herisko team which promised the owner of the Cadillac that it would be driven sedately across the country at 70, and then proceeded to dash across at speeds up to 110?

T. Rodman Wood
Alhambra, Cal.

I feel there is an unfortunate blemish on the Cannonball, and I am hopeful that the owner of the Cadillac will be able to make a pretty good case against Opert and Herisko using your reportage and the pattern of tickets on record. On receipt of the Cadillac, a verbal contract was entered—a contract grossly breached if your story is authentic.

James Selvidge
Seattle, Wash.

If I were the "stuffy New York businessman" whose Cadillac had been flogged across the country instead of trundled sedately as agreed, I'd be shopping around to let a contract on the clowns who drove it.

Hugh Birnbaum
New York, N.Y.

Any cop must have a lot of gall to stop a good American like Dan Gurney for doing a measly 100 mph in a Ferrari, even if Yates is with him. But a trio of long-haired Yankee lawyers in a practically stolen Cadillac is something else. I'd stop them for doing 60 and shake them down for dope.

David Bright
Winterport, Maine
Bet you'd be sure you found some, too. —Ed.

As a loyal supporter of the Polish Racing Drivers of America, I can't help but wonder if the results would have been different if *all* the road signs hadn't been in English.

Frank Laskouski
Brooklyn, N.Y.

I would just like Yates to know that I have cut out his March editorial and framed it on my wall . . . impeccably stated, m'boy.

Laura Maddock
Hemet, Cal.

Yates' continuous campaign against the futility of speed laws has made me a follower of his for some time. It's most encouraging to know that someone who knows what it's all about feels so strongly about this unjust situation.

Jim Adair
Seattle, Wash.

The most important thing done is the blow struck for individualism. It's a pleasant change to see those few people who are not afraid of the stares and whispers of the masses go out and do something that requires a little creativity and imagination.

James Brooks
Wilkesboro, N.C.

I have just canceled my subscription to your magazine because of Brock Yates' article on the Cannonball Baker. I'll renew my subscription when Yates is no longer affiliated with your publication. How can Yates justify his statement that: "We are willing to drive for excellence." Both he and Gurney are irresponsible, to say the least. The sad part of their ego trip is that they were not both arrested before they started.

Frank Moran
Oswego, N.Y.

Brock Yates . . . *C/D*'s answer to Abby Hoffman. How can he profess to crusade for "highway good sense" and then travel at 172 mph on California I-10?

James Hanson
Suitland, Md.

Does that mean we should change our name to Steal This Car? —Ed.

In Yates' Cannonball Baker article, there is a reference to the existence of a Brock Jr. Has the younger Mr. Yates shown any signs that it might be hereditary?

Harold Gislason
Spring Lake, Mich.

We're watching him closely. —Ed.

Great story. Cannonball Baker himself would have gotten a big bang out of it. It does raise a question, however. Mr. Baker once told me that when a manufacturer faced financial ruin and was about to fold, they called him in to make a transcontinental run for publicity purposes. Generally, a record-breaking trip helped, but only temporarily. As Mr. Baker put it, "It was usually the kiss of death." Would you say Ferrari and Cadillac are headed for bankruptcy?

Ed Macfarlane
Manlius, N.Y.
No, but those guys driving the Cadillac took a long step toward it.
—Ed.

Peter Lyons
AUTOSPORT REPORTS ON THE 1971 RACE

Dan Gurney, who was supposed to have retired last year, is still the fastest driver in the United States, writes Pete Lyons from America. He proved it last week when he won the first nonannual Sea to Shining Sea Memorial Trophy Dash from New York to Los Angeles. His driver was journalist Brock Yates, who very fittingly was the father of the event. Their time, which is a record, was 35 hours, 54 minutes. The distance is 2,950 miles, so their average speed, inclusive of eight refueling stops, works out to just over 82 miles per hour. As the highest level speed limit anywhere along their route does not exceed 75 mph, the actual cruising speeds used are shrouded in secrecy. Gurney did say, "We never exceeded 175." What car did they use? Kirk White lent them a Ferrari 365 GTB Daytona, which Paddy McNally tells us will do 174. . . . They drew attention from police just once, at dawn Tuesday in Arizona.

Coming in second, just 53 minutes later, was a Chevrolet van entered by the Polish Racing Drivers of America and driven by Tony Adamowicz, Oscar Kovaleski, and Brad Niemcek. Third by a mere 10 minutes was a Cadillac limousine not in any way owned or entered by its three drivers who are lawyers from Boston. A total of eight vehicles participated, leaving separately in no formal order from a parking garage in Manhattan in the minutes after midnight, Monday morning, November 15. The finish was at the lobby of the Portofino Inn, Redondo Beach. The other five entries: Yates' own Chrysler van, "*Moon Trash II*," driven by journalists Kim Chapin and Steve Behr, with a young lady named Holly along to keep an eye in the mirrors while the off-duty driver slept, delayed by chunking tire trouble; another car from Arkansas, coming in fourth, also with a two-plus-one crew; an American Motors AMX, which started with 91,000 miles showing on the clock and had not checked in at the finish by our press time; an MG TC, which retired with clutch trouble in Columbus, Ohio; and a 27-foot Dodge motor home, which arrived just a day later than the winners.

The preparation of the Daytona consisted of inflating the Michelins to 40 psi and stowing some ham-on-rye sandwiches, chewable vitamin tablets, and Gatorade. There was no mechanical trouble of any kind throughout the run, during which the car drank fuel at the rate of 12.2 miles per gallon (15.25 Imperial). Gurney himself did have some troubles as the Californian was not psychologically prepared for a blizzard encountered at 8,000 feet altitude in northern Arizona. At very high speed they ran on to a bridge that had frozen over with sheet ice; Yates says that had it not been Dan at the wheel they would never have made it through. "He made a bunch of lightning-fast minute corrections and the car never got more than about 15 degrees out of line."

The PRDA approached the race with a good deal more preparation. To make the distance nonstop they filled the van with five 55 gallon steel drums elaborately connected by the multiple fuel pump system, and then a bunk was stretched across the top. The mechanical troubles began a mere eight blocks from the start when the transmission jammed in second gear; that was fixed with a strategic blow on the linkage with a "Polish wrench" but the delay let two competitors by. Later a transfer pump backed up, so they had to stop for gas after all. As the trio were hurtling across Indiana, Niemcek was on the phone to a local radio station and forgot to help the driver, Adamowicz, with the Indianapolis by-pass, and they lost 25 minutes with a wrong turn. Kovaleski was asleep at the time, but he knows exactly what happened: "Tony got to Indy and immediately started turning left. It took us half an hour to stop him!" They were not molested by the police at all.

Yates has been planning this race for well over a year. After a long career on both highway and race track he has come to feel that "Speed limits are a farce and an abomination. There is getting to be too much order imposed on people's lives. Our individual rights are being closed within ever-tightening circles. Everything is going toward eliminating our aspirations."

We wanted to prove we can aspire to these things. That Ferrari is a dynamic car. At 100 miles per hour it feels so smooth and stable and so good that it's a disappointment to go any slower. At high speeds it's just incredible. We were holding an indicated 172 with just one finger on the wheel. What we are most proud of, Dan and I, is that at no point did we once scare each other, nor did we once scare anyone else. We were exceedingly respectful of the rights of others, but at the same time we exercised our own rights fully. The police? That's the first thing everybody asks. We regarded the police as just another natural hazard or factor, like weather or gas mileage.

We feel that by this run we have proved the capabilities of the existing road systems in this country. There are some sections that need improvement, but basically we can stop building more roads now and concentrate on using them better. We can stop, now, covering the earth with concrete and go on to something else.

Autosport is a prominent English weekly that covers automobile racing around the world. The story was submitted by well-known American correspondent Pete Lyons.

Dan Gurney
1971

I was a fan of Cannon Ball Baker long before Brock contacted me with the offer to do the race. I used to fantasize about the days when you could venture off and do things the way Cannon Ball did. I remember a story about him being involved in a motorcycle relay race where riders were exchanged at certain spots but continued on with the same motorcycle. In a town out west somewhere, one rider was waiting on the appointed street corner for the change all dressed up in leather, helmets, goggles, scarf, and gloves. The local sheriff spotting him, did not believe him when told the reasons for his waiting there and just threw him in jail as some sort of weirdo.

When Brock asked me to do this race with him, I was not so afraid of being thrown in jail (though the thought occurred to me!) as I had reservations about what kind of message were we signaling to the regular drivers on the road. How could this be done in a responsible way, adhering to the traffic laws, not frightening someone else into trouble and winning the contest at the same time? I had retired from driving only a few months before and had a new four-month-old son, and was trying to establish my business. I did not need this! But the temptation was there and I could not quite get it out of my mind. I thought of the time when Cannon Ball was in his prime. The roads and the cars were quite a bit slower than today. There was less traffic, more freedom all around, the tires were not very good, etc. I thought of my driving experience on regular European roads where they hardly had any speed limits at that time and tolerant police. There you could really concentrate on driving well and using good judgment in the process. Paris-Peking, New York-Los Angeles? I was pondering all this and came to the reluctant conclusion that I should not do it. If I got involved in a bad situation, it might put another black mark on racing.

And then fate intervened. My wife, Evi, was called to Germany, taking our baby boy with her, to be with her dad, who had been diagnosed with a virulent form of cancer and had only a short time to live. Sitting at her dad's bedside she told him about the planned Cannonball cross-country race. He encouraged her to tell me that he thought that was a splendid idea, that life is short. Carpe diem! Well it took only a phone call from overseas and I was on a plane to New York, determined that I was NOT going to RACE and would not drive any faster than was prudent under the existing conditions. I was going to be responsible and courteous at all times and concentrate on driving in a stealthy fashion. The latter, of course, was a little tough to do in a midnight blue Ferrari Daytona.

I arrived in New York just in time for a two-hour nap before the start at 11:30 P.M. at the Red Ball Garage in downtown Manhattan. I hardly met the other participants and knew nothing of their serious plans and hilarious schemes to get across the country. When Brock and I left we did not really know what pace would be required to win this contest, so for a long time we went right at the speed limit. My own "human radar" was certainly turned on and tuned up to full sensitivity. There were no race regulations to the best route, but Brock had worked it out beforehand and was busy reading maps with a small flashlight giving me directions. We were heading across Jersey on to Pennsylvania. I fondly remembered a story my Dad told me long ago about driving on the Pennsylvania Turnpike in 1940. He was passing a State Patrol car going about 85 miles per hour. The troopers on board just waved hello, as there were no speed limits at this time. Meanwhile Brock was providing both of us with nuts and cookies, potato chips and water. My human radar started to get more finely tuned and I started to pick up the pace gradually. We were approaching Indianapolis. It was exciting and scary. Then we hit a violent rainstorm for about 300 miles! Through St. Louis and on and on. I drove the first 18 hours and then Brock took over. He did an excellent job! Neither one of us got tired. The constant state of full alert for police speed traps and other forms of traffic control had an intensity that kept us very much on edge. Our top speed was probably in the 95 to 110 mph range and was dictated by our desire to remain stealthy. We had to make constant judgment calls as to how to proceed. Go too fast—go to jail! Go too slow—lose the Cannonball! Our scariest moment came when we hit a piece of black ice in Arizona. I saved it, but it was close. We had our feared encounter with the police finally.

Around 6:15 A.M. we were approaching the California border, cruising at about 110 miles per hour when an officer spotted us. He was just stepping off the porch of a ranch style restaurant about 100 yards from the highway and immediately jumped in his Dodge highway patrol car. Brock yelled, "He is coming after us!" and I thought, OK let's not panic, I'll take it up about 130 to 135 miles per hour, and I don't think his Dodge will go that fast. There was another problem: We needed fuel and the next town was 15 miles down the road. We would have to stop, because unlike some of our competitors, we did not have an extra fuel tank in the car. Brock was looking back and said, "I don't think we are getting away from him—he may even be gaining a little." The Ferrari was not straining at all, still loping along, but I was unsure of the tires' ability to withstand sustained high speed. As luck would have it, the gas station had automatic gas pumps that served you without help by accepting dollar bills in a slot. I just got the nozzle into the tank, and here came the Dodge with a very red-faced officer behind the wheel. I was at a loss for words, as was my eloquent writer-codriver. I kept pumping gas and the not too friendly officer started writing a ticket. I had the sinking feeling that our race effort was now in serious trouble, especially if he were to take us to see a judge, as is often the case. After I had signed the ticket, the officer showed the first sign of being a little bit more friendly. He finally asked how fast our car would go. Well, I was not in the mood for conversation at this time. I saw our possible victory disappear in the waves of the Pacific Ocean, and wanted desperately to get going. I felt my anger rising about our failed effort and naturally toward this officer. "It goes a lot faster than the thing you are driving." (Such mature behavior on my part!) I do not recall his reaction; I may have blocked it out. But I do know that in subsequent years our AAR race team trucks were sometimes subject to harassment by the authorities when they came through Arizona. . . . The officer's question of how fast our car would really go was ringing in my ears once we hit the open road again and Brock and I decided to find out. We took her up to 172 miles per hour without a problem.

We were the first to punch the time clock at the Portofino Inn in Manhattan Beach, California, where we received a great welcome. We had crossed the country in 35 hours, 54 minutes, which was the fastest time by a very narrow margin and made us the winner of the first Cannonball cross country race. Kirk White, owner of the Ferrari Daytona offered me the car at a price of $15,000—I could not afford it! Now 30 years later, the car is a priceless vintage piece in Bruce McCaw's car collection.

At the time Brock and I and the other participants had no idea that the Cannonball adventure would spawn countless caper movies and fire up the imagination of enthusiasts everywhere in the world. I knew only a few years after our win that this whole adventure resonated big time with young and old. In kindergarten my kids were asked whether their Dad had "really run the Cannonball." Spa? LeMans? Indy? Never heard of them! *The things one becomes famous for!*

Dan Gurney needs no introduction.

Brad Niemcek

PRDA VAN

1971

The concept was simple: We would not stop for ANY reason, even to check the oil. So, among the preparations we made was turning the tappet covers around on the van's small-block Chevy engine so that the dipstick was accessible from inside the van with the engine turned off on a long downhill grade. For some reason, the reversal caused a build-up of pressure under the tappet covers and, before we got very far into Pennsylvania, the gods sought relief. With a mighty "pop!" the rubber stopper on right tappet cover blew off and the van was filled with smoke. After a moment of panic, we determined that everything else was working OK, so we removed the engine shroud, found the stopper and replaced it. Whereupon, it blew out again a number of times. Finally, from our extensive cache of stuff, we grabbed some heater hose, taped the hose in place of the stopper and ran it out the passenger side wing window. Result: no more eruptions.

Swirling currents of a portable toilet:

I suspect there's no artful way of describing the use of an inexpensive portable toilet in a vehicle at speed. But, this is a Brock Yates book, so who's worried about being artful? The toilet (a camping model acquired from Sears) resembled the kind of "potty" used with toilet-trainers, except this one had the kind of nasty, blue chemicals in it that you see in toilets at America's finer race tracks. The unique feature of this toilet was the way the van's motion made the blue liquid swirl in a circular motion. Can you imaging "holding it" for 36 hours? Well, that's what both Tony and Oscar did, after one look at our portable toilet. I could never pull that off, so I ended the trip with a classic case of "blue butt."

Near-merger with a Jersey Transit commuter bus: The decision was to have me, the lone native New Yorker, take the first shift behind the wheel. I would have the best chance, according to theory, of negotiating our 1,800-pound load of gasoline out of Manhattan without incident. Alas, such an "incident" occurred barely 15 minutes into the event. As we approached the Lincoln Tunnel, which features the gradual merging, in stages, of about 67 lanes of traffic into just two, we nearly "merged" with a New Jersey Transit commuter bus. For some reason, the driver was not impressed with our van. I applied the brakes forcefully, and we avoided actual physical contact, but just barely. "Damn it, Niemcek, you're going to get us killed!" exclaimed Adamowicz. Obviously, he was a bit prone to hyperbole.

LeMans Rear-End, Courtesy of John Greenwood

It's inconceivable that a Chevy van could actually go 128 miles per hour. And we can't prove that it actually did. But, on a multimile downhill slope in San Bernardino County, we got going really fast. We calculated our speed from an rpm/mph chart that we made and taped to the dashboard. I don't remember who produced the chart, or how he did it. But, we produced it for use in lieu of a speedometer, for those rare moments we were worried about staying within the law. The secret to our speed was our rear-end gearing. Danny Zack, our sponsor at Brigg's Chevrolet in South Amboy, New Jersey, loved being involved with racers. The most notorious among these, excluding the PRDA, was a Funny Car driver by the name of Jungle Jim Lieberman. (He wore a mink-covered helmet in competition.) But the secret to our over-the-road speed in the van was not Lieberman, but another racer Zack supported named John Greenwood. Greenwood had taken a two-car Corvette team to LeMans that year and had, Danny Zack learned, some really nifty rear-end gears for the 2.3-mile Mulsanne straight. A Corvette with that rear-end was allegedly capable of close to 200 miles per hour. We had a set of those gears in our van.

Brad Niemcek is a highly regarded public relations expert with broad experience in motorsports

Kirk F. White
FERRARI DAYTONA
1971

In the spring of 1970, John Delamater called me from his home in Carmel, Indiana. John was one of the founding members of the Ferrari Club of America, incredibly knowledgeable about all types of automobiles and the most gifted salesman I ever knew. He called about an incomplete chassis and engine of a 1920s Supercharged Alfa Romeo 6C1500 in near-derelict condition. In the early 1970s little or no historic importance was attached to such nonsense. We had failed to raise a bid greater than $6,000 for a splendid 6C1750 Supercharged Roadster in our spring auction. John did it again and made this substantially incomplete heap sound irresistible. I paid him the pricey sum of $2,500 for it.

When it arrived, the Alfa was dismissed to a dark corner of the garage and I began to rack my brain as to who might want this somewhat sorry hunk of history.

In those days, I traveled at least once a week from our Philadelphia base to the sports car haunts of New York and lower Connecticut, including Luigi Chinetti's Ferrari distribution in Greenwich, Connecticut, where he also housed his extraordinary collection of early racing Alfa Romeos and Ferraris.

One bright Tuesday morning I arrived at Chinetti's with the best photographs I could take of the Alfa. After enduring the usual ritual of actually gaining an interview with him, I told him I had a treasure beyond words for him. He stared at me with that marvelously belligerent look he had, glanced down and took the photographs from me. He seemed to study them carefully, then slipped them into his pocket and in turning away dismissed me. "Go and have lunch . . . see me this afternoon," he said. I knew what was coming: he would offer to trade all of his remaining Lancia Aprilla doors and bumpers or some such nonsense for the Alfa.

I treated myself to a delicious lunch at one of Greenwich's waterfront restaurants and returned for whatever proposal he might have. "I shall trade you a new Ferrari 365 GTB/4 for this" said Luigi, holding the photograph in his hand. I was thunderstruck! Desperately I tried to feign deep consideration for the windfall. Finally I resignedly accepted his proposal.

Delivery was arranged for LeMans in June. We would bring the car home with the Penske/White 512 after the 24-hour race. Ferrari Number 14271 arrived in a sand beige metallic color with black interior. This color would never do, as we were in the midst of the 512 program and everything we owned had to be Sunoco blue. The Ferrari color was changed in less than a week and Penske's legendary pin striper, Larry Schoppett, did his magic in Sunoco yellow.

It was a splendid Ferrari and I immediately pressed it into service as my personal "driver" (demonstrating cleverly how youth and business acumen do not necessarily go hand in hand). Tom Conte worked his magic on the Webers and we recalibrated the advance curves on the distributors. Many a night after dinner with Tiny Gould, in Wilkes-Barre, Pennsylvania, I would boom down the Northeast extension of the Pennsylvania Turnpike at enormous velocities, usually smoking a Punch cigar with a small container of Drambuie on the console. Truly the very essence of debauchery . . . what a great time.

Brock Yates had been a good friend to our little organization almost since we opened in the spring of 1968. Early on he purchased an outstanding Ferrari 250 GT Lusso Berlinetta from us, which he used enthusiastically. We became good friends and he helped us immeasurably with Kirk F. White Motorcars, etc.

In early 1971 he called to relate this marvelous, but somewhat harebrained scheme of running a wide open, hunkered down, pegged pedal dash from New York to California. It will be the "Cannonball Baker Sea-to-Shining-Sea Memorial Trophy Dash," he said. What a grand idea with every ounce of it flying in the face of the law . . . and that, of course, was the reason it was hugely appealing.

He further mentioned, just in passing, that Robert Redford had apparently expressed an interest in codriving with him. If this was the case, could I provide an appropriate vehicle? Of course, I said. Take my Ferrari Daytona. Maybe I could even meet Robert Redford.

The winter passed into spring and more than a few enthusiasts allowed the cold light of day to cloud their thinking, including Mr. Redford, who may have seen himself cooling his heels in a small Texas jail.

Brock stayed hammer down on the idea, however, and ran a single-car event as a reconnaissance mission with his son in April 1971.

In the course of his enthusiasm for his totally bizarre, yet marvelous event, he mentioned it to Dan Gurney, who initially was quite excited about it. Once again however, rational thinking got in the way, and Dan felt his current sponsors, etc., may not be too keen on this type of adventure.

In keeping touch with Brock throughout the summer, I could feel his absolute determination to launch this event, and he would occasionally mention other potential codrivers.

Two days before the start of the race, Dan Gurney called Brock. It seems Gurney had decided that driving flat out from one end of the country to the other was "the American thing to do."

My phone rang at 11:30 P.M. that night. The Daytona was in the driveway, and we said we would have the car at the Red Ball Garage in New York the next evening for the start.

The next day we applied a few sponsor graphics around the car. (God forbid we should have asked them for some actual money!) We filled the car with gas, and checked the oil and tires. I told one of our drivers to have the car at the Red Ball by 6:00 P.M.

You know the rest of the story! Kirk F. White is a well-known dealer in exotic cars and gas-powered model race cars. In 1971 he ran a dealership for collectible cars in Philadelphia and was associated with Roger Penske in several motorsports campaigns.

The Travco Motor Home
1971

Is it practical? No. Is it profitable? No. Is it convenient? No. Will everyone think we're crazy? Yes. Then let's do it! This method of rationalization is typical of folks involved, one way or another, with auto racing. In no other segment of society is there a group with such a zest for living, that finds each of life's experiences an exciting adventure, and is so quick to find the levity in a given situation. Combining all of these was a recent event titled: "The Cannonball Baker Sea-to-Shining-Sea Memorial Trophy Dash."

Yates had decided to see if he could promote a timed transcontinental crossing with a number of entries, with verified starting and finishing times. He set a starting date of Monday, November 15, and put out the word. The rules? Practically none. Use any type of vehicle you wish, with any number of drivers (except that teams must be on board start to finish), choose your own route, and if you get a ticket the time lost is your own penalty. There was a gentleman's agreement that no duplicate vehicles would be "salted" at the end of the run and no one would piggyback their vehicles across via rail or air; also, you could start anytime from 12:01 A.M. to 11:59 P.M. on November 15.

A certain ex-president of a certain giant auto manufacturer was to provide a brand-spanking-new motor home from his present association. The rig's crew consisted of Bill Broderick, representing Union 76 gasoline; Phil Pash from the sports department of the newspaper *Chicago Today*; Pal Parker, a motorsport photographer from North Carolina; Joe Frasson, a hot NASCAR driver; and journalist Bob Carey.

Seven days before the starting time, the ex-president backed out when another department of his company got in the act and pooh-poohed the idea. Enterprising Bill Broderick got on the horn, and in a matter of minutes had the situation shipshape again. We now had a 1966 27-foot Travco motor home, provided by Lou Klug and sponsored by Lou's own Cincinnati-based Econo-Car Rental firm. Only one problem—Lou had just bought the used motor home and wasn't sure it would run, at least, not across 3,000 miles of desert, mountains, and prairie . . . through rain, sleet, fog, and snow. So, his crew went on a crash program. They tuned it, changed the oil, replaced the rear end, cleaned it, installed fresh propane tanks, filled it with fresh water, checked out the W.C., and repainted it. They also have a propensity for providing sponsors—in this case, four of them. One of them, Mrs. T's Kishkies, was also responsible for the first official event on the Cannonball calendar—a gathering at the Auto Pub five hours before starting time.

The Auto Pub had race cars glued to the ceilings—upside down— real full-sized race cars. In fact, the first time they set it up, workmen forgot to drain a crankcase. The oil leaked out and was accidentally ignited. The whole place was gutted. The waitresses wore little more than signs reading: "Give me a hug and a Kishkie." The Kishkies were delicious—sort of a tube of firm mashed potatoes that had been browned on the outside. Oscar Kovaleski, Brad Niemcek, and Tony Adamowicz, the three founders of the PRDA, were holding forth in a group about 100 strong, most of whom had no idea what the gathering was for. Meanwhile, somewhere west of . . . Abilene? . . . No, the George Washington Bridge, Unit 1 of the Travco team, Broderick, Frasson, and Pash, were tooling eastward, having picked up the motor home in Cincinnati. Frasson was getting his first taste of real driving. He wasn't doing something as commonplace as battling race cars at 200 miles per hour on a 34-degree banked turn; what he was doing was battling semitrailers at 70 miles per hour for whatever space on the highway that the truck drivers reluctantly allowed him.

Following a driver's meeting at *Car and Driver* staffer Steve Smith's apartment, the entourage retired to the roof of the Red Ball, vehicles and all, where they whiled away the time waiting for midnight by posing for official photos. Everyone went except the Travco Unit 1, which was still playing trucker tag on the George Washington Bridge.

Jockeying the vehicles and posing the crews for the various photos took more time than most people realized. However, sharp Dan Gurney was keeping an eye on his watch. When the photo called for another change of vehicle positions, Gurney roared across the roof and into the car elevator, pushed the "down" button and was gone. It was then that all present realized that it was one minute to midnight, and all vehicles tried to be next in line for the elevator creating a rooftop traffic jam. Kovaleski immediately was up in arms.

"We Poles are appalled by the perpetration of this perfidy. We protest! The pole for the Poles," he shouted.

The vehicles backed off, allowing the PRDA van to be next on the elevator. Down on the street level they met Gurney. "What's everyone so upset about? I just wanted to get a sandwich at the delicatessen before it closed," stated Gurney in mock perplexity.

To verify the starting times, the Red Ball's timing clock was used, although it was located well inside the garage. Half a block up the street was a traffic light. It became a battle of wits to time one's takeoff so that he hit the light green. It soon developed that one crew member would stand at the light then blow his horn. On the horn signal, the clock was punched, the crewman would vault out the door, leap into the open door of the vehicle just as it roared off.

This worked fine until the Caddy's turn. Someone else blew a horn, the crewman punched the clock, sprinted out the door, leaped into the car, and away they went in a cloud of dust with screeching tires. The light turned red. They almost upended the car getting it stopped. After a moment's pause, they ran the light.

Once under way, we neatly cleared New York City via the Lincoln Tunnel and headed down U.S. 22 and I-78. Parker had disappeared. We soon discovered him in the W.C., making full use of it orally. We don't know what he had, but whatever it was, none of us ever want it. He was completely bed-ridden for about 30 hours.

Next, the generator went out—no TV and no hot water. Nobody wanted to take a cold shower. It didn't make any difference anyway; Broderick was using the shower stall for storage of about 752 cubic yards of PR paraphernalia, and you couldn't even get a toe in.

Now we began to work in teams; while one drove, another rode shotgun on the flight deck while the other pair relaxed. Pash and Frasson relaxed by indulging in a little game of chance, with Frasson soon owing Pash his shirt. Soon Broderick began a procedure that he repeated so many times that we could all join in unison. He'd call a radio station on our mobile telephone. "This is Bill Broderick. We're driving cross-country in our motor home to set a new transcontinental record, and we've just stopped at one of those great Union 76 truck-stops and filled up with Union 76 gasoline."

Every morning, Broderick did a live broadcast over Chicago's No. 1 morning radio show. As we came out of the dawn in Oklahoma, Broderick was telling the audience that we were about to make a pit stop at the Oklahoma City Union 76 truck stop. On his way to work in Chicago, listening to the broadcast, was the president of the giant food chain that leases the restaurants in the Union Oil Truck stops. This enterprising gentleman rushed to the phone, called his vice president, who happened to be staying in a motel in Oklahoma City, and gave him some instructions. As we rolled up to the gas pumps and threw open the Travco door, we were greeted by five hot breakfasts of ham and eggs and about 50 pounds of fried chicken. Now that's what you call organization.

Shortly after we got rolling again, we heard a great cacophony of auto horns and yelling voices as the AMX passed us. Evidently their good night's sleep had them in fine fettle. Before you could say "there goes the AMX," they were out of sight.

Parker's wife, Ginny, had supplied us with delicious trays of nice, gooey, baked lasagna. All we had to do was stick it in the oven, and eat it piping hot. Broderick served, the Travco swerved; the lasagna skated—plop! Have you ever tried to clean a gooey cheese lasagna from the nap of a shag rug?

The Travco was powered by a 318-cubic-inch Dodge engine that had a few miles on it. Our speedometer was a digital tach, and we drove by rpm, as the regular speedometer was disconnected. Maintaining good speed was no problem, nor was worrying about gendarmes. All you had to do was hold the accelerator to the floor boards and let 'er rip. The upgrades, regardless of how slight the grade, controlled the speed. The tired 318 was giving it all she had. Midway in the trip, we computed and found our average speed to be 52.5 miles per hour. Not bad, and should we continue that average, we stood a good chance of completing the voyage in under 60 hours, which was our goal.

Travco

During one night, it was my job to ride shotgun for Frasson. Instead of keeping him awake, I fell asleep. When I awoke, all I could see was this blank whiteness. I couldn't tell how far away it was or what I was looking at. I looked over at Frasson. He was sitting up there with an idiotic smile on his face, wearing his famous floppy black hat and puffing on a big cigar. "Look at me," he says, "I'm drafting." The blank whiteness was the back end of a moving van about 4 feet away. "What gets me," he laughs, "is the way the suction pulls the radio aerial right straight forward." I was too speechless to answer. Another truck barreled by; Frasson changed his draft to the passing truck and got sucked right by the moving van. We did this most of the night with Frasson sitting up there giggling and cackling like a hen that had just laid a dozen eggs.

Pash woke up and came forward to the flight deck. "He learned that on the George Washington Bridge. The guy's a madman." When we drafted, we could get the rpm indicator to go 300 or 400 rpm higher than when running by ourselves, but madman Frasson was the only one either with guts enough or mad enough to try it.

Parker came to after we crossed the Mississippi. After he got his sea legs, he took his turns at the wheel. We also got a bigger game of chance going.

Coming down out of the highlands of eastern California, the interstate is a downgrade for maybe 100 miles. Frasson was elected to bring us on in, being the only professional driver on board. He let her rip, and the gravity pull gave us a nice boost. The closer we got to L.A., the heavier the traffic became. Our level, up in the Travco, was real great looking down on and into passing cars. My, the skirts are short in California. "Look at that one! Look over here! Wow, wow, wow." Frasson tried to stay alongside the more interesting sights—for all our benefits.

Broderick had pulled the coup de grace of the trip. Coming off the San Diego Freeway and into the heavily trafficked city streets for our final run to the Portofino, we met our prearranged police patrol, right on time. With sirens screaming and red lights flashing, we roared through traffic lights and packs of cars like there was no tomorrow.

We pulled up in front of the Portofino in a cloud of dust and smoke. Brock Yates was standing there, dumbfounded, just leaning on a post for support and shaking his head from side to side. Unknown to any of us, Broderick had also secreted an ice-cold bottle of champagne on board. Yates had no sooner recovered his composure than we were pouring him a toast—right out there in the middle of the street.

We had done it—set a world's record for a transcontinental crossing of a motor home. Our time was 57 hours and 25 minutes, for an average speed of 50.8 miles per hour. We even obtained acknowledgement from the *Guinness Book of World Records* that no one else had done it.

Bob Carey, a friend of Bill Broderick who ran in three Cannonballs, was the editor of a small motorsports magazine in Virginia. This story, in part, first appeared in that publication. Broderick represented Union 76 for several decades at major motorsports events across the nation.

1972: The Secret Is Out

WITHIN HOURS AFTER the stories of the second Cannonball appeared in *Car and Driver* and *Autoweek,* my phone began to ring around the clock. Seemingly every sports car nut, hot rodder, closet anarchist, and general Hell-raiser in the nation was ready to run if another race was organized. We had to go again. While I was in midst of finishing up my book *Sunday Driver* for Farrar, Straus & Giroux, any such madness would have to be delayed at least until late 1972. A November 13 start was chosen, in the main to coincide with a publication party for the book that was to be organized by Roger Straus III, the scion of the publishing company and a volunteer to codrive with me in the Cannonball.

Roger decided that the party ought to be held at the Red Ball Garage as part of the start. Generally such functions involved gentile clusters of New York literati nibbling on canapés and sipping Chardonnay in the suite of a midtown hotel. The thought of dragging the same crowd into a dingy midtown parking garage mightily amused the iconoclastic Straus.

My first challenge was to find another automobile. Kirk White had sold the Ferrari and it was unlikely that

Fake ad run in Hot Rod *in 1972.*

he would be able to replace it with one as potent and reliable. I spoke with Moon Mullins, my old Dodge pal who had provided the original *Moon Trash II* van, and he suggested a heavily modified Challenger. I had learned that long range, at least 400 miles, and an easy 90–100 mile-per-hour cruising speed were the keys to winning the Cannonball, provided the highway patrols could be avoided and a quick, efficient route was chosen. At the time, Dodge was heavily involved with Spartanburg's Cotton Owens, a great ex-stock car driver who was preparing David Pearson's machines for the NASCAR Grand National (now Winston Cup) wars.

Mullins had a 340-cubic-inch Challenger in the press fleet that could be converted by Owens into a proper Cannonball car, and we made a deal to have the car transformed into a latter-day liquor hauler set up for cross-country running.

As the start approached, a driver problem arose. Business obligations forced Straus to withdraw. *Car and Driver* editor Bob Brown had a change of heart about the Cannonball, prompted in part by the departure of his publisher, who was the central source of angst at the magazine. Brown volunteered as my second driver. But he was under enormous pressure in the editor's chair and I believed it entirely possible that he, too, would be forced to back out. Therefore, I enlisted a reserve in the form of H.K. "Bud" Stanner, a close friend and senior

The Yates Challenger as built by Cotton Owens.

agent for Mark McCormick in his International Management Group, a worldwide sports management agency that represented such motor racing luminaries as Jackie Stewart and Mark Donohue. If Brown was forced to withdraw, Stanner was a ready replacement, although any thoughts of taking them both made no sense. Cotton was removing the rear seat of the Challenger in order to mount the spare tire—which in turn had been hauled out of the trunk to make room for a 35-gallon auxiliary fuel tank. One or the other, Brown or Stanner, would codrive.

Among the myriad phone calls from wannabe competitors was one from a California screenwriter named Eugene Price. He produced the amazing news that he had been assigned the job of writing a script about the Cannonball. The director would be John Avildsen, a young, hot talent who had just finished *Cry Uncle*—and was considered a major talent in the business. Price said that Avildsen had signed a two-picture deal with Universal Studios to do the Cannonball movie and *Serpico*, the story of a tough, rebellious New York cop who bucked the old boy system. A major motion picture. Cannonball goes Hollywood. Price announced that he and Avildsen would be at the start in Manhattan to gather information and color for the script.

Entries began to pour in. It was clear that the stakes were getting high. Brad Niemcek announced that while his old teammates Kovaleski and Adamowicz would not be able to run with him, the Polish Racing Drivers of America would come loaded for bear. He was teaming up with Steve Durst, an aspiring pro driver, to run a Vega wagon that had been stuffed with a Chevy small-block and a larger fuel tank. Steve Behr, who had run well with the old *Moon Trash II* the year before, was returning with two Indiana enthusiasts, Bill Canfield and Fred Olds. They planned to copy the drive-away Cadillac scam employed by the Opert team in the last Cannonball. Wes Dawn, the Hollywood film technician who had teamed with New Yorker Bob Perlow in his MGB GT, only to suffer clutch failure in Columbus in 1971, was hooking up with *Indianapolis Star* motorsports reporter Robin Miller to run a Chevy Vega of indeterminate lineage. The Bruerton brothers, Tom and Ed, were returning from their Sandy, Utah, haunts to run their battle-scarred AMX one more time. Union Oil's Bill Broderick was on board for a reprise with a Travco motor home, teamed again with stock car ace Joe Frasson and a pair of good ol' boy journalists, Pal Parker and Tom McGrail.

The guys at *Hot Rod Magazine*, although they were owned by the arch-rival Petersen Publishing Company, were game for the

Size doesn't count. The huge Travco Motor Home of Bill Broderick and crew dwarfs the mite-sized Honda 600 of Stan Stephenson and Ed Gallagher prior to the start of the 1972 Cannonball.

Auxiliary gasoline tanks were added in a variety of ways. The Hot Rod Magazine *team of John Fuchs and Clyde Baker made a rather tidy installation of fuel cells in their AMC Hornet.*

Cannonball. Two staffers, John Fuchs and Clyde "Cannonball" Baker, entered a tweaked-up, 401-cubic-inch V-8-powered AMC Hornet.

At one point the entries swelled to 37 teams, although several dropped out prior to the start. One noteworthy absence was Edsel Ford II and Kenyon & Eckhart advertising exec Jack Falla, who announced plans to run a 2-liter Capri. At that time Edsel was a student at New England's Babson business college and a major car enthusiast. Presumably Ford public relations types in Dearborn got wind of the plan, and Edsel's entry was canceled.

I flew to Spartanburg to pick up the Challenger from Owens. I had known Cotton well since doing a story with him and David Pearson several years earlier. He was a leathery little man, with a quick smile and a deeply competitive streak that had carried him to a number of major NASCAR victories prior to his retirement during the gritty, fender-bashing years of the 1950s. Cotton was confident the Challenger would run the distance without breathing hard, based on his years building stock cars and the local knowledge that he had gleaned from illegal earlier, high-speed experiences. "Just imagine you're haulin' 50 gallons of white liquor instead of high-test and you'll be fine," he mused in his laconic South Carolina drawl.

...and then there was the hardware-store engineering to be found on the Dawn/Miller Chevy Vega.

Straus' idea to hold the publication party for *Sunday Driver* at the start of the Cannonball was a total distraction. He had arranged for the party to be catered by Nathan's Coney Island Hot Dogs, a famed local fast food purveyor that would, he claimed, add a déclassé element to the party that would be long remembered.

I had by now created a logo for the event, which I had sketched out and had drawn up formally by *Car and Driver* art director Gene Butera. It depicted a highway leading to the horizon and the setting sun—symbolizing the westward rush of the Cannonball and the great east-to-west migrations toward the nirvana of California, its legendary streets paved with gold and the intoxicating aura of Hollywood.

Within two days of the start, the teams began to gather in New York. Many of them appeared at the offices of *Car and Driver,* housed in the Ziff-Davis Publishing Co. building at One Park Avenue, three blocks away from the Red Ball garage on East 32nd Street.

Some serious iron rolled in. Danny and Hoppy Hopkins of Asuza, California, appeared with a new Pantera entered by Pacesetter Homes, a construction company then active in sports car racing. Two 911s were on hand, one driven by Sewickley, Pennsylvania, friends Dick Scott and Leo Lynch, the other by East Coasters Bill McFaul and Spike Nunn. Both cars appeared to be potential winners. After all, Porsches were noted long-distance tourers with great reliability. Ironically, both would break before clearing the western Pennsylvania border.

Airline pilots Richard Harris, Dick Cannata, and Fred Feiner arrived with a neatly prepared 1951 Studebaker hot rod powered by a modified Chevy V-8. A bit of glamour was added to the affair when Judy Stropus, a well-known personality in motor racing who timed and scored for major teams, SCCA racer Donna Mae Mims, known as the "Pink Lady," and Brad Niemcek's wife, Peggy, rolled in with a stretched Cadillac limousine entered by Atlanta sportsman and race-car owner, Bobby Rinzler. The trio would run as the "Right Bra Racing team," decked out in neatly tailored white coveralls.

Then came another serious challenger. Pete Brock, the much respected designer of the Shelby Daytona coupe and a former prodigy of GM Design chief Bill Mitchell, entered a new Mercedes-Benz 250SE sedan with his codrivers, Jack Cowell and Dick Gilmartin. Cowell was a former *Car and Driver* ad salesman who had moved on to Wall Street, while Gilmartin was known far and wide in the motorsports world as a sometime racer, writer, and general hell-raiser. All three were skilled drivers, and the car seemed perfectly suited for long-distance high-speed running.

In all, 34 cars were entered in the 1972 Cannonball Sea-to-Shining-Sea Memorial Trophy Dash. I had dropped the "Baker" from the title, concerned that somewhere, somehow a relative of the late endurance driver might take umbrage at our use of his name, although he had always spelled it "Cannon Ball," which, in legal terms separated my event from his legacy, according to people who knew the law better than I.

As the starting hour approached and the Red Ball began to fill not only with the entered cars, but with members of the New York literary elite—most of whom had never ridden on a freight elevator of the type that led them to the third-level party site—a serious complication arose. Both Stanner and Brown said they were going. The Challenger's back seat had been removed and the space consumed by the spare tire and a roll bar. Somehow a few pillows would have to suffice for a grown man in a space better suited to small Fox terrier.

The publication party was something of a success, with all manner of media biggies appearing at the Red Ball to munch chili dogs and

The Right Bra Racing Team (left to right) Judy Stropus, Peggy Niemcek and Donna Mae Mims, "the Pink Lady."

ogle the collection of madmen about to drive nonstop to California. I rode the freight elevator up to the affair with Gene Shalit, the wry, hirsute, lavishly mustachioed *NBC Today Show* media critic, who appeared totally baffled. Jim Bouton, the ex-Yankee pitcher who had gained fame with his book *Ball Four*, was on hand and totally amused—and slightly baffled—with the whole affair.

John Avildsen quietly examined the scene while Stanner, Brown, and I rolled the Challenger out of the Red Ball for the start. I had decided to leave second after the Niemcek-Durst PRDA "pole" Vega, reasoning that the publicity surrounding the Cannonball might have alerted the cops. Justifying my position on being the former winner and also the organizer who could set the rules, I figured an early start might permit an escape from Manhattan before some nut triggered an all-points bulletin across the entire East Coast.

Such problems were unlikely to happen to the Brock/Cowell/ Gilmartin team. They had appeared at the prerace party decked out in rented priest's costumes, reversed collars and all. Their intended scheme was to explain to any officers trying to make an arrest that they were merely simple padres delivering their monsignor's Mercedes to him at San Juan Capistrano. This would be the first—and most outrageous—of several disguises employed in the Cannonballs to delude the highway patrols.

The Flying Fathers (left to right) Dick Gilmartin, Jack Cowell, and Peter Brock check results with California PR specialist Deke Houlgate.

A small crowd had gathered in the heavy rain outside the Red Ball for the midnight start as Brown wedged himself into the nonexistent back seat and I took the wheel. The weather to the west looked terrible. Rain swept across the Midwest as a giant late-autumn storm was lashing the nation's midsection and roaring eastward. I decided that the normal St. Louis-Route 66-U.S. 40 route was a potential disaster, recalling the storm that Gurney and I had skated through the year before. I chose instead to run south along newly completed interstate 81 through the Shenandoah Valley to pick up U.S. 40 westbound—or at least as much of interstate 40 as existed in those days. (The interstate system, which now totals almost 40,000 miles, was less than three-quarters complete in 1972).

Again, the rules would be elemental. The competitors were given a time card, and the departure time was recorded on the Red Ball's electronic timer. Any route west could be taken, at any speed, with the simple proviso that the same car would be driven (not flown, or replaced with a duplicate at the finish) to the Portofino Inn in Redondo Beach, California, where the arrival time would be recorded at their check-in desk clock. The lowest elapsed time between the two points would determine the winner. This formula would later be the theme for the Cannonball: "There is only one rule. There are no rules."

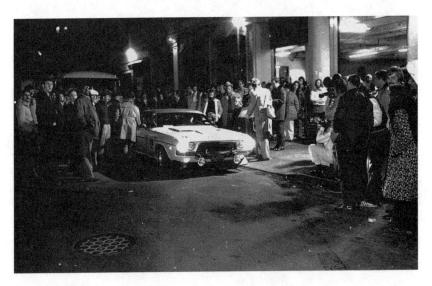

The Yates/Stanner/Brown Challenger ready to start from the Red Ball Garage. The bearded man in the black sweater and sheepskin jacket is movie director John Avildsen.

My scheme to dog-leg south around the bad weather in the Midwest was a failure. Not only did we run into monsoonlike rain in Virginia ("like running through a car wash," mused Stanner in the blinding slush) but the route was well over 100 miles longer than the more direct route. Worse yet, we overshot an off-ramp exit in Memphis and became bogged in a tangle of downtown streets before breaking loose and crossing the Mississippi.

Rumbling across the flats of Oklahoma, Stanner employed the elemental car phone that we had packed on board. He was trying to reach his client, Jackie Stewart, in London. Amazingly he reached an operator who quickly connected him. We would take that for granted today, but it bordered on a technological miracle 30 years ago.

As the second night fell we poured through the darkness at a steady 100 miles per hour, the giant Cibie driving lights arrowing through the gloom. The night was clear and the road, a scramble of interstate and two-lane, was utterly devoid of traffic. The west in those days was vacant and a half-hour would normally pass before another car or truck appeared, poking across the vast, blackened landscape.

Then up ahead, the arcing lights of a patrol car on the roadside. Surely somebody was being arrested. We slowed to a prudent speed

The interior of Yates/Stanner/Brown Dodge Challenger: Scheelk Bucket seats, a Halda Speed Pilot, a special map light, an early radar detector, and a state-of-the-art 1972 mobile telephone are visible modifications.

and eased past. The Mercedes and the bogus priests! We laughed, wondering if their preposterous tale of serving their monsignor would actually work.

For reasons forgotten, I discarded the Ash Fork cutoff and ran straight west to the California border, crossing at Needles then on to Barstow and interstate 15 into Los Angeles. Exhausted, our bodies cramped by the nonexistent back seat, we surged into the parking lot of the Portofino and checked in. One car was already parked. The Cadillac Coupe DeVille of Steve Behr, Fred Olds, and Bill Canfield had clocked in with a time of 37 hours and 16 minutes—exactly 10 minutes quicker than our time. Then came the Brock/Cowell/Gilmartin Mercedes-Benz team. They had taken the conventional route through St. Louis and had, as expected, hit horrendous weather. But in the end they had essentially run the same time, coast to coast as the Challenger—all three cars finishing under a time blanket of a mere 17 minutes and all averaging about 77–78 miles per hour.

The winners. (left to right) Bill Canfield, Steve "Yogi" Behr, and Fred Olds.

Fourth home was the Pantera of Danny and Hoppy Hopkins, as the others trailed in during the remainder of the afternoon. Motor heads from southern California, hearing about the race through all forms of the grapevine, began to gather. More and more cars staggered in, each spilling out weary, grizzled drivers with mad tales of high-speed pursuits, rain-dashed hopes and nighttime hallucinations. Then came news of the frustrating failure of the Durst/Niemcek Vega. Apparently reeling off a record pace and, according to them, far ahead of the winning time of the year before, the little Vega's rear end was finally overpowered by the lusty torque of the Chevy V-8 and broke somewhere in the western reaches of Arizona. (See table page 98.)

Word drifted in about a crash. The reports indicated that the Rinzler limousine with the Right Bra Racing Team rolled in El Paso, Texas, breaking the arm of Donna Mae Mims and wrecking the big Caddy. This would be the *only* serious accident in all five Cannonballs. An amazing statistic considering the tens of thousands of high-speed highway miles covered.

In all, 26 starters in the 1972 Cannonball straggled into the Portofino, the last being a modified Corvette driven by Rick Jellison and John Jessen in 57 hours and 19 minutes. The pair of Tampa Florida drivers

The second place Challenger team members sport their fancy racing jackets. (Left to right) Bud Stanner, Bob Brown, Brock Yates, while the amused winners Fred Olds and Bill Canfield look on.

had taken the advice of American Automobile Association travel experts and tried a northern route through the Rocky Mountains, there to be stranded in a snowbank until freed by a Colorado highway crew. Eight other cars, including the Durst/Niemcek Vega and the Right Bra limo, failed to make the finish, suffering various mechanical maladies.

After a few days of catching our collective breaths and an ad hoc victory celebration for Behr, Olds, and Canfield, the competitors began to drive out of the Portofino and head home. Plans were discussed for a 1973 running, but dark clouds on the horizon internationally and domestically made the resumption iffy at best.

Not only was the Watergate scandal shaking the very foundation of the American political structure, but the Vietnam war continued in all its mindless brutality. The Middle East was soon to explode in the Yom Kippur War that once again saw the Israeli army repel the combined forces of the Egypt and Syria. This conflict resulted in the intensification of the Organization of Petroleum Exporting Companies (OPEC) to tighten the screws on oil pricing and production that was to lead to a two-year "oil crisis" in the Western world. Suddenly gasoline supplies were squeezed to the point of strangulation, and long lines formed at gas stations around the nation.

A motley crew of finishers poses for a group photo in the Portofino Inn parking lot. Identifiable are Peter Brock second from left, winners Olds and Behr (seated on left), Yates in the center, Stanner seated at the right, Brown and Canfield are standing at the right.

As the world shuddered with the economic and military impacts, it somehow seemed inappropriate to launch yet another blast across the nation in the name of sheer fun and light anarchy. A 55-mile-per-hour national speed limit was soon to be implemented as an energy-saving measure, and suddenly the notion of recreational driving for any reason became unpatriotic. The Cannonball was indefinitely put on hold.

OFFICIAL RESULTS
1972 Cannonball Sea-To-Shining-Sea Memorial Trophy Dash
November 13–15, 1972

Pos.	Car	Drivers	Time	Av.mph
1.	Cadillac	Steve Behr/Bill Canfield/Fred Olds (drive-away)	37:16	78.04
2	Dodge Challenger	Brock Yates/Bob Brown/ Bud Stanner	37:26	77.8
3	Mercedes 280 SEL	Jack Cowell/Richard Gilmartin/ Peter Brock	37:33	77.6
4	Pantera	Danny Hopkins/ Hoppy Hopkins	38:02	76.2
5	Alfa Romeo Guilia Sedan	Richard Jenkins/Bob Rost	38:37	75.5
6	Mazda RX-2	Fred De Van/Paul Solski	39:29	73.8
7	Vega	Wes Dawn/Robin Miller	39:35	73.6
8	AMX	Tom Bruerton/ Ed Bruerton	39:42	73.5
9	Chrysler	Pete Locke/Charles Chapman/ Jesse Pitt	40:11	72.3
10	Chevy Van	Dick Roder/Rainec Dainko/ Scott Dennison	40:55	71.5
11	Ford Torino	Tom Morton/Dave Moody/ Paul Fischer	41:01	70.7
12	Vega	Bill Henry/Tom Denner	41:06	70.6
13	Hornet	John Fuchs/Clyde Baker	41:15	70.4
14	Datsun 510	Spike Nunn/Pete Marget	41:41	70.0
15	Citroen DS19	Joe Fergusson/Alice Fergusson	42:08	68.9
16	Ford Van	Jack Cady/Duane Unkefer/ Chauncey Martin	43:02	67.4

Pos.	Car	Drivers	Time	Av.mph
17	Torino	John Ramsey/Jon Trefethen	43:28	67.0
18	Bradley GT	Bob Taatjes/James Miller	43:45	66.7
19	Travco	Bill Broderick/Joe Frasson/ Pal Parker/Tom McGrail	44:42	65.2
20	Mustang	Dick Leib/George McMeekan R.A. Talbert	44:54	65.1
21	Opel Rallye	John Thibeau/Paul Crabbe	45:39	63.8
22	Opel Rallye	Larry Houge/Morris Erickson	46:17	62.8
23	Pinto	Bill Spreadbury/S. Pfeifer	47:28	61.3
24	Datsun 240Z	Steve Garbarini/Wm. Garcione	48:25	60.1
25	Monte Carlo	Doug Scribner/Sam Lincoln/ Doug Blue/Tom Corrozoni	49:04	59.1
26	Corvette	Rich Jellinson/John Jessen	57:19	50.7

DNFs: Durst/Niemcek—PRDA Vega—Corona Del Mar, California
Stropus/Mims/Niemcek—Cadillac Limousine—El Paso, Texas, crash
McFaul/Hammil—Porsche 911—Pennyslvania
Scott/Lynch—Porsche 911—Pennsylvania
Missing: McPherson/Johnson—Austin-Healey
Kenny/Kepler—Camaro Z-28
Coumo/Feiner/Harris—1951 Studebaker—Late Departure
Stephenson/Gallagher—Honda 600—Stopping En route

Steve "Yogi" Behr 1972

I originally wasn't sure what vehicle would be used. There was an MGB from Long Island that was offered to me as a codriver, but I could not fathom riding coast-to-coast nonstop in such a vehicle.

With just a few days remaining before the start, Brock mentioned that there were a couple of guys from Michigan who were coming with a Cadillac. Something was better than nothing and the car would at least be comfortable, so I signed on with Bill Canfield and Fred Olds. Obviously, it would not be as fast as some of the other entrants, but this was the Cannonball, where a low-profile vehicle would not as likely be noticed as a red Corvette, Porsche, or Jaguar.

Bill and Fred arrived at my apartment in New York City the night before the start. My micromanager for motorsports, Hawley T. Chester III, had arranged for sponsorship from Gleason's Tavern with locations on York Avenue and First Avenue. The fact that the event was in the spirit of civil disobedience did not allow Wayne Dulley, the manager and primo wine connoisseur, to purchase signage on the vehicle, but not only did he provide dinner, he provided excellent traveling provisions to sumptuously feed Bill, Fred, and me during the next day's transcontinental journey. Gleason's Tavern sure beat the C-rations and cola, which sustained John Buffum and me on the Rallye Monte Carlo.

Here it was the autumn of 1972 and these two guys showed up with a glistening new 1973 Cadillac Coupe DeVille. With 500 cubic inches, I thought we would really be able to stretch its legs when we got outside of any metropolitan area. They told me the car ran fine, but that the speedometer was not working.

That night Bill and Fred camped out on the floor of the apartment after we had gone over the maps, the overall route, and the philosophy as to how to handle the unforeseen challenges. They asked me to be the initial driver to get out of Manhattan and head west.

Since I lived in Manhattan, I had the opportunity to put in some time evaluating which was the best way to get out of town from the starting point at the Red Ball Garage on 31st street.

The Red Ball was the corporate parking garage for Ziff-Davis and its various magazines, including *Car and Driver*. It had a time clock that printed out the time of day. Each entrant punched out from the same clock at intervals of their choice. Some entries headed cross-town to the Lincoln Tunnel, others headed downtown for the Holland Tunnel, and others went uptown to go over the Hudson River via the George Washington Bridge. Bill, Fred, and I went over the bridge and headed westward on Route 80 through New Jersey and into Pennsylvania.

A hurricane was belting the eastern half of the United States. Rain was coming down in sheets and we were starting at night. Vision was limited, the roads were not draining completely, and we were thankful for the invention of Rain-X. Yates scheduled the event during the week so as not to encounter heavier weekend traffic with possible Friday or Saturday night celebrants.

Prior to the start we had prepared ourselves with proper food and sleep, and we had maps, food, and pillows in the car. The fuel tank filled, we were as prepared as we were going to be. The Cadillac was bone stock. The only thing we ever changed was radio stations! There was no large or spare fuel tank, no CB radio, and no radar detector. We were on a wing and a prayer with God as our copilot.

All the way across New Jersey, the torrential rain continued, with rooster tails coming off every vehicle on the road. We got gasoline for the first time in Stroudsburg, Pennsylvania, which is just west of the Delaware Water Gap, where the New Jersey-Pennsylvania state line is. My eyes were strained, but I told Bill and Fred that I'd do one more tank of gas.

We continued westward on Route 80 for another 25 or 35 miles. The rain was worse than German Autobahn fog.

At the fuel stop and driver change on the Ohio Turnpike, Bill said to Fred that it was time to reconnect the speedometer cable. Back in New York they had said it was broken. It was then I learned that they had signed up with a drive-away company in Detroit to deliver the fresh-off-the-assembly-line 1973 Cadillac Coupe DeVille to Los Angeles. By reconnecting the speedometer, the mileage would read about right for a trip from Detroit to L.A. In the previous Cannonball another drive-away Cadillac had been entered by Larry Opert and Ron Herisko.

Driving on the Ohio Turnpike with the rain as intense as ever, we passed a Corvette and an Alfa Romeo, each of which had started ahead of us. I recall that during that stint I again lost the feel of the front tires through the steering wheel due to aquaplaning. I looked down at the speedometer and we were going 80 miles per hour. There was probably a good quarter-inch of water everywhere with an occasional 1 inch or more in places. The lighter cars with wider tires were not suited to the absolutely miserable hurricane conditions.

By the time we got to Illinois, the rain had tapered off enough that there was no more aquaplaning. Soon we would find out how fast the potent 500-cubic-inch V-8 engine would move our stealthy, comfortable Cadillac. Space and traffic conditions only allowed us to safely reach 90 miles per hour.

The wide-open spaces of the Southwest finally gave us the opportunity to hold the "pedal to the metal" for a prolonged period of time. The engine would propel the Coupe DeVille up to about 105 miles per hour and no faster. That 105 miles per hour was with wide-open throttle with obvious increased fuel consumption. I brought the pedal back to about 70 percent of its travel and was still able to maintain 95 miles per hour. The Caddy was still quiet, comfortable, and smooth at 70 percent throttle, so I drove 60–70 percent as often as possible.

When Bill Canfield suggested I stay behind the wheel for an extra stint or two because I was cruising the fastest of the group, I was definitely up for it. I did a long stretch of four to five tankfuls. Elapsed time was the bottom line, so the faster we went, the better our chances of finishing in the top half of the field. There were some potent vehicles entered that could definitely blow our doors off. In our favor was that we had a low profile, stealth approach, which is of high value in the Cannonball.

I was running about 70–75 miles per hour in light traffic and came up behind a cluster of cars running at 65 miles per hour. In the midst of the cluster and slowly working its way through was the red Chevrolet Vega Monza station wagon of Brad Niemcek and Steve Durst. Their entry was from Briggs Chevrolet of South Amboy, New Jersey. This was not our ordinary grocery-getter station wagon. With the blessing of Danny Zack, the boss man at Briggs who was very helpful with the John Greenwood racing Corvette, a 454-cubic-inch big-block Chevrolet engine sat in the engine compartment! Other than the red paint, the Niemcek/Durst duo had the best "sleeper" and highest performance potential of all entries. I was surprised to even have a view of them, since they should have been long gone over the western horizon. The hurricane conditions must have held them back.

Just before the Chevy Monza wagon was about to sedately break loose from the traffic cluster, I got a rolling jump and built up momentum to pass by them at about 90 miles per hour. I didn't think that they had seen us till then, so my thought was to have them think we could do 90 miles per hour all the time and convince them they would have to go faster. I figured the "arrest me red" Monza would never make it to California without getting pulled over and losing time. Devious thinking, but hopefully at least a good psych job.

About 30 seconds after passing them, they blew by us at an effortless 110–115 miles per hour. We didn't see them again until the Portofino Inn finish line at Redondo Beach, California.

We never saw another entrant the rest of the trip. Since the rules of the Cannonball were "no rules" and route choices were entirely up to each vehicle, there was no way to judge how we were doing.

At the next fuel stop, Bill again suggested I drive even though he was next in rotation. By now, the hurricane was far behind us and we enjoyed the pleasant, dry nighttime air. We ran in the cool evening breeze at about 70 percent of pedal travel. I was expecting that Smokey would eventually nail us. I balanced the time it would take him to write a ticket with the time we would gain by cruising at good speed, and figured we would still be ahead after receiving the ticket— provided the officer didn't take us to the courthouse. (I had already gone through the scenario; I would tell Bill and Fred to carry on to L.A.

while I spent a few hours in new surroundings. Besides, the Cadillac was being delivered to California and I was going to fly home anyway.)

Kingman, Arizona: The back seat of the Caddy was a welcome respite after trying to define by the light of night where a Smokey might be lying in wait. Bill and Fred brought us into California. When the light of dawn began to appear behind us we were about two to three hours from Los Angeles.

Since I had scoped out the various routes to the finish line in Redondo Beach, I drove the final tank of gas. The freeway was building up and getting denser as we got closer to L.A. The early morning commute appeared to be as bad as the Long Island Expressway on a summer Friday night. As we approached the metropolitan area the traffic would come to a stop and then inch along again. Finally, the traffic wasn't even moving. There was an exit about a half-mile ahead, so we looked on the map to see just where the exit would drop us onto the surface street. The original route was for a few miles on the freeway, but since there was complete blockage on the freeway we decided to at least keep moving—even though we would be passing through a couple of towns.

We still had to get to the exit about a half-mile away. I straddled the curb, went on the shoulder and slowly made it the exit. We made as much haste as cautiously possible and eventually reached the surface streets we had originally planned to use.

When we drove under the arch for King Harbor where the Portofino Inn was located, Fred Olds was in the front passenger seat with Bill Canfield in back. As we briskly drove up to the entrance, Fred appeared to immediately run in the front door to have the Portofino receptionist time stamp the card, which had our beginning time from the Red Ball garage in New York.

As we sat there with Fred disappearing through the front door of the Portofino Inn, Bill and I looked over the parking lot to see how many Cannonballers had already arrived. There were none! I really couldn't believe it. The others must have already checked in and parked near their rooms.

Fred came back with the stamped time card and said no one else had arrived yet. I cautioned the guys not to presume we had won since this was an elapsed-time event. Anyone starting behind us could still beat our time. As we sat there in the Caddy pondering if we might have won, another entrant rolled in. We didn't know if they started in front of us or behind us. Then as we were starting to compare notes with them, another entrant came in—we thought they had started ahead of us.

Cars were now arriving at different intervals, but we wouldn't know who had the lowest time until all the cards were tallied. Even though all the participants were fatigued from the transcontinental trek, the parking lot was totally energized with enthusiasm and the swapping of tales.

The official chart of results was finally posted. The first three cars had traversed the United States within 13 minutes of each other, with the first-place car beating the second place by 8 minutes. The second-place car beat the third-place car by 5 minutes.

Our Cadillac Coupe DeVille had come first!

The second-place Cotton Owens-prepared Dodge Challenger of Yates, Bud Stanner, and Bob Brown had taken the southern route to avoid the hurricane conditions.

The third-place car, which we had never seen the entire trip, was the very fast Mercedes-Benz of Jack Cowell, Dick Gilmartin, and Pete Brock. They had lost time with two speeding tickets.

The big-block "arrest me red" Chevrolet Vega of Niemcek/Durst received a traffic citation, went to the courthouse, and eventually arrived at the Portofino Inn on the hook of a tow truck. Their rear end had failed.

Cadillac is the only American car to have ever won the Cannonball Sea-to-Shining-Sea Memorial Trophy Dash.

The McKesson trophy for winning the Cannonball was entrusted to Mo Campbell to bring back to the East Coast. It was too large and fragile to be entrusted to airline luggage. We never saw it again.

The Cadillac was taken to a car wash and then delivered to the L.A. address as per Bill and Fred's commitment.

Steve "Yogi" Behr was a Wne amateur sports car driver in the 1960s and 1970s and with John BuVum formed the highest-place all-American team to ever finish the Monte Carlo Rally.

Peter Brock
"THE FLYING FATHERS"
1972

We'd left the Red Ball Garage in Manhattan about 9 P.M. *Car and Driver*'s au revoir party was in full roar, way up there, on one of the top floors where the Cannonball entries were staged. With all the celebrities, press mooches, and name drivers, with their decal-plastered, tricked-out special Cannonball racers getting all the attention, our plain, dark brown Mercedes 280 four-door looked pretty mundane. Perfect for our game. My codrivers Dick Gilmartin and Jack Cowell had returned about an hour earlier from the mysterious quest to find what Gilly had said would be "the proper vestments" for our adventure.

In the shopping bag they'd handed me with a knowing look, I was surprised to find a pair of black slacks and a matching shirt with a reversed collar. Without question I followed them into a side room where we quickly transformed ourselves into three pious young men of the cloth. Properly attired as Papal attachés we reemerged to some questioning glances as we quietly slid into the Benz. Gilmartin, with his gold wire-rimmed glasses, balding pate, and angelic face had suddenly acquired a perfect South Boston Irish accent. He'd also gone us one better with an appropriately sedate black straw fedora. I struggled with the urge to confess all my sins. There were few goodbyes, as we didn't know many people at the party.

The huge vertical door on the garage's freight elevator closed behind the Benz, and we silently dropped away from the noise and lights. We had the Red Ball's attendant stamp our ticket with the exact time of our departure and eased out onto the poorly lit, rain-slicked streets. It was coming down so hard the raindrops were bouncing on the mirrored pavement. Jack, being the Gotham local, was at the wheel, carefully but quickly navigating his way through the now lessened traffic as we headed west, out over the river toward Pennsylvania. We tried in vain to find a weather report on the radio that might advise us how to avoid the storm that had increased in intensity.

I was scheduled to take over from Jack at our first stop. While we refueled, Gilmartin went into the station's store to buy some extra munchies and practice his new Irish parish persona. He dived back in the car, soaked from the rain, giggling quietly as he emptied the soggy paper sack that contained our sustenance for the next several hours. "Amazing," he laughed, "I've never encountered such respect. These guys," he said, gesturing to his all-black garb, "have a really cool gig." Jack and I had noticed the same thing when servicing the car. The attendant had quoted a price for the fuel and then never counted the bills as we prepared to drive off.

After several hours the rain hadn't abated so we'd elected to alter the course, to run south in a long westward arc that would, hopefully, clear the rain and ensure that we didn't have to cross the Rockies in the snow. We hadn't had enough foresight to bring chains. The weather, now being announced on the radio as "The Worst Storm of the Year," was blanketing the entire Eastern seaboard. The new route would be longer, down through Kansas and Oklahoma, but the rest of the racers tried to go straight west across the plains and fight the weather. We knew we'd make better time. Our plan was to use the interstates only when necessary, trying to time our major city-crossings, if we had to go through, to off-peak hours. Where possible we'd use the ring roads to go around. By keeping to the secondary roads we could run as fast as the car would go when there was no other traffic in sight.

It was amazing how fast you could run in those days. There was little traffic off the interstates, so we kept increasing our averages, learning the practical limits as our speeds climbed but still playing it very carefully with even the most distant bogey.

As we headed further south and west on the first full day, the weather gradually eased off and our averages continued to improve. The most interesting thing we noticed, once we lost the weather and got west of the Mississippi, was that fast road-travel speeds far exceeded the averages we had ever achieved on racetracks. All of us were SCCA competition license holders with enough experience to feel comfortable at high average speeds, but this type of racing was completely different than having to haul the car down off a quarter-mile straight to a sharp turn. Racetrack averages for production cars in those days seldom exceeded 50 miles per hour . . . we were now averaging 80-plus. The car was remarkable because it, too, seemed poised at speeds well over the legal limit. Although its top speed was a bit less than the 120 indicated, on the level it could run there comfortably all day.

We streaked across Kansas as our first sunset of the trip began shutting down the western light. The road had been empty for miles, and I felt confident that I'd make the 100 miles per hour average I'd set for myself on that fuel leg. I was constantly monitoring the fuel gauge and checking the road map with Jack, trying to stretch as much distance as possible from this tankload but still looking for a small town with a gas station that wouldn't be closed by the time the sun disappeared. At night we'd have to slow to a less obvious speed. A rural hamlet with a familiar bright fuel station logo appeared just as the needle neared the empty mark. We slowed to enter the station and then the three of us leaped out to begin what had now become almost as well choreographed as a NASCAR pit stop. The attendant, who had ambled out expecting a leisurely conversation with his evening visitors, was baffled as it became obvious we had no time to talk. The sight of three priests in rotation racing for the men's room while servicing a heavily bug-splattered Benz at warp speed was obviously not something that had ever been observed in those parts.

Late that night as we crossed over into Oklahoma we encountered our first real delay. Gilly was driving, Jack was reading the maps in the front seat, and I was in back checking the side roads for traffic. It was almost dark with just a hint of moon to give some idea of the surrounding area. We'd just cleared a railroad crossing, and at the speed, the car had settled heavily on the far side of the grade with a solid "whoopmp," as the suspension bottomed out. Just past the tracks there was what appeared to be a side road and the glint of moonlight on chrome . . . obviously a parked car. I watched it closely and suddenly its lights went on and then just as suddenly went out . . . but it was moving! "Cops." I shouted. Gilly eased off, never touching the brakes, and we dropped down to about 50 miles per hour. The car was behind us, lights-off, tracking our speed. After about a mile the troopers eased up alongside and checked us out. As they moved up, Jack and I feigned sleep, leaving Gilmartin to deal with the situation. They dropped back and followed up some more, as if trying to decide what to do, and then the red lights came on.

Gilly eased over to the edge of the road and stopped. Flashlights probed the interior as one huge trooper came to the driver's window and the other stood at the right rear. "And a foine good evenin' to ye, officer," said Gilmartin in his best Boston Southie accent. More flashlight . . . the trooper could now see that Gilmartin was a man of the cloth.

"Good evening sir . . . is there some emergency?" He had a strong Oklahoma country accent.

"Why no," replied Gilmartin, "We're just . . . well . . . is there a problem now, officer?"

The trooper politely asked Gilmartin to step out of the car. "We're concerned with your safety and your speed, sir. Have you been drinking?"

"Speed?" asked Gilmartin incredulously, "Liquor?" Anyone could see that was just . . . impossible. We were priests, for Christ's sake . . . total innocents! I think we'd begun to believe our own scam. "I've been driving the legal limit," fibbed Gilmartin. "I should think you would know that, as I noticed that you've been behind us for some time."

"Yes, sir, that's true but we clocked you at more than 85 over the crossing back there."

"Oooh, did ja now . . . that rise was a bit of a surprise, wasn't it? Didn't expect that. I'm sure it must have looked faster than it was."

"Yes, 87 miles per hour, sir . . . on radar," replied the mountie. Gilmartin and the trooper walked back toward the cruiser to verify the speed. The other officer again probed the interior with his light. The conversation between Gilmartin and the arresting officer drifted back. "You have New York plates, Father. Is there a reason you are traveling across Oklahoma?"

"Well, it's the monsignor's car," Gilmartin said apologetically, intimating that a man of his lowly stature could never hope to own such a luxurious foreign car. "We're delivering it to California. There's an ecumenical council of prelates there and the monsignor is attending."

The trooper seemed suspicious now, unimpressed with Gilmartin's story. "I'm going to have to cite you for excessive speed, Father, but I'll write it for less. Otherwise, I'd have to take you to jail for reckless driving."

"Reckless driving? I'm sure you must realize that's just not true. You've followed us for some time, we were driving the legal speed."

The trooper looked at Gilmartin and said, "I'll write it for 70 and you'll have to pay the miles per hour!"

"Pay? At this hour? Ah . . . Just how much is that officer . . . in dollars, I mean?" The lawman explained some complex formula that the fine was so much per mile up to 10 over the limit plus $100 at that point plus another $20 per mile up to the cited speed.

"That'll be $310, sir; otherwise, you'll have to explain it all to the judge in the morning."

"Morning?" replied a dazed Gilmartin.

"Yes, sir, if you choose to contest the speed. It's VASCAR." The rather diminutive Gilmartin tried to peek over the big trooper's shoulder.

"Ah . . . about the speed officer. Could ya make it 60 instead of 70?" Gilmartin implored. "The monsignor would never understand . . . " His voice trailed off.

The trooper stopped, looked up from his citation and stared quietly at Gilmartin for a few moments. "You wouldn't want me to *lie*, would you, Father?"

We followed the troopers back the way we had come, at a very sedate speed, for what seemed an eternity, watching the clock eat away at our precious time. Finally we turned in to a small town and counted out the cash for the troopers on the hood of the car, which we then put in an envelope and deposited in a mailbox. "Thank you," said the trooper. "Now you boys have a good evenin', ya hear?" It was pretty obvious by then that they didn't quite believe we were priests, but then they weren't quite sure just what we were.

Our legal detour had cost us more than an hour and a half. We knew it would hurt us badly time-wise, and there was a natural reaction to be more cautious while in Oklahoma, in case they had radioed ahead, but we were soon over the state line and realized our game plan had been pretty successful so far. We were soon up to speed again.

We didn't have any more run-ins with the law until we arrived at the Arizona-New Mexico border. As we came over a slight rise we could see a lot of flashing red lights up ahead so we slowed to be greeted by several patrol cars forming a road block and a couple of what turned out to be Cannonball racers parked by the side of the road. We drove slowly through the gauntlet of black and whites. The troopers inspected us closely but never motioned us over. There wouldn't have been any reason to do so, we thought, but we recognized some faces and cars from the Red Ball party and they, obviously, couldn't have all been running together, so we wondered what was going on.

They weren't being cited but they obviously were being delayed! Well, we thought, their misfortunes is our good luck! With all the law structures in one spot, our odds of getting stopped farther on were diminished. A couple of miles on down the road we came up on another car from the party. We immediately recognized Cannonball veteran Steve Behr and his Cadillac! He had left New York before us, so that meant that we were in front of him on time! We were elated that, even with our Oklahoma delay, we were still running fast enough to beat one of the top competitors in the race. We rolled down the windows and talked. Behr explained that the other cars were being held at the border as a lesson to the racers. Evidently the law felt that the best way to discourage all this illegal activity was to make sure those caught would have no chance to win. Evidently enough racers had converged on this area for the law to know there was some kind of illegal speed contest, so they were stopping all suspicious cars and questioning them if they looked even remotely guilty. The Benz and Caddy, with no identifying race or sponsor decals, had cruised through the blockade without suspicion.

Our totally unmarked car and disguises had evidently saved us. We pressed on, still wary because Behr was obviously going slower than race speed. He undoubtedly knew something we didn't (and hadn't told us) and was using us as a front-running lure to be captured so he could run clear if we were stopped. We eased up for several miles, thinking there might be more trouble. Nothing suspicious occurred so we pushed our speed back up to what we felt would still be a race-winning pace. By now we were west of Flagstaff and ready to cut south on the Ash Fork cutoff that would keep us off the main interstate into California. We'd heard about the Arizona cutoff from others who had raced previously. We weren't disappointed. The road was fast, empty of traffic, and relatively clear of spots that might hide a trooper. We came down out of the mountains at good speed, meeting the desert and the road west to California within an hour.

Since I was living in Riverside, California, at that time I knew all the back roads into L.A. The major freeways running east from the coast hadn't yet been completed, so knowing a fast back route into the city would be the key to setting fast time on our final leg. All went perfectly until we came to a railroad crossing near Riverside. A long freight was across the tracks and there was nothing we could do except wait. It took 12 precious minutes to clear the track. We raced on into the city, finally merging into a freeway that took us toward the coast and our intended goal, the Portofino Inn in Redondo Beach.

We made an almost perfect run, down toward the beach, catching all the lights in sequence for miles across the L.A. sprawl. As we angled south toward our destination we began to sense that we might have won. As we pulled up at the Portofino's entrance we scanned the parking lot for other cars. There seemed to be no activity or any expectation of our arrival. Either we were so early that no one else had checked in or so late that it didn't matter. We raced into the hotel's office to get our Red Ball ticket stamped with our official arrival time. The subtracted difference between the New York stamping and the Portofino's would determine our total time for the race. We asked if anyone else had come in yet. "Why yes, a couple of cars are in," the girl behind the counter replied. Gilly, Jack, and I looked at each other. Not good, we thought, but an early arrival didn't necessarily mean we'd lost. The launch window from New York was up to each team's discretion. Some teams had left earlier than we did, and a whole lot had left later. It would be hours before all the racers were in and the times tabulated.

We lost by exactly 12 minutes, the time the train had held us up in Riverside. We were third overall, behind Behr's Cadillac and Yates, Stanner, and Brown. Both had taken the conventional route into L.A. from Flagstaff. If . . . (always the big IF) we hadn't been stopped in Oklahoma, we would have won by more than an hour and a half.

Peter Brock is a brilliant car designer (Shelby Daytona coupe), race team manager (Datsun Trans-Am championship cars), and a world-class photojournalist in motorsports.

Donna Mae Mims
1972

Judy Stropus' guy friend borrowed a brand-new limo from the owner of a limousine service for three gals who were in town for a few New York fun days. No problemo, and Mark Donohue saw to it that the brand new-Caddy was well shod—brand-new Goodyear racing tires all around!

We dutifully made a note for the limo owner that rear seatbelts were absent and that the privacy window refused to go up. We thought this would rob our off-duty driver of peace and solitude during snooze time, relaxing from the terrors of highway driving and peer critiquing of navigational skills.

One sponsor was the Right Bra Company, and I brazenly elected to go braless in those really shocking braless days! I also elected to wear a racing helmet—well, hey, this was racing USA! Number-three driver, Peggy Niemcek, along for the ride because she raised some sponsorship stuff, demonstrated how her hubby had advised her to properly steer—pushed way back in the seat with arms stiffened straight out onto the steering wheel. Hmmm.

Judy and I, on the upper level of the soon-to-be famous Red Ball Garage, enjoyed the racy fraternizing with the drivers we'd met throughout the United States, which came to a halt as our car was next down the elevator and on to the starting line. We punched our time card and Judy, knowing the way out of New York onto our southern route, took the green flag as we peeled off in front of the TV cameras, stopping one block away at the red light.

Visibility was worse than horrible as we got onto a turnpike in a downpour and sped by a slower vehicle—sudden blinking lights and a screaming siren announcing that the slower vehicle was a state trooper touring in the fast lane as we passed him on the berm. Judy handled the situation by simply opening up our official cigar box—which housed $700 for just such situations—and paying the fine pronto to a happy trooper right at the scene of the crime. Like the other gendarmes, he was nonplussed by the array of advertising affixed to the limo's exterior. Nor did our very high-tech dash equipment—three stop-watches duct-taped to the dash and a tachometer hanging off the steering column—bother him. We explained to the trooper that we were rushing this limo to Hollywood where it was needed for an MGM movie. He opined that it would behoove us to slow down to ensure getting it there in one piece.

Most memorable is the ticketing event in the wee dark hours as we were pulled over by a Barney Fife look-alike who claimed that he'd been chasing us for 15 minutes at 115 miles per hour. No bribe could corrupt this pure-hearted Don Knotts, and we were doomed to follow him to the magistrate, earning more points as he was quite effectively blinded by our aircraft headlamps.

At fuel stops, three of the doors simultaneously flew open as we raced around the limo, unhitching the hood safety chain, checking oil, radiator, and cleaning windows. One of us attacked the gas pump while another unceremoniously threw the gas money on the ground as we leapt back in, slamming doors, to screech off in pursuit of the unknowns along the southern route.

We managed to get lost in Texas and I brilliantly navigated our limo back on course. During my turn to nap, while dreaming that I was in a clothes dryer, I awoke standing up all hunched, realizing that we'd rolled the thing and landed right side up. I observed, "Gee, the window fell up!" and the aircraft lamps revealed that it was raining money. I hadn't yet figured out that the official cigar box had escaped and that my messed up brain and bod had apparently been beaten up by the Snap-On tool box with which we shared the rear quarters. No surprise that, as Judy navigated, our stiff-armed third driver decided to doze off about 30 miles east of El Paso, rolling us way off the road, just short of a great Texas ravine. It was nice that the big fuel can in the trunk remained inactive.

This event led to my first ever real cowboy encounter. A cowboy who was driving an 18-wheeler full of horses on the way to Oregon appeared and dug down into the sand or whatever to release my door. Mr. Cowboy got the paramedics on the scene. My rattled brain conjured up the fantasy that I was a guest on the TV series *Emergency*, but my wrecked bod and broken collar bone only permitted me to sit up front with the med guys instead of theatrically getting hauled away on a stretcher.

No one in the emergency room spoke English until a blue-eyed, blond kid showed up—his claim to fame being that he smuggled Joshua trees across the border. My helmet sent the message that I was a biker and, in reality, we knew from racing that, hey, if we removed it, my head might explode or something. The doctor grimaced in horror as he looked at me and stepped back—only to learn from the smuggler that my green face and hands were due to the dunking I'd received from the official porta-potty which, happily, Judy had sanitized at the preceding pit stop. When I was released the next afternoon from the hospital, it was only necessary to put on my shoes, since the hospital guys economically dumped me in bed with all my own clothes on.

Sans any proof of ownership, Judy sold the wrecked limo to a used-car dealer for money for us to fly home. The aircraft pilot came back to visit me, as the stewardess apparently mentioned to him that someone back there was rambling on about crashing.

Judy's New York friend creatively told the limo guy that the gals really liked the limo so much that they wanted to buy it and he paid for the thing! Way to go!

Donna Mae Mims gained fame in the 1960s and 1970s as "the Pink Lady" of sports car racing, competing in SCCA races in an Austin-Healey Sprite painted ... you guessed it.

Judy Stropus
1972

Talk about the agony, the ecstasy. What I thought was going to be one of the adventures of a lifetime turned into a total disaster . . . and not a whole lot of fun. In the midst of my earning my 15 minutes of fame back in 1972 as a professional timer and scorer for the world's greatest race teams, I decided to put together a team to run the Cannonball Sea-to-Shining-Sea Trophy Dash. And, although I wouldn't be caught dead doing something so politically incorrect in 2001, I was delighted to put together an all-girl team. We were so all-girl that we were even sponsored by a bra company—the Right Bra Company. Of course, our star driver, Donna Mae Mims, arrived not wearing one— she didn't have to. To be sure not to offend the sponsor, she proceeded to ask the sponsor's PR guy if he had an extra one on hand. Don't all PR people carry the client's product with them? He didn't. Our third driver was Peggy Niemcek, wife of PR guru Brad Niemcek, who was driving in another Cannonball entry. She was fresh from the delivery room after giving birth to her and Brad's child. Peggy was too busy to help because of severe motherhood, so I offered to put the entire deal together. Luckily, we had the help of some famous folk from that era—Bobby Rinzler, the Atlantic race team owner, who obtained a Cadillac limo for us, and Mark Donohue, who convinced Goodyear to give us good tires. Roy Woods, the race driver and race team owner, had a friend in the financial business who wanted to see his name plastered on the side of a race car . . . (well, it was *almost* a race car). In honor of "Think Pink" Donna Mae Mims, whose race cars to this day are painted pink, we decked ourselves out in pink stretch bodysuits and pink hip-hugging bell-bottoms—at least for the launching party in the Red Ball Garage in New York City. We were too, too adorable, especially Donna Mae, whose perky breasts, sans bra, caused quite a sensation in the not-quite-so-liberal 1970s.

With a bag o' bucks and Donna Mae with her helmet in tow for safety, off we dashed to California. We decided to outwit and outsmart the competition and take the southern route through Georgia, Texas, and so forth. After being stopped for speeding three times in the first few hundred miles by state troopers dumbfounded by the sight of this limo with sponsor's names emblazoned all over it and a platinum blonde with a helmet on in the back seat, we settled in for a long and boring ride. Not even circling Atlanta on I-285 several times when I, the navigator, was taking my sleep stint, would keep us from our goal of reaching the Portofino Inn in Redondo Beach ahead of the others, whom we envisioned trapped in snowdrifts up north. What did finally keep us from our goal was a totally broken-down Cadillac limo on the side of the road outside of El Paso, Texas, in the middle of the night. By then the alignment was out of whack, the heater stopped working, and the vehicle had had just about enough of the torture we bestowed upon it as well as ourselves. We were done . . . and on an airplane the next day home to New York. It took me years to finally watch the *Cannonball Run* movie, which depicted some of our experiences, although in a Lamborghini. I could laugh then.

Judy Stropus gained fame in motorsports as a timer-scorer for top teams in Indianapolis-style, major sports car, and Formula One competition. She is now a public relations specialist in the racing field. Her version of the Cannonball does not mention the crash.

Robin Miller
1972

Brock Yates had no idea who I was, but my hook was that I was to deliver at least one Indianapolis 500 biggie.

It was October of 1972 and as a neophyte journalist and pseudo race driver, I had become possessed about competing in the Cannonball Baker Sea-to-Shining-Sea Memorial Trophy Dash. So I called Yates and convinced him that America would be a better place to live if he allowed me and Art Pollard or Johnny Parsons to be part of his coast-to-coast madness the next month. He agreed and that set the wheels in motion. Pollard, who had taken me under his wing and convinced Andy Granatelli to sell me a Formula Ford, was always up for an adventure, so he agreed to be my codriver. I then approached local car dealer Jim Campbell about lending me a Datsun 240Z for a few days of "road testing." He gave me the OK.

I cleared a week of vacation at my workplace, the *Indianapolis Star*, and started counting the minutes until I could mix it up on the nation's highways with Dan Gurney and Tony Adamowicz. But, when Pollard found out the Cannonball was a nonpaying event that required little or no sleep for two days, he told me to find somebody else. I begged Parsons, and he laughed at me. So I vowed to go to New York City solo, figuring I'd pick up a codriver when I got there.

The night before leaving I received a phone call from Campbell's attorney, informing me that because of insurance concerns I wouldn't be taking that Datsun anywhere and it was being towed back to Campbell's lot as we spoke. Now, losing your codriver and your ride the day before the show would have likely discouraged most people, but not me. Hell, I'd flunked out of Ball State Teacher's College, and my IQ wasn't much higher than the number on Gordon Johncock's Indy car. I bought a one-way ticket to New York the next morning and arrived at the parking garage (where the race was to start) looking for a car to drive. As fate would have it, I ran into a friend named Bill Henry, an eclectic fellow who had invented the first really good fireproof shoes and gloves. Henry said he'd just purchased a Vega station wagon for his mother-in-law and wanted someone to drive it to California (honest to God). I volunteered and he paired me with a part-time stock car driver (and full-time Hollywood makeup artist) named Wes Dawn.

Because the Vega had a 5-gallon fuel tank, Dawn suggested we find an auxiliary fuel tank or else we'd be stopping every hour for gas. Of course Manhattan, isn't exactly brimming over with speed shops, and we had to go to Brooklyn before we could find an auto parts store. We bought four 5-gallon cans, a piece of hose and a toggle switch. Considering I was a mechanical moron, Wes explained that we could run the line to our main tank, and when it went dry, the guy who wasn't driving would simply crawl back and put the hose in one of the cans. Colin Chapman would have been impressed.

Yates, obviously experimenting with assorted drugs in those days, had everyone assemble at this parking garage and invited local TV stations to make sure this insanity could be documented. On Monday night, teams started five minutes apart and punched a time card. If you reached 75 miles per hour in midtown Manhattan you could make 20-some lights in a row.

Wes started and we had the first of our five tickets 20 minutes into the race—on the Jersey Turnpike. Immediately, we both noticed the fumes from our "spare fuel tanks" were about to overcome us, so we decided to roll all the windows down. Nothing like running 100 miles per hour in 20-degree weather for the first 30 hours.

Our first mistake came when I tried to catch a short nap in Ohio. When I woke up, I saw a sign that said "Cleveland . . . 25 miles." Not being a student of geography, I nonetheless realized that my California teammate had taken 80 North instead of 80 South. We got turned around but it cost us a couple of hours. Because our Vega was meant for Bill's mother-in-law, it didn't come equipped with too many bells and whistles. There was no cruise control so naturally we invented one—taking a snow scraper and jamming it between the seat and gas pedal. We ran most of the race at 110 miles per hour (top speed) and used the median a couple of times to avert multiple-car pileups.

When we stopped for gas it looked like the Wood brothers at Daytona as we scrambled to fill our tanks and our stomach and empty our bladders. Wes had brought along a "Fuzz Buster" radar detector, which turned out to be perfect for spotting airplanes but a complete failure at alerting us for The Man. We acquired speeding tickets in Ohio, Indiana, Oklahoma, and California. (More about that later.)

As the sun came up to begin our 30th hour on the road, we were storming through Needles, California, and saw a white Pantera at a gas station. I screamed at Wes and told him that was one of our competitors and we had to be in contention. Wes said he knew a shortcut to L.A., so we took it and shortly thereafter got another ticket. Our final ticket was given across from the Riverside Raceway (we thought that was ironic) but we still managed to roar into the Portofino Inn on the Pacific Ocean in 39 hours and 35 minutes—good for seventh overall.

Naturally, there was no prize money, but we had a wonderful dinner and everyone shared their horror stories. I flew back home the next day—$500 poorer, but richer for the experience. I've not talked to Wes since we parted company but I did get an engaging postcard from him a few months after the race. Turns out since we used his address on our last two tickets (and didn't show up for court) he got to spend six weekends in the slammer and wanted to "thank" me for sharing. I went home and wrote a full-page story in the *Indianapolis Star* (titled "Cannonball was 90 miles per hour Jailhouse Rock") that sent the Indiana director of motor vehicles over the edge. He tried to have my license suspended. Yates, who somehow avoided prosecution, penned a wonderful play-by-play for *Car and Driver* and used a group photo (of the people who weren't maimed, killed, or lost in action), which still resides on my wall today.

There were only two more pure Cannonballs before Brock wisely opted to throw the red flag and go for a more docile exercise in man, machine, and time. But I'll always be honored that I got to be a part of it. Sure, it was stupid, dangerous, costly, and exhausting. And I'd do it again tomorrow. In a New York second.

Robin Miller is a world-class motorsports journalist and sometime race driver based in Indianapolis, Indiana.

Brad Niemcek, Steve Durst
1972

Everything was fine until they offered us money. The guys at Briggs Chevrolet of South Amboy, New Jersey, (drag racers all) created a nifty little rocket for the PRDA's running of the third Cannonball: A Chevy Vega Kammback wagon, fitted with a small-block LT1 V-8 and Camaro drivetrain. Remarkably, the vehicle handled quite well. It did, that is, until we were offered an indecent amount of money to run Rodger Ward Indy Champ tires on our trip. The tires arrived, already mounted, only 36 hours before we were due at the Red Ball garage. They turned out to be seriously oversize. So, we had to not only rearc the wheel openings (with some sort of air-powered cutting tool), we also had to raise the car, front and rear, to accommodate these behemoths.

It apparently is not nice to raise a powerful car's center of gravity. But, once on the road, Steve Durst and I quickly learned how to cope. We had only to anticipate things. When accelerating, we learned to expect the Vega to jump one lane to the left; when decelerating, it will jump back to the right. Steve Durst agreed to codrive the 1972 Cannonball because Oscar and Tony seemed to have something else to do that week. Durst was a publicity client of mine, and he believed me when I told him that doing the Cannonball would be good publicity for him. Turns out his confidence in my abilities as a publicist did not translate to confidence of my ability behind the wheel. Or perhaps Durst is normally a white-knuckled rider. In any case, Durst decided to pull his helmet out of his case soon after I had motored into Pennsylvania and put it on. Fortunately, this unspoken commentary about my driving lasted only through the first set of driving shifts. But all through the event, I noticed his tendency to wipe his hands on the thighs of the white jeans he wore. By the time we got to Redondo Beach, those jeans appeared to be hopelessly stained.

You can say what you want about our strategy to run slow and make no stops in 1971; it did apparently save us from any confrontations with the law. Such was not the case in 1972. We went much faster, and we got nailed five times. Fortunately, I was only stopped once, near St. Louis, and released with the warning to go more slowly until we were in the next county. Durst was not so lucky, especially as we entered Gallup, New Mexico. Cresting a hill in the late afternoon sun, I saw what I thought was a "Smokey" at the end of a long decline in the distance. I issued a warning to Durst, and he hit the brakes, but it was already too late. The New Mexico state trooper ordered us to follow him to the local justice of the peace. I'll never forget the bright red numbers flashing on the trooper's dashboard display: "106-106-106."

It is not good psychology, I learned, to interrupt a justice of the peace in the middle of his "speed kills" harangue. But all I wanted to do was to tell him that we'd be glad to pay our fine and be on our way. So, as respectfully as I could, I pulled a small Tupperware container from the pocket of my jacket and asked, "Do you know what the fine will be?"

The spluttering JP raged on some more. Finally, after peeling $240 from the roll I kept in the Tupperware, we were allowed to continue, but not until we had been warned, "You will be stopped by every state patrolman you encounter between here and L.A.." Yep, we were stopped three more times (if memory serves). One of those times, in Arizona, two troopers converged on the scene, and asked to see what we had under the hood. We obliged. They laughed, and sent us on our way.

The advantage we felt we had as far as Gallup (we got there in 25 hours flat) was obviously trickling away. By the time we reached Riverside County, Durst and I were in near total despair. We could not possibly still be leading at this point. So we just resolved to soldier on. And, then, on a fast downhill right-hander west of Riverside on Highway 91, disaster struck, at about 85 miles per hour. It felt like something let go at the right rear. The tail of the Vega slewed viciously to the left. Thankfully, my instincts saved us. I cut the wheel sharply into the direction of the skid, and the Vega straightened. We slowed quickly and took an exit ramp. And, as we coasted toward the stop sign at the end of the ramp, Durst said, "That was a nice catch." Whatever relief I felt was short-lived. We stopped in front of a gas station and got out to see if we could identify the problem. It wasn't hard. The right rear wheel was tilted in at the top what seemed to be at least 10 degrees. We summoned the gas station's tow truck, and when it picked up the rear end of the Vega, that right rear wheel fell off!

This was the second of three Cannonballs in which Brad competed.

Doug Scribner
LONG-HAIRED WEIRDO RACING TEAM
1972

I spoke with Brock Yates after the results of the 1971 Cannonball event were published in *Car and Driver*, and he extended an invitation to run in the next one, planned for November of 1972. Since it was a singular honor to be invited to participate in the madness, my friend (and later brother-in-law) Doug Blue and I spent the next few months trying to put together a competitive car-sponsor package. We thought a souped-up Cadillac ambulance in full Red Cross trim might have a certain "stealth" ability, but in the end we settled on a 1970 SS-454 Chevrolet Monte Carlo owned by drag and stock-car-racer Sam Lincoln who had a Sunoco station in our hometown of Rochester, New York. The Monte Carlo was built by Sam and ace mechanic Tom Corrozoni, who became the other two members of our team. Extensive preparation produced a machine that would do an honest 140 miles per hour at 4,000 rpm. Koni shock absorbers and big Goodyear steel-belted radial tires were tuned into the suspension. The tires were pre-production prototypes, and Goodyear wanted them back after the event. Big Cibie Super Oscar driving lamps (with 100-watt bulbs) were mounted between Cibie quartz-halogen headlamps, for a total of 1.1 million candlepower of nighttime illumination. A second fuel tank was installed in the trunk, so we had fillers on both sides and a total of 42 gallons for extra range.

On Sunday, November 12, 1972, the four members of the Long-Haired Weirdos Racing Team made our four-hour shakedown cruise into New York City. We arrived at the Red Ball Garage on East 31st Street early enough to choose a parking spot on the third floor where a minimum of concrete dust would clog the pores of our black vinyl roof. It was in this dingy atmosphere that hundreds of beautiful people gathered on Monday evening to attend a catered party thrown to celebrate publication of Brock Yates' new book, *Sunday Driver*, which featured a chapter devoted to the 1971 Cannonball.

At 10 o'clock that night, amid the glow of ABC-TV camera lights, a street full of curiosity seekers and well-wishers sent up a tumultuous cheer as the first cars left the garage for California.

We left at 10:25 with Sam Lincoln driving. Twenty minutes later, having made excellent time out of New York, we encountered a monumental traffic jam caused by a fire in Parsippany, New Jersey. The cops had stopped traffic on interstate 80 because the smoke was so thick. After sitting motionless in traffic for nearly 20 minutes, we worked the big Chevy through and around the jam, passing the AMX, the Travco, and possibly others. Only minutes later we were stopped for speeding by New Jersey State Police in an unmarked car and lost 10 minutes. Around midnight, the AMX caught up to us, and stayed with us, keeping a smooth, moderate pace. We then encountered rain and heavy fog on 80 through the Pennsylvania mountains. We allowed the AMX to pass in order to have taillights to follow through the fog; we then repassed the AMX to keep a faster pace. At 1:00 A.M. we were passed by a Porsche in the rain and followed it at a comfortable 90–100 miles per hour cruising speed for some time. At one point, both cars were passed by a Ford station wagon! We made our first gas stop at the Pennsylvania-Ohio border at 4 A.M., elapsed mileage 400, getting 10.3 miles per gallon. We wasted no time at gas stops. We would slide to a stop between two rows of pumps. Our doors would fly open and four people would burst from the car. Two immediately began filling the fuel tanks, one would open the hood and check the fluids, the fourth would drag the attendant out—this was before the days of self-service—and stand there with him counting out dollar bills as fast as the bells on the pumps were ringing. "We don't have time for you to count this," he'd explain, "and we're not waiting for change."

Off we went, leaving a dazed attendant standing in a haze of tire smoke, clutching a fistful of money. I was driving in Ohio, for three hours, in the rain. At one point we passed an unmarked police car. We didn't have a clue it was a police car until I caught a glimpse of his uniform shoulder patch as we went by. His high beams came on and he was obviously making some effort to catch up, but we were at least a mile ahead of him. Then 2 miles ahead, a couple of tractor-trailer trucks in tandem were starting up a long grade. The one behind started signaling to pull out and pass. We started working the lights. (Two toggle switches on the console controlled the Super Oscar lamps, which worked wonders to clear traffic). The second truck pulled back over and we went by. The truck then pulled back out, and we never saw the cop again.

We reached the Ohio-Indiana border at 7 A.M.; it was still raining. At 8 A.M., we were forced to follow a patrol car for 40 miles past Indianapolis, speed held at 70 miles per hour. We had our second gas stop at 774 miles; Corrozoni took over driving, was followed by another

Indiana patrol car 54 miles, and again held to 70 miles per hour, with it still raining. At 10 A.M. we were stopped for speeding (75 miles per hour) after another 75-mile "following session" by Illinois State Police. Ten minutes lost: Lincoln took over driving; in hopes of staying in competition, we decided to "up the pace." At 11 A.M., we arrived in St. Louis; heavy overcast but it had finally stopped raining. At 12:40 P.M., we made a gas stop at 1,195 miles. We had made excellent time. In Springfield while we were stopped, the PRDA Vega cruised past. Excitement renewed, the pursuit began.

At 12:55 the throttle broke; 3 1/2 minutes lost in repair. At 1:40 P.M., entering the Will Rogers Turnpike (interstate 44—a toll road), we questioned the toll attendant about the PRDA Vega, he reported no sign; we concluded they must have stopped for gas and been passed.

Doug Blue was now driving; the team was on full four-man alert, cruising; at 2:30 the sun came out. At 3:15 we overtook the PRDA Vega on Route 44 west of Tulsa. We came over the hill, and there they were, at the end of a line of cars in the right lane. We passed the Vega, passed the other cars in the line. The car at the front was a police cruiser . . . but he had started onto an off-ramp!

The Vega pulled out, accelerated down the hill after us, and we raced for the next 135 miles, consuming nearly an hour. We left the Vega behind, but not before Sam Lincoln showed them a hastily made sign, "Bad Valve—Can't Exceed 150 miles per hour!"

Finally, we were forced to stop for gas. After the quickest fill-up yet, I took over driving. At 5 P.M. with 1,580 miles elapsed, we limped into Elk City, Oklahoma, with third gear in the automatic transmission slipping badly. We pulled into Gene Smith Chevrolet just as a line of mechanics were filing out the back door at the end of their workday. We explained our situation. They were all aware of the Cannonball— they all came back in, turned on the lights and set to work in our car. They dropped the pan and determined the transmission was shot.

We knew it was over for us. The owner's son rushed in and offered to trade us his nearly identical Monte Carlo on the spot, but we decided to change the transmission. They made some calls, located the nearest available replacement unit 120 miles away in Texas, and we waited. It's not for nothing that we were known as the Long-Haired Weirdo Racing Team. Here I was, with my hair stuffed up into a hat, hanging around with redneck Oklahoma cowboys, listening to hippie jokes and watching them do rope tricks. But they were all incredible guys, and they had us back on the road in eight hours. Having exhausted Lincoln, Corrozoni, and most of our cash, we continued to Amarillo to spend the night in a Holiday Inn. The next day, Lincoln and Corrozoni returned with the car to Rochester, while Doug Blue and I caught a flight to Los Angeles. We spent the day hanging around with a friend of ours at his Porsche shop, then in the evening we all got dressed up and drove to Portofino Inn in a borrowed Rolls-Royce. We punched in our special time card, and ended up the 25th finisher, with a total time of 49 hours, and an average speed of 59 miles per hour. (Although it should be noted that we were officially a DNF.)

Without getting into a lot of "If only . . . " bench racing, suffice it to say that our goal was to make the New York to Los Angeles trip in 32 hours. We had a very realistic chance of doing that.

As the PRDA team admitted in the March 1973 issue of *Car and Driver*, our Monte Carlo was their most serious competition. We were leading when the Chevy broke—leading a professional team that had started 25 minutes ahead of us, and leading all others by at least an hour. All together, we covered 1,580 miles in 18 1/2 hours. That's an average speed of 85 miles per hour.

To quote Yates, "The Cannonball is run for two distinct reasons, one frivolous, the other quite serious. Essentially I view it as an adventure for people who really care about cars and drivers in the real world environment (as opposed to the laboratory environs of the race track). But the more weighty purpose of the Cannonball is to prove the validity of high-speed interstate travel (as opposed to the oppressive lunacy of the 55-mile-per-hour speed limit), both in terms of safety and economic efficiency."

Personally, our attitude in running the Cannonball was one of serious determination. There is no other way. Call it a journey, a trip, a tour, a vigorous jaunt (anything but a race), and no matter how loose the rules, or how much fun the event generates, it must be taken seriously. Danger is everywhere. Losing is nothing. All the axioms are true. But, what the hell, it'll be a long time before anyone dreams up a better excuse to go to California.

Doug Scribner is the proprietor of Mini-City, a Rochester, New York, firm specializing in Austin and Morris Mini-Minor sales and repairs.

H.K. "Bud" Stanner
1972

Brock Yates is the first real racer I ever met. When I arrived at Mark McCormick's International Management Group in 1971, fresh from Head Ski Company, where I was deeply involved in skiing and tennis, I was assigned to handle Jackie Stewart's account. I will never forget the Questor Grand Prix at Ontario, California, my first race. When I arrived I met Brock, who was absolutely the nicest and smartest journalist I had met. I am sure after the first few minutes of our conversation, Yates was aware that I knew nothing about motorsports. We quickly became good friends and did a lot of exciting stuff together, most of which should go unmentioned.

When Brock decided that the "Cannonball" should be an annual event, he invited Bob Brown and me to participate with him in a wonderful car—a two-door Dodge Challenger. I will never forget the start of the race. Earlier that day I took a 7 P.M. flight to Toronto and then a 4 P.M. flight to LaGuardia. I showed up at the Red Ball Garage about 6 P.M. and changed clothes in the mechanics' changing room. When I saw some spare tires in the rear of the car instead of a back seat and looked at the fuel cells packed into the trunk, I knew it would be an uncomfortable ride. (Unless you were driving the car!) When I saw the series of radar detectors and checked out the halogen lights and heard the roar of the engine, I knew it would be a fast ride.

My recollection is we left the Red Ball Garage about 9 P.M. and arrived in Marina del Rey about 37 1/2 hours later. I was starting to consider myself a racer. After our celebration at Marina del Rey, I had to take a red-eye flight back to Cleveland for some meetings, which I couldn't avoid. That means I had been up for about three straight nights! When I got to the office my eyeballs were squeaking every time I blinked, but I knew I had one of the best times of my life.

My thanks to Yates and his amazing idea, as well as his thoughtfulness in inviting me to participate. I will be forever grateful, and I will never forgive him!

Bud Stanner remains an executive vice president of the International Management Group and one of the most powerful and influential men in worldwide motorsports.

Richard Leib

MUSTANG

1972

In 1972 the Cannonball cross-country outlaw automobile race hit its peak of silliness. It was probably the most Disney-esque, live-out-your-fantasy race that has ever occurred in the United States.

That's the year I was part of a team that drove it, and though it seemed all the drivers had their own secret equipment and plots to win, I soon found we were part of a field of mongrels. There were professional drivers, experienced amateurs, con men, and Walter Mittys. It was postlogic time. This was the almost ruleless Cannonball, and soon we would be blasting cross-country, from sea to shining sea, tethered to reality by only the thinnest thread.

Let me tell the story as it happened to me, from "everyman's" point of view, the way it might have happened to you, and you be the judge.

Early in 1972 I read a story in *Car and Driver* about the 1971 Cannonball that had just been run. It was a light, humorous article, but it contained the stuff that dreams are made of. The Cannonball, it explained, was a race from the Red Ball Garage, in downtown New York City to the Portofino Inn in Redondo Beach, California. It was, of course, illegal to use highways for a race, and so its start was never announced. The race was just confessed to after it was over.

Somehow a few people learned about the race, and when the time came, they secretly met at the Red Ball and made history. Finally came the part that stopped me cold. Anyone could run it. No special licenses were required. God, think of it. Anyone. Naturally you'd have to somehow figure out when it was being run again, but if you could, just think . . . anyone.

I've got these three wacky friends, George, Kaa, and Dave. Kaa is not his real name, but he has a Marty Feldman way of crossing his eyes and looks like the Python Kaa from the movie, *Jungle Book*. Somehow the nickname stuck.

The four of us call ourselves "the Lawyers." Why we do so is a long story I won't bother you with. Anyway, I was sitting with George in a local night spot, and George had a really bored look on his face, so I figured I needed a sentence with real shock appeal to get his attention.

"George," I mumbled, "know what we oughta do? We oughta drive the Cannonball."

"What the dickens is the Cannonball?" asked George drowsily. I should point out that George doesn't use profanity. One day he decided that he should have at least one good habit, and the easiest, as well as one of the most impressive of all good habits, was not cussing. So that's the one he chose.

I told George what I had read and said the Lawyers ought to give it a shot. George was sitting up straight now. His eyes were clear, and there was no drowsiness in his voice when he said, "Gees, what do we do first?"

"We'll take it step by step," I said. "First I get someone to sponsor us a car, then you phone Yates."

The next afternoon I stopped by the local Pontiac dealer to talk to Dick Choler. Choler was a good friend, an autophile, and the leading Pontiac salesman in the area. He was familiar with the Cannonball. I told him my plans and said I'd like a new Pontiac to drive.

"Just think of the publicity," I muttered. I waited for him to laugh me out of the showroom; the laughter didn't come. "OK," he said, "you get in the race and I'll give you a car."

It took an hour for the shock to wear off, and then I picked up the phone. In the most relaxed tones I could muster, I told George we had a new Pontiac. "Give Yates a ring and set it up," I said. "Let me know what you come up with."

Not too bad, I thought. Not only did I really have a cool idea, but also I accomplished the first step. Now it would be George's failure that would stop the adventure. I mean, you don't just pick up the phone, call the editor of a leading magazine and tell him you'd like to break the law with him, right?

A couple of weeks went by with no news, then one day George stopped by. "I got tired of waiting, so I called Yates," he announced. "Yates said he got the letter and he wondered if we were for real. Anyway, we're in. We've gotta be at the Red Ball on November 13."

I thought we should stick to a maximum speed of 85, and if we avoided arrests, breakdowns, getting lost, and found the best route, we could finish with our heads held high. We weren't going to be able to outdrive top-notch professionals, so the likelihood of our winning was not great.

George mostly agreed. He felt the maximum of 85 was a little slow, though, and suggested 130.

Over the next few weeks we drew up plans for car modifications, route choices, and driving strategies. For car modifications we'd need a big fuel cell to minimize stops, a pilot relief tube for the same reason, a reclining seat for sleeping, and some spare parts for road maintenance. We discussed the pros and cons of various routes and finally gave up and phoned Chicago Motor Club. It turned out we probably had the best route in the race.

Finally we checked with Dave. He was too busy to get too involved, he said, but told us to do whatever we felt was best. So, with our finalized plans in hand, we headed off to see Dick Choler about our car.

"Are you guys putting me on?" was not the reaction we expected from our Pontiac rep. "Hell, I had no idea you were serious."

Ten minutes later at a small table at Jim and Chink's Foundry Lounge, we discussed the fact that not having a car to race was going to really slow us down. I had a two-place AMX; Dave, a Corvette; George drove a Firebird; while Kaa's transportation was renowned for undependability. We were in trouble. George and I were also getting strong vibrations that Dave was not going along.

The summer disappeared into futile attempts to get a car from every conceivable source.

We were considering renting one from Hertz when, as luck would have it, my job handed me a trip to Mexico, thereby offering me a colorful, coward's way around the problem.

"George, my man," I proclaimed, "we're burned out on this thing. Let's give it a rest. It's time that Kaa did something; let him figure it out. I'll be in Mexico the week before the race, and I'll return directly to New York on the 12th. You meet me at the airport and tell me what we're driving then. Any way you two handle it is fine with me." I should have known better.

On the 12th I deplaned in New York City and was greeted by two beaming faces. Dave hadn't come. He decided to stay home and get a divorce instead.

"What are our wheels?" I asked.

"Come on, we'll show you," babbled Kaa. "It's actually kind of a funny story," offered George.

There in the parking lot sat a tired green Mustang with a Mexico sticker on the side window. It seems George and Kaa had answered an ad in *The New York Times* for someone who wanted their car driven to California. They had met a man in the hotel room who gave them the car, an L.A. address, and a week to get it there. I stared, incredulous, at the car and then my friends.

"We think it's hot," they said in unison.

As we drove toward the hotel, it became painfully evident the car would never make it.

"We need shocks and a wheel alignment if we ever hope to get this thing to 100 miles per hour," I sighed.

"OK," said George, and we set off to find a suspension shop. We had been turned down by a bunch of places and George was getting pretty nervous about the winos who kept jogging beside the car and wiping our windshield, when we spotted the Lafayette Tire Company, just closing up.

"Just keep taking pictures," Kaa told me. "I'll do the talking." So while Kaa explained the race and his hopes that we would be famous, I just kept aiming my camera around the shop. The shop manager balanced the tires, aligned the wheels, put on all-new ball joints, and periodically posed for my pictures.

That night we had a great meal at an old college chum's home in New Jersey. He was, at the time, a driving instructor for the New York City school system.

In the morning we went on a shopping spree and loaded our car with pillows, candy, bottled water, and Spam, then drove to the Red Ball. At the garage, we and our car were lifted to the top floor on a rickety wooden elevator and unloaded amidst a collection of fantastic cars and people.

There was Yates and his special Challenger; *Car and Driver*'s project car, the 240Z Omega (which was not entered); a Pantera set up for the Cannonball by a Can Am team; the PRDA's V-8-equipped Vega station wagon; the Right Bra-sponsored black Cadillac limo with its all-girl team, dressed in pink jumpsuits; an exotic-looking Bradley GT; an Excalibur; a steel gray Mercedes with Rev. Tom Thuck lettered on the door . . . and our dirty green Mustang.

"We've gotta go back down," whispered George.

"Why?" I wondered.

"We forgot to gas up," he replied.

As we were entering the Red Ball for the second time, we bumped into ex-baseball star Jim Bouton and an ABC camera crew. "Is this where the secret race is starting from?" asked Bouton.

"How did you know about the race?" asked Kaa.

"Where's Brock Yates?" asked Bouton. Then he saw the girls in the pink jumpsuits and bounded off, putting an end to his questions.

It seems Yates was having a publication party for his book, *Sunday Driver*, from 7 to 9 P.M. on November 13 at the Red Ball. The race was no longer a secret. All three networks would carry its running, and police across the nation would be looking forward to thinning our ranks.

We got outside the city quickly and were heading down interstate 80 when we came upon a long stalled line of traffic. George slipped over on the shoulder and inched along the right side of the line till we came face to face with a state tropper who was directing traffic around a fire truck that was spraying a barn fire.

"Pardon us," smiled Kaa, as George slipped through the traffic, around the truck, and into the night.

"Christ," I mumbled.

"Geez," said George.

Kaa started singing, "California, Here We Come."

It was raining, and the roads were a touch tricky. George was holding it around 90 miles per hour. I was about to tell him that seemed a bit fast for the conditions when the Can Am Pantera screamed around us and disappeared over a hill. "Maybe we should go a little faster," I offered.

The first gas stop was a masterpiece of teamwork. I jumped out of the 'Stang and started pumping gas. George shoved a Xeroxed article on the Cannonball into the attendant's one hand, while I transferred the pump nozzle to his other hand.

"Fill it up, we're in a race," shouted George as the Lawyers ran for the rest room.

We were back on the road in almost no time, complimenting each other on a perfect pit stop.

The next 15 hours or so we were not very eventful, except for one gas stop when Kaa announced he was heading for the john. After waiting anxiously in the car for 10 minutes, George and I headed into the building to hurry him up.

We found Kaa sulking by the door.

"Some big drunk is locked in there," he said, "and he told me he's not coming out till he's good and ready."

"Lord," I mumbled. George knocked on the door to the ladies' room. "All clear," he shouted.

So while Kaa used the ladies' restroom, George and I stood by the door like palace guards and wondered if this was really what big-time racing was all about.

After a while, when our turn came to rest, we learned how to tune things out and fall into kind of a cross between a hypnotic and natural sleep. It was so effective that I still don't know for sure what happened when we ran out of gas in Texas. It was during my sleep shift, and I remember asking why we weren't moving.

"We're out of gas," I heard.

Seeing no buildings, I asked where the hell civilization went.

"It's a big state," George told me.

"What are we doing?" I wondered drowsily.

"Waiting for help," Kaa replied.

I drifted off to sleep, and when I awoke, we were pounding down the highway at 110 miles per hour as our right rear tire was starting to make unnatural sounds.

We left our tire and wheel (we had brought an extra spare) near the Texas border. Somehow it had become more square than round.

A bit further down the road, we saw the exotic-looking Bradley GT, empty and obviously broken. "At least we won't be last," Kaa announced.

About 2:30 in the morning, I saw a Cannonballing van and decided to take him. It wasn't as easy as I thought, but about 20 minutes later he slowed for a moment, and we flashed by. That's when we saw the speed trap. The van had a radar detector; we didn't even have common sense. The New Mexico patrolman looked at us, all dressed in black (we thought we ought to dress alike to look like a team), and almost fell over laughing. "You guys wouldn't be cat burglars, would you?" he asked. He kept my license as assurance I would pay the fine and sent us on our way. George got arrested 15 minutes later.

There was a song on the Top 10 that weekend called "Take It Easy." Some of the words went, "Standing on a corner in Winslow, Arizona. . . ." It was playing on the 'Stang's radio when we blazed into Winslow, Arizona. 'What the hell," Kaa asked, "how much time can it cost us?"

So we squealed to a stop, all jumped out, then popped back in the car and sped away, just so we could say we had stood on a corner in Winslow, Arizona. We were very punchy by this time.

When we hit Flagstaff, it was snowing, so we put Kaa at the wheel. He was from Wisconsin, and we figured he'd know how to handle the snow. He did, but the mountains scared him to death. He clamped his hands on the wheel and maintained a steady 20 miles per hour. We couldn't get him to talk or yield the driving. He finally broke his silence when, halfway through the mountains, a car passed us. It was the Bradley.

"Should have flattened their tires when we had the chance," Kaa mumbled.

"Welcome to California" is a very nice sign when you've been driving as long as we had been. Kaa, out of the mountains and back to his old self now, started singing, "From the New York Island to California's water . . . "

Our first gas-up had been a masterpiece of teamwork; our last was a tribute to total exhaustion.

"Fill 'er up," George said.

"Hot food," I said, as I focused on a McDonald's across the street.

By the time we had gotten gas and hamburgers and shakes, we had blown almost 20 minutes; but our heads began to clear as nourishment oozed its way into our Cannonballed bodies.

We pulled into the Portofino Inn 44 hours and 53 minutes after we had punched out in New York.

George was driving. Kaa was curled up in the back seat making sounds like a sonar receiver. I was looking for fame and glory.

"Where's the photographers?" I asked.

"In the bar," I was told. "They didn't think anybody else was coming."

Later we found we had placed 20th out of 28 finishers, out of 34 teams that has started the race. Some big-time racers like Donna Mae Mims didn't finish, so we could always say we'd beaten some pros . . . and, we had stood on a corner in Winslow, Arizona . . . and, we would forever be a part of the band of certifiables that had driven the Cannonball Sea-to-Shining-Sea Memorial Trophy Dash.

Richard Lieb is an Elkhart, Indiana, businessman. His recollections are typical of the relaxed, ad-hoc efforts put forth by nonprofessional enthusiasts in the Cannonball races.

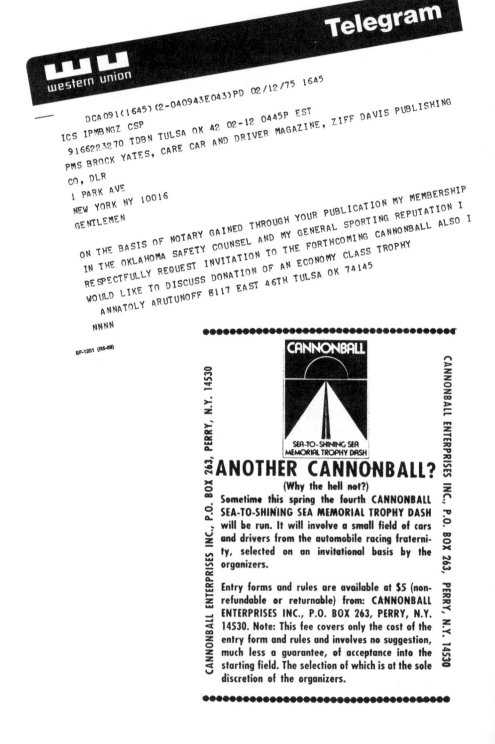

Telegram

western union

DCA091(1645)(2-040943E043)PD 02/12/75 1645

ICS IPMBNGZ CSP
9166223270 TDBN TULSA OK 42 02-12 0445P EST
PMS BROCK YATES, CARE CAR AND DRIVER MAGAZINE, ZIFF DAVIS PUBLISHING
CO, DLR
1 PARK AVE
NEW YORK NY 10016

GENTLEMEN

ON THE BASIS OF NOTARY GAINED THROUGH YOUR PUBLICATION MY MEMBERSHIP
IN THE OKLAHOMA SAFETY COUNSEL AND MY GENERAL SPORTING REPUTATION I
RESPECTFULLY REQUEST INVITATION TO THE FORTHCOMING CANNONBALL ALSO I
WOULD LIKE TO DISCUSS DONATION OF AN ECONOMY CLASS TROPHY
ANNATOLY ARUTUNOFF 8117 EAST 46TH TULSA OK 74145

NNNN

SF-1201 (R5-69)

CANNONBALL

SEA-TO-SHINING SEA
MEMORIAL TROPHY DASH

ANOTHER CANNONBALL?
(Why the hell not?)

Sometime this spring the fourth CANNONBALL SEA-TO-SHINING SEA MEMORIAL TROPHY DASH will be run. It will involve a small field of cars and drivers from the automobile racing fraternity, selected on an invitational basis by the organizers.

Entry forms and rules are available at $5 (non-refundable or returnable) from: CANNONBALL ENTERPRISES INC., P.O. BOX 263, PERRY, N.Y. 14530. Note: This fee covers only the cost of the entry form and rules and involves no suggestion, much less a guarantee, of acceptance into the starting field. The selection of which is at the sole discretion of the organizers.

CANNONBALL ENTERPRISES INC., P.O. BOX 263, PERRY, N.Y. 14530

CANNONBALL ENTERPRISES INC., P.O. BOX 263, PERRY, N.Y. 14530

1975
In the Face of the Double Nickel

RUNNING THE FOURTH CANNONBALL Sea-to-Shining-Sea Memorial Trophy Dash in 1974 seemed like the height of madness. The nation was in turmoil. Richard Nixon had fled the White House in shame in August and within a few months Saigon would fall, ending the decade-long debacle in Vietnam. The OPEC embargo on petroleum production instituted two years earlier was mercifully over, but its long-lasting residue—the universally ignored 55-miles-per-hour national speed limit imposed by the Nixon administration on January 2, 1974, was in full effect.

In the autumn of that year, I went with fellow *Car and Driver* staffers Jim Williams (a veteran of the first solo Cannonball) and John

One of the rolling chicanes commonly encountered on the Cannonballs. Here the Atwell/Stanton Porsche (CB handle "Little Beaver") and the Olds/Fernald/Hourihan Volvo obediently dawdle behind a Missouri "County Mounty." The photo was taken by Tom Kozlowski from the front seat of the E-Z Wider Mazda RX4 with its highly appropriate handle "Rolling Gold." The trio were forced to hang behind the cop for 50 frustrating miles.

Eberhardt on a 7,000-mile tour around the United States in a Mer-cedes-Benz 450SEL sedan. This trip resulted in a story in the February 1975 issue of *Car and Driver* titled "One Lap of America." (A bit of acci-dental prescience that would lead to the event of that name being started in 1984.)

The story examined the impact of the so-called "double nickel" and grappled with the phenomenon of citizens band radio. "CB" had been discovered and popularized by long-haul truckers to defeat the speed limit. By late 1973, Channel 19 was a coast-to-coast early warn-ing system against the so-called "Smokeys" (a reference to the car-toon character Forest Ranger Smokey the Bear, and the flat-brimmed felt hats favored by the nation's highway patrol officers.)

Two years had passed since the last Cannonball. But suddenly a groundswell of support rose up to run again. The 1973 John Avildsen movie project had died, although he would later win a Best Picture Oscar for *Rocky* and would enjoy a distinguished career as a director. Another movie was attempted by a pair of struggling producers but went nowhere. In the ensuing 24 months the nation's attention was riveted on the Watergate scandal, the Vietnam mess, and the OPEC

Former co-winner Fred Olds ominously aims toward California while team rally ace Bob Hourihan and Steve Fernald, contemplate the long drive ahead. They brought their Volvo 164E home 10th in 40 hours and 35 minutes.

shutdown. In the face of such unpleasantness running a cross-country automobile race seemed to edge toward the treasonous. Still, chase movies involving madcap driving remained a basic part of the Hollywood production cycle. Steven Speilberg, fresh out of film school, directed his first feature, *Sugarland Express*, a film about a couple being chased across Texas as they try to rescue their son. The picture, while not a classic car movie, involved serious road action and starred ex-*Laugh In* luminary Goldie Hawn. Schlock director Paul Bartel released the 1975 drive-in classic, *Death Race 2000*, starring Sylvester Stallone—a gory, campy comedy about cross-country race involving, among other pleasantries, running down pedestrians. The picture was successful enough to prompt Bartel and Stallone to follow up with *Death*

Sport two years later. But this was just the beginning of Hollywood's fascination with the Cannonball coast-to-coast theme, no matter how perverted their versions might be.

But now, with Nixon gone, gasoline loosening up, and Vietnam close to being settled, one more trip across the continent seemed possible, if dodgy. The date was set for April 23, 1975, and entries began to pour into the magazine.

Wes Dawn, the Los Angeles film technician, came again, this time with California sportsman and vintner Gil Nickel and his steamy 450SEL Mercedes-Benz. Wes, now deceased, will be remembered as the only person besides Yogi Behr and myself to have competed in all four of the full-tilt Cannonballs. Fred

American pro rally champion John Buffum had troubles on his one and only Cannonball. He and his co-driver ex-wife Vicki were unable to run better than 9th in their much-raced, ex-factory Porsche 911 Carrera—a veteran of the African Safari rally. His resemblance to Peter Fonda was entirely coincidental.

Olds, who had won with Behr in 1972, reentered with a Volvo, and teamed with Bob Hourihan, at the time the top pro-rally driver in America. Brad Niemceck was back again with his PRDA team (minus Kovaleski and Adamowicz) and a modified Ford van. Bill Broderick was returning with a Travco motor home, this time sponsored in part by the Bolus & Snopes racing team, a creation of talented writer and humorist William (Don't call me "Bill") Jeanes, who had recently been hired by *Car and Driver* as a feature editor. Then came some really serious players. John Buffum, perhaps the best pro-rally driver ever produced on these shores, entered a lightweight Porsche 911 with his ex-wife Vicki (still friends), while Sandy Satullo, a Cleveland-based offshore powerboat champion, brought along a low-key Buick Electra sedan for himself and his son, Sandy II.

Three Porsches, all modified Carreras, were entered by SCCA pro racer Tom Nehl and racing photographer Bill Warner; Leo Lynch and Dan Rowzie from Pittsburgh, Pennsylvania; and the much-decorated retired U.S. Army Colonel Jim Atwell and Porsche salesman Chick Stanton of Virginia Beach, Virginia. Three General Motors engineers, Dave Shugars, Dennis Weglarz, and Ron McConkey, brought along a tweaked 1974 Pontiac Trans Am. In the vintage category, Fred Feiner was back with his 1951 Studebaker/Chevy, while well-known sports car racer Anatoly "Toly" Arutunoff entered a 1969 Chrysler-powered Bristol 410 saloon.

Airline pilots Richard Harris, Richard Cannata, and Fred Feiner leave the Red Ball Garage with their hot-rodded 1951 Studebaker.

Then came a serious Florida entry. Jack May, a successful real estate broker, enlisted the aid of Rick Cline, a well-respected sports car driver and race mechanic, to prepare and codrive his creamy-white Ferrari 246GTS Dino. We immediately knew that the little Ferrari would pose a formidable challenge.

While the flashy Dino attracted much attention, no one considered a 1973 Chevy pickup that rolled in from Modesto, California, much of a threat. But its driver, Jack McCoy, was one of the best stock car racers on the West Coast, and he and pal Gary Johnson had packed their truck with a 454-cubic-inch Chevy motor and extra fuel tanks. Jack's wife, Peggy, would serve as the third driver in the machine, which was not given much chance against the seemingly quicker competition.

Eighteen cars and 52 drivers appeared for the fourth running of the Cannonball. The start and finish would be the same—Red Ball Garage to the Portofino Inn. "There would be one rule—there are no rules." Lowest elapsed time would win. Breaking the record appeared iffy. While more interstates had been added west of the Mississippi, through Oklahoma and Texas, the new 55 mile per hour speed limit offered a serious barrier. Enforcement had increased to insane levels in Ohio, and the power and sensitivity of police radar had been notched up in the years since the last race.

I planned to run the Cotton Owens Challenger again, with updates that included a 22-gallon NASCAR fuel cell and the exchange of the original Detroit locker rear-end for a conventional Posi-Traction differential. Bob Brown had moved on to *Sports Illustrated* and Bud Stanner was too busy for a repeat as a teammate. Yogi Behr had become an obvious choice. He was an excellent driver who had won the 1972 Cannonball and I knew him as a stable, resourceful friend. Better yet, he was friendly with the guys who ran the Gleason's, an upscale New York pub. They planned to supply us with the lavish provisions for the cross-country run. Skilled driver, great food, fast, reliable car. Experience. What else did we need? More brains, as it turned out.

Running across interstate 80 in Ohio on the first rainy night, we attracted the attention of truckers, who began to shout about our high speed on the CB. Our "early-warning system" was backfiring. We heard the Ohio Highway Patrol respond. They had already established a reputation as utterly ruthless in the enforcement of the double-nickel. We knew we were hunted men. We ducked into a rest stop and sat, surrounded by big rigs, in the darkness for half an hour until the road seemed clear.

Always jiggering with the route to find the perfect high-speed way west, I decided to run 80 to71, then South to Columbus and interstate 70 west to Topeka. There we'd jump on the two-lane U.S. Route 54 to Tucumcari, New Mexico. Friends in Indianapolis had told me this was the favored route of USAC regulars from California traveling back and forth to the Speedway. I had also discovered what appeared to be a secret shortcut from interstate 17 north of Phoenix that would slide us into interstate 10 and Los Angeles. This was typical of all competitors in the Cannonball, all of whom sought the magic route like the Holy Grail—the hands-down key to success being wide-open roads with no cops. That secret route remains to be discovered.

Once clear of Ohio, we were rolling. The next morning, near St. Louis, we decided to partake of our first nourishment since leaving the Red Ball. I reached into the cooler mounted behind the seats. Empty. One bottle of Coca-Cola rolled in lonely isolation on the bottom. Otherwise we were without food or drink. In our haste to depart, we had left a mouth-watering hamper of Gleason's finest roast beef sandwiches and other delights on the Red Ball curb.

We pressed on, snacking on candy bars at fuel stops, but haunted by the culinary delights now no doubt being savored by one of New York's homeless.

I was stopped by a county sheriff outside Topeka, Kansas, but not arrested. This marked the only time in five Cannonballs, nearly 15,000 miles averaging better than 70 miles per hour, that I personally encountered the law. And only one codriver, Dan Gurney in 1971, received a speeding ticket. Call it dumb luck. But the old submariner's adage, "Run silent, run deep," also pertains to fast driving.

More troubles on the fast, flat, relatively open U.S. 54. We slowed behind a gray Plymouth with twin antennas sprouting from its rear deck. It was surely an unmarked patrol car dawdling along at 50 miles per hour. We cautiously hung behind him for well over half an hour before he turned off. It was then that a label on the door revealed the Plymouth as belonging to the United States Bureau of Mines.

Nightfall brought more wasted time. My secret shortcut north of Phoenix was a dead end. Behr and I charged across the desert, only to find the road dwindling into a cattle path and finally ending completely on the edge of an arroyo. We got out, stood in the silent, starlit darkness, and cursed my idiotic navigation.

Once westbound on interstate 10 we hit a vicious sandstorm that pitted the windshield, leaving us to grope through the night half blind.

At that point May and Cline passed us and we knew we had lost. A quick chat on the CB with May gave them a suggested route to the Portofino and we headed into the finish, knowing full well that bogus short-cut in Arizona had ended all chances of victory.

At the Portofino we discovered we had also been beaten by Jack McCoy and his team in the Chevy pickup. Their margin over us in third place was a mere 13 minutes, although May and Cline had won easily, making the run over 2 hours quicker than both the McCoy team and Behr and myself. Wes Dawn and Gil Nickel brought their Mercedes-Benz 450SEL home fourth, another 13 minutes behind us, while Leo Lynch and Dan Rowzie rounded out the top five finishers in their Porsche RSR, crossing the country in 38 hours and 39 minutes.

Arutunoff and Pryor were the last team to finish, straggling into the Portofino in their battered Bristol 410 some 14 hours after the winners. They brought with them a hilarious tale involving a weird arrest in Tennessee after they picked up a young female hitchhiker. When the cops spotted a loose license plate on the Bristol, Arutunoff and Bill Pryor had been pulled over and briefly charged with the Mann

Colonel Jim Atwell re-checks his map to determine how he and co-driver Chick Stanton managed to make the run in their new Porsche Carrera over an hour slower than their pre-run a year earlier.

Act, an obscure law involving transporting underage females across state lines for immoral purposes. The misunderstanding took hours to clear up and produced the most unusual and humorous excuse for a poor finish in all Cannonballs.

Mechanical ailments dropped John Buffum and ex-wife Vicki to ninth place in their Porsche Carrera—a modified ex-factory rally car that, stripped of insulation and other niceties, produced noise and vibration on the long haul that caused unexpected fatigue even for an expert like Buffum. Ironically, for all their vaunted capabilities as long-distance haulers, the best finish for a Porsche in the five Cannonballs was the Lynch/Rowzie fifth place in 1975.

Then came the calculations that May and Cline had beaten Gurney's and my coast-to-coast record by one minute. I called Dan with the news. "Check the clocks," he demanded half in jest. "There are no clocks," I answered, knowing that the "what if" factor had once again come into play. Virtually every man and woman who ever ran the Cannonballs has been haunted by the "what if" syndrome. What if there had been no encounters with the cops? What if there had not

The winning Ferrari with the second place Chevy pickup of Jack McCoy and the third place Yates Challenger in the background.

been that detour? What if the car hadn't broken down? What if we had taken a different route? What if everything had gone as planned?

The general chaos involved in driving as fast as possible over 2,900 miles of public roads offered the strangest, most unusual set of challenges in all motorsports. Nearly everyone who competed in the Cannonballs believes that had a few things gone their way, they would have won with ease. "What if?" haunts us all.

The Cannonball had created a small buzz in the motorsports community (some of it negative from quarters who believed that such madness would only generate anger among potential sponsors for legitimate racing efforts), but it took a story in the May 5, 1975, issue of *Time* to launch the race into the public domain. In fewer than 1,000 words, the article, titled "Cannonball Dash," told the woolly story of how the competitors had faced the challenge of the cops and their radars, lousy weather, and other road hazards to complete the race. Calling the event "unsponsored, illicit, and carrying no prize money, the Cannonball etc. does not exactly compete in the public imagination with the Indy 500 or LeMans. Yet among the dedicated speed freaks, the nontelevised, nonspectacular has become something of a legend in the five tenuous years of its existence."

By the time the Yates/Behr Dodge Challenger drifted to a third-place finish, the winning Dino had been parked for over an hour and the local press had been alerted to the entire affair.

The story was amazingly positive, considering the hopeless illegality of the race, with the *Time* writer noting that "many other racing aficionados worldwide stoutly believe that the Atlantic to Pacific dash represents a blow for sanity." The reference was to the 55-miles-per-hour speed limit that, I was quoted as claiming, "made criminals of us all." The story noted that the participants: "Made no public nuisance of themselves, suffered no loss of life or limb and racked up a total of 12 tickets."

The story ended with a breezy comment about the Broderick Travco Motor Home, noting that the "three drivers, who between turns at the wheel, were served soufflé Romano, fettuccini, and cannelloni by an Italian chef. They made the trip in 45 hours and 36 minutes and celebrated with chianti."

The *Time* story opened the floodgates. Calls came into *Car and Driver* from all manner of writers, columnists, and media elites demanding comment on the Cannonball. The editor at the time, Steve Wilkinson, was undaunted by the potential criticism and went forward with a story, written by himself. It trumpeted on the cover of the August 1975 issue "Cannonball! Coast to Coast in 35 hours and 53 minutes." The cover photo included some of the assembled teams on the roof of the Red Ball Garage with the caption, "These men are wanted for breaking the dumbest law since prohibition."

Pierre Honegger spills out of the Mazda RX4 wagon and heads for the Portofino desk with his time card to check in. The winning Dino can be seen in the background, already washed up from its gritty run.

Hollywood was immediately back in the game. International Management Group, the worldwide sports marketing firm that was representing me at the time, entered into a deal with Paramount Pictures for me to write a screenplay for a picture tentatively titled *Coast to Coast*. But at the same time, ex-stuntman-director Chuck Bail announced that he was doing a picture for 20th Century Fox to be called *Gumball Rally*. It was blatantly based on the Cannonball. Worse yet, a Hong Kong production company, Run-Run-Shaw, had hooked up with the aforementioned Paul Bartel to produce a quickie picture called *Cannonball*, starring David Carradine. The picture would also offer bit parts for Sly Stallone, plus Bartel buddies director Roger Corman, the king of B-pictures, and oddly enough, Martin Scorcese, prior to his ascendance as one of the greatest directors in motion picture history.

Gumball Rally seemed the biggest threat to *Coast to Coast*, and I attempted legal action to stop the project, only to be told that an open-road car race was in the public domain, and that I had no legal rights. (Other legal minds later advised me that an "intellectual property" claim might have been made.) Nonetheless, the *Gumball* project was well ahead of the Paramount script, and *Coast to Coast* was canceled. (The title would be later resurrected and employed in a 1980

Rick Cline (left) and Jack May display their winner's wreath, courtesy of an unidentified fellow competitor, in the parking lot of the Portofino Inn.

movie starring Dyan Cannon and Robert Blake about a mildly demented divorcee escaping a sanitarium and embarking on a transcontinental trip with a truck driver.) Furious over what I considered a theft of my idea, I refused to see *Gumball Rally* (to this day), although it was, by all accounts, a reasonably solid comedy about the race I had created. The picture did well at the box office, although for years thereafter it was a source of personal irritation when the Cannonball races were referred to in the press and elsewhere as the "Gumball"—as if the bastard child had created the parent.

It was during the middle 1970s that my life entered into a crisis mode. My first marriage was unraveling, and a deteriorating relationship was developing with old friend David E. Davis Jr., who had returned in late 1976 to resume the editorship of *Car and Driver.* I was doing work more and more outside the magazine (a novel, *Dead in the Water*, and cowriting the autobiography of NFL star Fran Tarkenton) and CBS Sports television, which caused internal frictions and jealousies. Davis hated the idea of the Cannonball and I was told that any resumption of the race would result in my immediate dismissal.

Until my personal life could be reordered, any thought of another Cannonball left my fevered brain, although word filtered in that no less an eminence than Hunter S. Thompson wanted to run another Cannonball from Big Sur to Key West. I deferred to the Doctor and let the Cannonball Sea-to-Shining-Sea Memorial Trophy Dash be seized by the movie moguls—at least temporarily.

OFFICIAL RESULTS
1975 Cannonball Sea-To-Shining-Sea
Memorial Trophy Dash
April 23–25, 1975

Pos.	Car	Drivers	Time	Av.mph
1	1973 Dino 246GTS	Jack May/Rick Cline	35:53**	81.0
2	1973 Chevy Pickup	Jack McCoy/Peggy McCoy/ Gary Johnson	37:50	76.7
3	1972 Dodge Challenger	Brock Yates/Steve Behr	38:03	76.3

Pos.	Car	Drivers	Time	Av.mph
4	Mercedes 450SL	Wes Dawn/Gil Nickel	38:16	75.8
5	1973 Porsche 911RSR	Leo Lynch/Dan Rowzie	38:39	75.1
6	1975 Buick Electra	Sandy Satullo/Sandy Satullo II Jack Howlett/Jack Pearson	38:45	74.9
7	1975 Porsche Carrera	Jim Atwell/Chick Stanton	38:56	74.5
8	1974 Mazda RX4	Tom Kozlowski/Jeff Martini/ Pierre Honegger/Ray Walle	39:22	73.6
9	1974 Porsche Carrera	John Buffum/Vicki Buffum	40:19	71.9
10	1975 Volvo 164E	Fred Olds/Steve Fernald Bob Hourihan	40:31	71.6
11	1974 Ford Van	Brad Niemcek/Tim Carlson/ Bob Turkovich/Ken Regan	40:37	71.4
12	1974 Pontiac Trans Am	Dave Shugars/Dennis Weglarz Ron McConkey	40:43	71.3
13	1974 Ford Torino S/W	Tom Morton/Vern Menke/ Paul Fischer	40:53	70.9
14	1971 Porsche 911	Tom Nehl/Bill Warner	41:32	69.9
15	1974 Olds Cutlass	Richard Gould/Robert O'Brien John McGovern	41:35	69.7
16	'51 Studebaker	Richard Harris/Richard Cannata Fred Feiner	44:23	65.3
17	1975 Travco 270	Craig Ammerman/Bill Broderick/ Wm. Jeanes/Tom McGrail/ Pal Parker/Jerry Scarlato	45:36	63.6
18	'69 Bristol 410	Anatoly Arutunoff/Bill Pryor	49:32	58.6

Jack May
WINNING THE CANNONBALL

I had first heard of the Cannonball Baker Sea-to-Shining-Sea Memorial Trophy Dash from an article in *Sports Illustrated*. The magazine reported that Brock Yates, senior editor of *Car and Driver* magazine, and racing driver Dan Gurney had established a world's-record time driving from New York to Los Angeles in 35 hours and 54 minutes in a Ferrari Daytona. There were subsequent articles and even a book about the record of Yates and Gurney. I almost routinely clipped the articles, filed them away and went about my business, but the germ of an idea grew in my mind.

In early 1975, it all began to crystallize. It was possible, *really possible*, to go for the record. One of the trade journals stated that Brock Yates was considering his antiestablishment Dash over again. He would again flout the law, break all the rules, evade the police, and run free. I excitedly dashed off a personal and confidential letter to Yates, advising him that I was prepared to join him. I, too, could be the best, the fastest.

A spring issue of *Car and Driver* carried a small cutout that, when filled in and accompanied by $5, would possibly get an entry blank for Cannonball 1975. I risked the money and, in due course, received an entry form.

I had no way of knowing whether Yates would personally read my completed form. But I carefully cited my experience, which involved a lifetime of driving at high speeds, including some organized and legal racing with Sports Car Club of America. I did not list my codriver. I didn't have one. Strangely, the entry fee was $250 ($200 of which was payable to the charity of your choice.)

I mentioned to several potential codrivers the possibility of the Dash, but had not chosen or asked anyone . . . besides, submission of an entry form was no guarantee of acceptance, as was stated in bold print on the form itself.

I left my home in Gainesville, Florida, for almost a week and tried to get on with routine business—but what was Yates to think of my qualifications? Finally, I was notified. An acceptance from Yates, who could obviously drive better than he could type. Needed: A prepared Ferrari Dino. I happened to have one. So, now to find a codriver. It took only a word with my friend, fellow SCCA race driver (National Champion quality), and National Racing Mechanic of the Year 1974, Rick Cline.

"Yes, I'll do it," he said without hesitation.

We were committed. Now, to service and prepare the car for the competition! First, we cannibalized a 15-gallon fuel cell from one of Rick's racing cars, increasing our total capacity to 36 gallons. Next, we constructed brackets on the front bumpers for the 100-watt Carello driving lights. Then we serviced the engine: new Shell oil, new air and oil filters, new Champion plugs. Finally, we mounted the best Goodyears on the road, and installed a CB radio and a radar detector to warn of delays and cops. (Cops—a word that would come to dominate much of our conscious thoughts.) Then boxes of high-energy candy, chewing gum, chewable Vitamin C tablets, Gatorade, raisins, and other junk-type munchies, first aid kit, flashlights, binoculars (to scan far-off horizons for . . . cops), driving glasses, a couple of shirts each, driving gloves and shoes, and a complete set of road maps courtesy of AAA. (AAA tried to help us by marking a route, but really didn't seem to grasp the basics of high-speed highway transit.)

A drivers' meeting was held in the nondescript headquarters of *Car and Driver*. What a collection we 20 or so entrants were! Car nuts all, lots of race drivers (amateur and professional), writers, pilots, business and professional men, doctors, lawyers, photographers, truckers, stockbrokers, a U.S. Army colonel. I didn't know a soul, though I'd heard of many. And no one knew me, either.

Lots of pictures were taken. If this race were secret except to all of the news media, maybe it would be equally secret to all the highway patrolmen out there.

Regulations of the motor race were incredibly simple: "Entrants must drive a land-based vehicle of any configuration, with any size crew, at any speed they deem practical, between New York and Los Angeles. The car covering the distance between the start and finish in the briefest time will be the winner. There are no rules."

We would leave at different hours and run against time. Yates elected to depart first. "It's not my preferred time of departure, but due to all the anticipated press coverage, I need to be at Redondo Beach first." Who was I to dispute him? Besides, our limited experience indicated that 9:31 to 10:45 P.M. would be prime departure time, after the early evening rush and prior to the after-theater crowd. We agreed to leave after a steak . . . and too much coffee!

Yates teamed up with "Yogi" Behr, a well-known racer with the distinction of being the highest American finisher in the history of the Monte Carlo Rally. After snapping a few photos of Yates and Behr getting into their trick Dodge Challenger, Gainesville's Cannonball entrants hailed a cab . . . just as the Dodge, sporting small but neat *Car and Driver* labels on the sides, pulled away with chirping tires from the crowd gathered around the Red Ball Garage. Our taxi pulled alongside Yates and Behr.

I yelled, "Hey, Brock."

Yates, navigating, glances over, but with one eye peeled on the still red stoplight. "Yeah?"

I chortled, "Rick and I will save you a place at the breakfast table in Redondo."

The light turned green. We would meet Yates later.

Our nerves ajangle from too much coffee, it was our turn. I was to drive the first shift. I started the Ferrari and pulled onto 31st Street. The V-6 engine was hardly to stop until it faultlessly revolved more than eight million times! The odometer registered 9,571 miles. Juan, the garage man, suggested we wait until the light at Lexington turned before punching our ticket.

Driving lights on, chewing gum a-go-go, driving gloves snug. The light turned green! Mark Jones, my longtime friend and blood brother New York City resident, stamped our official ticket at the Red Ball clock . . . 10:07 P.M., EDT, Wednesday, April 23, and with a wave from our well-wishers, we accelerated away, around potholes and taxis, under an ominous sky. Adrenaline was rushing as if driven by superchargers. The Lincoln Tunnel at high speed was psychedelic . . . zip, zip, zip . . . and then the rain, along with the sad discovery that we two seasoned race drivers had failed to check the intentionally overinflated tires and adjust pressures! No time. Press on, third gear, fourth, fifth, fourth . . . the responsive double overhead cam engine hummed its melody up and down the scale as I carefully but speedily maneuvered through the heavier-than-expected traffic, 90 miles per hour . . . 100 miles per hour. No cops, no problems, just more and more rain. My confidence grew; I relaxed, concentrated. Rick had the radio going, confirming directions and highway patrol locations. All was smooth, and as we settled down to a day and a half of racing, we welcomed the monotony of the wipers, and we worshipped the happy response of the great, exciting work of mechanical art, the 246 GTS Dino Ferrari.

The rain stopped. We were listening now to our CB. ("Tijuana Taxi moving east near Exit No. 12.") Your "handle" is your call name. There are all sorts: "South Whippoorwill," "Shadow," "Dirty Nick," "Lula Belle" (a female). We changed our handle frequently. Also, we learned soon to listen lots and talk little!

Our selected route was ours alone so far as we knew. After avoiding six "Smokeys taking pictures" (patrolmen with radar) on the New Jersey Turnpike on my trip into New York City, I was certain the Turnpike should be bypassed. Thus, the more northern route across Pennsylvania on interstate 80 was dictated. We would then cut south to Columbus and on to Dayton and Vandalia, all in Ohio. Then our route would lead us into Indiana on interstate 70. Terre Haute was next, then to St. Louis and over the Mississippi River—Gateway to the West!

10:07 A.M. EDT, Thursday morning, April 24. Twelve hours and 961 miles from the Red Ball Garage, averaging 83.3 miles per hour, approaching St. Louis. We are gaining back our average speed and, equally important, our confidence. Then, a navigational mistake takes us into the center of St. Louis. Our average speed gain is partially lost. Time, our competitor, ticks on.

Gas stops were handled with the urgency of the Indianapolis 500 race. The driver popped open the gas cap and trunk and engine lids with the inside latches. The navigator would pump the gas, with two pumps if they'd reach, check the oil (the Ferrari only burned one quart in the entire 8,000-mile trip!) We usually cleaned the windshield and lights with our own bottle of Windex and paper towels and got out a wad of dollar bills. We took turns running in to whiz and grab an occasional soda, then stuffing dollar bills into the usually startled attendant's hands and without waiting for change, we leapt in and peeled away back onto the "course." Seldom did a stop take as much as five minutes.

One stop in Kansas didn't save us much time. It was the coffee station for the Highway Patrol, and no fewer than seven cars were pulled in. Our pit stop activities were viewed with interest by most of the troopers, and we pulled out at 55 miles per hour, followed by two Smokeys . . . for the next 20 miles! Were they really seeking to protect the citizenry or was it the smug harassment of heavy-handed nondescripts toward the world's hotdogs?

In our 18th hour, we covered 40 miles. Forty whole miles! A serious blow to our average speed and to our spirits.

The heretofore perfectly performing spark plugs did not adapt to the sudden change in internal engine temperature. They began to foul. We lost the tail at the outskirts of Wichita—exactly where we encountered a construction detour. The sweet Ferrari now began to run on five cylinders! While it probably runs better on 5/6 power than other engines at 100 percent, it would have been frustrating and impractical to risk continuing without mechanical correction, for fear that other plugs would collapse.

A serious pit stop was in order. A Western Auto looms ahead in a shopping center. Screech! Stop! Rick dashes in to buy six Champion N6Y plugs. I assault the superhot engine, extracting the near glowing red plugs. Fast! Time is the race! Time is everything! Five plugs are OK—one is black. I screw them in, replacing the bad one, burning myself without feeling it. Concurrently, we discover the connection between gas tanks and fuel cell leaking. Rick jacks up the car, crawls underneath, with tools. Gas floods on him, his clothes, my feet, and the parking lot. Hurry, hurry! Time is all! Old ladies with filled grocery buggies stop with their mouths agape. It's fixed. We slam down the engine lid, throw the tools in the trunk. The engine fires with a nice, new, yet familiar, clean roar. The old ladies stand back. The clutch is engaged. The rear Goodyears spin in the puddle of gas, catch, smoke, and we fishtail at full bore in low gear and back on the course. We lost 43 miles this hour. Can we get it back? Have we lost all chance? Press on.

9:37 P.M., EDT, Thursday—April 24, Tucumcari, New Mexico: With the odometer registering 11,488 (1,916 miles from the Red Ball) and an average speed of 81.6 miles per hour, Rick takes over at a fuel stop. At 24 hours we passed through Santa Rosa, New Mexico, 1,971 miles from Manhattan. Moving on!

The machine is right and with almost no traffic we continue to cover nearly 100 miles in each hour. We wonder, "Will the other drivers press on like we have?" Will they be willing to put themselves through this? We think they will.

3:07 A.M. until 4:07 A.M. EDT, Friday—April 25, Arizona: A trucker talks to another on his CB: "A little white car just zipped past me with the hammer down (truckerese for "wide open throttle") Darn near sucked off my belly pan! Wait till he hits one of those big jackrabbits. It'll roll that little car up in a ball and they'll never find it!" Rabbits. Ha! Who's afraid of rabbits?

The odometer advances to 12,070 from 11,871: 99 miles covered during the hour. We leave I-40 and cut south through Prescott National Forest, heading for the desert and the I-10 route to Los Angeles. This was the route taken by Yates and Gurney in their world-record run. It was supposed to be mountainous and slow—and it was. But between curves were frequent high-speed stretches. It was a nice two-laner.

We zip past a sign. "Watch for animals." Punchy by now, we laugh that the animals had better watch for us! They did a poor job. We had six quartz-iodine bulbs aglow for our nighttime racing. This total of 490 watts seemed about the equivalent of the landing light for a 747 jumbo-jet. Then, far in the distance we saw a tiny shining light on the road. An eye. A rabbit's eye.

Rick: "Wish we could call that trucker and tell him the rabbit lost." But the rabbit war wasn't over. At 4:55 we tear through Yarnell, Arizona, at an indicated 4,782 feet above sea level. It's cold, in the thirties. Nineteen minutes later we were confronted with another jackrabbit. We're not sure, but we guess at a little over 100 pounds! At least that's what it seemed like at 140 miles per hour! It sounded like hitting a coconut with a Louisville Slugger bat! Crunch! The car jolted. We knew the rabbit was beginning to score. The wiring for the driving lights were definitely rabbitfied. The six lights flicked on . . . and off . . . and on . . . randomly. The effect was confusing and, at our speed, very dangerous. Please God, no more rabbits. "Thunk!" Listen to the car. A new rattle? What had been damaged? Then the road began to narrow and we started out of our first mountains.

Were we lost? Minutes, tens of minutes, passed; we were still in the mountains, hairpin after hairpin, "25 miles per hour" speed limit signs, on and on it went. Rick was driving now and I watched in admiration as he smoothly and masterfully conducted the Ferrari apex to apex. We might be falling below our average speed goal, but we were maintaining at least 70 miles per hour. We were tired, but strangely swept with waves of exhilaration. Such motoring is a joy, an art, indescribable to those who have never tried it, and unlike anything else in my experience. Ahead: the red pin pricks of taillights and further the oncoming lights of another car. A passing situation. It will be safer to prevent alarming the oncoming driver, to zip past on the right. We do. At 135 miles per hour. I look past Rick, who was concentrating intently on driving, to see what it was. Dodge Challenger. *Car and Driver* lettered on the door. "Yates! It's Brock Yates! Whoopee!" We had not only passed him, but on the right. On a two-lane road! And at 135 miles per hour! Hooray! And it didn't even cost the hundred we no longer had anyway!

In radio contact Yates (CB handle "Silver Bullet") had little to say about our departure time of 10:07 except to acknowledge we had a good shot at the record.

At Blythe, California, on the border just past Arizona, we stopped for our last tank of petrol and prepared for the final leg. We knew the world's record was within our grasp. It was possible. But, as experienced race drivers, we were also aware that the race isn't won until you get the checkered flag. What could delay us? The car was without fault, all gauges registering at optimum operating levels throughout our run. So, only Smokey or bad navigation could foul us.

While we were tanking up, Brock and Yogi pulled in to get gas. We coordinated on our CB's.

It dawned on me that there one small detail I should attend to. "Brock, how do we find Redondo Beach and Portofino Inn?" I asked.

"Jack, the simplest route is to follow I-10 to San Diego Freeway, turn south, off at Western to 190th street and straight in," he replied. The map showed that this was the least confusing route, but it was many miles farther. We debated. We didn't want to risk getting lost, and we had no time to spare. Or so we thought. So we followed Yates' directions. A mistake.

Cautious in the face of the awesome reputation of the California Highway Patrol, we headed across the desert in the eastern part of the Golden State keeping our speed just over 100 miles per hour.

9:07 A.M. EDT, Friday, April 1975, Los Angeles, California: Two thousand, nine hundred and eight miles and 35 hours from the Red Ball Garage. How much farther? As if by magic—black magic—traffic began to stream onto the six-lane highway, and each entry ramp seemed to be jammed with vehicles of all descriptions, moving out to join us. We held to 80 miles per hour as long as safe, then gradually our speed dropped as our maneuverability was lost. We fell in line reluctantly at 50 to 55 miles per hour, anxiously looking for openings to dart and gain even a precious 10 yards.

Was this really happening? We became choked with apprehension. So this is how we would lose it. This is the story we would have to tell. Speech was difficult. We were scared and now acutely aware that there was no room for error. One wrong turn and we could just lose our chance at fame. We grabbed at every opening in the traffic, press ahead. I hit the deck with my official card in hand. It was taken and stamped by the ball clerk and handed back, along with a bottle of champagne due all finishers.

The time punch said, in slightly smeared ink, 7:00 A.M. It fell from my shaking hands . . . I was speechless. The world's record. The World's Record! We had it. We made it. Whoopee! "Rick, we did it! By damn."

Jack May is a successful Florida real estate executive, and still owns his winning Ferrari Dino.

Jack McCoy
1975

Back in 1971 and 1972, I had closely followed the Cannonball Sea-to-Shining-Sea Memorial Trophy Dash. Brock Yates and Dan Gurney had won it together in 1971, driving a 4.4-liter Ferrari Daytona V-12, running the trek from Red Ball Garage in downtown Manhattan to the Portofino Inn in Redondo Beach in 35 hours and 54 minutes. In 1972 the Cannonball was won by Steve Behr, Bill Canfield, and codriver Fred Olds, in a Cadillac. It sounded like a wonderful lark to me, driving as fast as you could from the Atlantic to the Pacific Ocean, and what would make this especially challenging, is that now we were under the nationwide 55-mile-per-hour speed limit mandate. With the new-found time on our hands, I thought this would be an exciting and challenging event to take part in.

I called Brock to inquire about the feasibility of entering the event and was told that it was going to be limited to 22 entries, depending upon the perceived notoriety of the vehicle and/or pilots. He would make some determination as to who the entrants would be, and that they would have to make a "sizable donation" to some specified charity, if selected. There was no prize money, and the promise of plaques or trophies for those of us in several categories turned out to be barroom promises. But that didn't matter, for the only reason a person would enter such a crazy event like this was for the pure fun and excitement of seeing how fast you could cross the country under a 55-mile-per-hour speed limit. I didn't have a vehicle. I thought it would take one with lots of power, and I didn't cherish the idea of riding cross-country in some cramped-up, high-powered sports car, I guess that was mostly because I didn't know anybody who had one, and couldn't afford one myself.

Ivan Baldwin had a relatively new 1973 Chevrolet pickup truck with a 454-cubic-inch engine with a special cam, carburetion, et cetera, that was his tow car method of transportation. I eyed Ivan's Chevy truck and being the true racer and kind of loose guy that he was, he readily agreed that's what we should use. There weren't many parts you could hustle for a project like this, but McCreary was making a passenger car radial tire. They were hoping to eventually expand on the radial line, so we got a set of them and shaved the tread down to about 50 percent, so they would live under sustained high speed. We got a camper shell, one that would fit sleekly behind the cab of this Chevy truck, and opened the windows, so that we could crawl back and forth and stretch out. And we installed a huge 32-gallon fuel cell in the back bed, in addition to the two saddle tanks the truck was equipped with. All we did to the suspension was add the proper Carrera shocks. We decided not to change rear end gears, as the truck would run 115–120 miles per hour the way it was, and Ivan insisted that at that speed, we wouldn't hurt his engine. We knew that our competition would be in vehicles capable of 150 miles per hour or better, but felt areas where you could run wide open would be so few and far between, that it wasn't really going to make that much difference.

The next thing I had to do was talk to my wife, Peggy, into the idea, and she readily agreed on three conditions: first, she could go with me; second, we would go by Tres Mesa, Arizona, and visit with the Hopi Indians, one of whom we had met on a recent trip home from Florida (he made fabulous Hopi jewelry); and third, that we would get someone to help who could run fast and safe, but whose personality would not wear thin after a couple of days of steady, tense association.

We both knew just the guy, Gary Johnson. We had worked with Gary on some stock car endeavors before. He was a former Formula Ford champion, but most significantly, his personality seemed perfectly suited for the job. We approached Gary, and he gladly agreed, saying he thought it would be a ball and that he would pay his own airfare to New York City if we'd pay the entry. Such a deal!

I bought the book *Sunday Driver* in which Brock Yates recounted his 1971 triumph with Gurney, right down to the best time to leave the Cannonball garage and his newly found secret route. We studied roads and maps and strategies, and planned the entire trip. We got gigantic maps and marked them and were prepared to make corrections as Peggy and I drove the route backward cross country. We would note hazards, areas of road construction, and other situations that might call for an altered route. We obtained a powerful citizens band radio and a new state-of-the-art radar detector. We were now ready to go on a somewhat leisurely trip to New York to chart the course backward and visit our newfound Hopi friend.

We convinced ourselves that going clear to the Portofino Inn and back up through Los Angeles to San Bernardino would be a long way out of our way for such a short portion. We agreed to go on Highway 40 straight to Flagstaff, where we would rejoin the predetermined route, and we'd be able to visit our Hopi friend.

A recent national truckers strike seemed to unite all the truckers, and they were running convoys to be able to traverse the country at high speeds. We found out that if you cooperated and asked for help they would help you, but if you did something foolish like getting in front of a convoy and leading without knowing what you were doing, you soon were admonished heartily. We were advised of the towns with speed traps, the radar traps, and the cops who sat in the corn-fields on the little roads. This was important, because we were going to take many little roads where we thought we could run faster rather than certain interstates that would be heavier patrolled. We also planned to avoid all toll roads.

Our game plan was to leave the Red Ball Garage at midnight sharp, just as Brock Yates had done. That would get us through Manhattan after the theaters were out, and with the minimum of traffic, get us through eastern Pennsylvania and around Indianapolis and Kansas City at non-rush-hour times. And if we were on schedule, we'd get into Los Angeles early enough in the afternoon to avoid heavy L.A. traffic. Once the cars were allowed to leave, about 8 P.M. in the evening at a pace of about one car every two minutes or so, most of the people got anxious and took off, including Brock himself, from whose book we had gotten the game plan! Even the new Ferrari Dino of Jack May and Rich Cline, who had announced their departure would be at midnight also, left about an hour earlier, leaving us in a very big, empty garage. It was lonely and eerie feeling.

We streaked rather carefully through New Jersey on a particularly dark and foggy night. However, in Pennsylvania, especially along I-80, a stretch that we had selected, we noticed during our prerun that most of the patrol cars parked on the median strips so that they could take pursuit in either direction. Those were the only cars you saw on the median. So we could click along pretty easily, around 85 miles per hour until we would see any vehicles sitting in the median strip, and by the time we were there, we were running a nice, smooth 55 or 50 miles per hour. I'm sure our innocent-looking Chevrolet truck with camper shell was one thing that helped avoid the high-buck tickets that many others received.

Daybreak came as we entered Ohio, supposedly home of the most stringently enforced traffic laws in the country and we could verify that. On our trip over, there were Smokeys taking pictures (police with radar) over about every third or fourth crest. So we tiptoed through Ohio at about 80 that brisk morning, relying on our CB to warn us of the Smokey environment. It had been raining rather heavily most of the time through Pennsylvania, and our windshield wipers and headlights would allow no more than about 80 miles per hour anyway. We didn't want to have driving lights or any other external appearance on the vehicle that might indicate that it was anything other than an innocent truck.

Plenty of publicity had gotten into the press and we wondered how Brock Yates, who organized this whole thing, could possibly escape the liability if any of these 18 vehicles got into a wreck, let alone if they hurt or killed someone. To this day, I admire his courage for organizing what would certainly seem to most an expression of antisocial behavior. By midmorning, when we got to Indianapolis, the road was blocked and a detour slowed us down dramatically. It was still raining, although somewhat lighter, so we opted for our first fuel stop, premature to our planning but still allowing for two more stops. We tried to figure out our way around the tremendous traffic jam that existed on the loop on I-70 around Indianapolis. That worked—we bypassed traffic on a frontage road and were on our way again about 20 minutes behind schedule.

Our method of filling this truck was what we'd like to call NASCAR style—the fastest and most efficient pit stop possible. Our plan was to pull into gas stations that were not busy, and pull in between two pump islands. We had three tanks; the two side pods and the fuel cell. So each person was in charge of getting a nozzle started and completing their own tankful. Picture pulling into the middle of a pump island, jerking two gas nozzles from one side and one gas nozzle from the other side, and getting them all running simultaneously. Oftentimes before the amazed attendant could get up out of his chair to come over to see if we wanted anything, we were ready to go. One person was assigned to the underhood monitoring, the second person was assigned to cleaning the windshield, and the third person got to use the facilities (even though we did have emergency facilities in the back of the truck). In the three planned stops, each person had a turn at one activity or another. Since we knew about how much gas we were going to buy, we would have the ample amount of money ready without requiring any addition or change-making.

The rest of the trip was going exactly as planned until we came to Kansas City. A route that took us around the city itself was pretty fast, but there was more traffic than we anticipated. Still, we were moving right along. We saw a radar patrol car approaching from the other side of the highway and we knew that we had been had. We slowed immediately, but to no avail. The officer flipped a "U" and pulled us over. He asked, "Where are you going?" I replied that my family and I were just on a holiday trip and that we were so into sights and the beauty of the countryside that we had let our speed get away from us momentarily. The friendly patrol officer let us go with a warning and a smile. It was if he had sensed something—maybe the Cannonball decal on the fenders gave him a clue. Anyway, he warned us not to speed, at least not while in the state of Kansas, with a twinkle in his eyes, and sent us on our way with a mere warning. This belied our worst fears and made us exude confidence.

Our driver changes were to coordinate with pit stops, with me driving the first leg, Gary the second, me the third, and Gary bringing it home. We also planned to put Peggy behind the wheel for a while too, so she could gain her claim to fame in the Cannonball, but that never took place.

There were several stretches where you could open it up, as fast as it would run, and the truck felt very comfortable running its top speed, which was about 115 miles per hour. However, we soon noticed that it began holding back a little and the speeds on these wide-open stretches slowly declined. This panicked us because we felt the engine might be seizing up, so we immediately backed down to 70 or 80 cruise for a while. Then I remembered a problem that we had on the prerun—driving at much slower speed, we had a fuel supply problem and traced it down to a plugged fuel filter. One of the original steel tanks we were using probably had something in it that would cause the fuel filter to plug and now we were facing the same problem. We were afraid if we ran a full throttle with the engine starving for fuel we would damage it or even blow it up. So we eased back up to see how fast it would run without fuel starvation. Top speed was now down to about 110 miles per hour on the fast stretches, so we decided to run about 5 miles below top speed, or about 105, to keep from starving the engine of fuel. Now this wasn't too important in the early stages, because there wasn't very much country that you could run at full speed. Later on, as we progressed west, and there were longer and longer stretches of wide-open road without police enforcement, this 10-miles-an-hour handicap was going to be crucial. We only hoped that it didn't get worse.

Since our fuel range was estimated to be 800 miles per tankful, and we had stopped a couple of hundred miles prematurely in Indianapolis, our next stop would have to be stretched about as far as we could go—which was a little town called Pratt, Kansas—about 80 miles west of Wichita. The stop went off as planned and we were out of there.

Tearing down Highway 54, across the panhandle of Oklahoma and the northern tip of Texas into Tucumcari, New Mexico, about midnight, 24 hours after we had started, we witnessed an enormous wreck just as we got into town. We held our breath hoping that it was none of the Cannonballers. As we proceeded by slowly we were relieved that there was nobody involved that we knew. By 3 in the morning, we had cleared Albuquerque on Highway 40 and were well on our way through New Mexico. There was beginning to be more and more stretches where you could run the truck wide open, but we felt like we were crawling at 105 miles per hour. The truck became too comfortable at that speed. The roads in Arizona were lightly populated, excellent freeways, seemingly designed for wide-open runs.

We had determined that the shortest route on this trip was to turn off at Flagstaff toward Highway 10 for our final run into California. This is the area that we bypassed when prerunning, thinking all we had to do was follow a map and take it a little bit easy. It was about 5 in the morning when we turned off on this shortcut route heading south. I was driving the truck, Peggy was reading the map, and Gary had crawled through into the back to stretch out and rest in preparation for the last stop in Arizona and our final run into California. Suddenly we found ourselves winding through steep hillsides, some of them seemingly without road signs. The road became slower and slower, and I became more vociferous about Peggy's ability to read a map.

Then it happened. When I saw the same scene appear before us, the same place we had been 10 minutes previously, I realized, my gosh—we were lost! An argument erupted about Peggy's seeming lack of map reading ability and we both loudly called for Gary to resolve the matter, insisting that he show us where we were, but his calming demeanor soon made us both slow down and figure it out. Now we were hopelessly mired in a time-loss on this so-called "short cut"—it seemed as if it took us hours to get straightened out and back on the road, but in reality we probably lost only 30–40 minutes. But in a race like this, where 10 miles per hour off your top speed already throws you clear out of sync, we were beginning to feel that the entire event was a total disaster and we were hopelessly going to place dead last. Gary was fully awake now, had us both calmed down, and we were on our way again. To make matters easier, it was beginning to turn daylight and the lighter it got, the better we could see and the faster we could run.

As morning dawned, Highway 89 became a better two-lane road and we streaked along at about 85—as fast as you could, not being familiar with turns and the terrain. As we got onto Highway 60, though, we picked up the pace and got it right back up to 105 and there we stayed until we were about a mile or so outside of Quartzsite, which was to be our last fuel stop. As we crested a knoll, we saw a patrol car parked on the side of the road heading in the same direction that we were, and there was a patrolman out in the center of the road, sweeping up what appeared to be broken glass. By the time we saw him, there was nothing we could do but continue to run at full speed. We knew Quartzsite was only a couple of miles away, and so our only possible plan would be to pull onto a side street to do our refueling, better than on a main highway, and hopefully if he radioed ahead or streaked through town in pursuit, he wouldn't find us. We weren't even sure of the speed that we were going if he was going to take pursuit. We didn't really want to wait and find out. We gassed up in Quartzsite with our typical center-of-the-pump islands technique and Gary piled into the driver's seat in preparation for our final run.

Though the California Highway Patrol at that time was deemed to be the second most diligent in the nation, topped only by Ohio, from Blythe to Indio we saw virtually no CHPs. Beyond there and through San Bernardino, traffic started to get a little thicker and our speed dropped measurably as we entered the Los Angeles area. Peggy's job was to sit in the back with the binoculars and scan the overpasses. In California, the Highway Patrol and local police would often sit on elevated frontage roads or overpasses to observe the traffic below. From the vantage point at the rear of the camper with the binoculars, we were going to be able to spot the potential "spoilers of fun" and blend into traffic.

Gary drove very smoothly, not using the brakes excessively, not weaving in and out of traffic, but using his headlights to move people over in a manner that shouldn't be too obvious to observing police. We had mixed emotions. We knew that we hadn't obtained our goal of crossing the country in less than 37 hours. We could see that we weren't too far off, but then a small disaster struck again.

We had local maps of the Redondo Beach/Los Angeles area, but the route that we planned to take had been detoured. We found ourselves in such a hurry to get around the detour, we wound up getting lost again—a second mistake made by not having prerun the entire course. That little fiasco cost us about 15 minutes, but we finally roared in Portofino Inn.

Plans had been to get to the Los Angeles area after the lunch-hour rush traffic. However, due to our lack of top speed and our getting lost in Arizona, we got there well after about 2 P.M. When we did pull up to the Portofino Inn, we stopped as fast as we could and I ran up and punched the time card on the time clock. Since we had left last, it was 1:50 in the afternoon and the fastest cars were already in.

Jack May and Rick Cline of Gainesville, Florida, in their 1973 Ferrari Dino 246 GTS, had already been declared the winners. They made the trip in an amazing 35 hours and 53 minutes—the new record. Steve Behr and Brock Yates were already celebrating second place as they had made the run in 38 hours and 3 minutes, with an average speed of 76.3 miles per hour. So needless to say, there was vivid disappointment when we showed up 1½ hours later, having made the trip in 13 minutes less than Yates and Behr. It took us 37 hours and 50 minutes total time, at an average speed of 76.7 miles per hour. Obviously, we were dog-tired but jubilant for having made a good, safe record across the United States.

Jack McCoy remains one of the finest stock car drivers ever to come out of California. His story is excerpted from his excellent autobiography Racing's Real McCoy.

Steve Fernald
CAPTAIN AMERICA ALIAS BEAVER CLEAVER ALIAS MUDFLAP

It started out fine! We were out of the Lincoln Tunnel in 8 minutes and 42 seconds, and we only ran two red lights to do it.

The "Colorado Kid," "Rubber City Plowboy," "Skinflint," and the rest of the gang took our Volvo 164 EO, affectionately known as the *Beaver Cleaver*, through New Jersey and Pennsylvania, helping us avoid Smokey. We hit the Ohio border (390 miles) in 5 hours and 10 minutes (75.5 miles per hour).

Hourihan turned the driving over to Olds, and the "Smoke Watch" became very alert. Ohio's reputation, the rain, and all the Smokeys spotted in transit see us exit Ohio holding a 70-miles-per-hour average.

Indiana border and Fernald gets the driving program on at 110 miles per hour across the whole state. We let up only while circling

Indianapolis. Halfway around Indy, we picked up a police escort that took us full tilt to the county line. Buffum had been right behind us when the officer blew by him and approached us with all lights on— "Capt'n, Capt'n there's a Tijuana taxi com'in after ya, Capt'n." He lost sight of us as he groped on the Carerra's floor for his teeth. His frantic calls over the CB had us rolling with laughter in the Volvo. Incidentally, we did Indiana, border to border, in 1 hour and 17 minutes.

We pick up a commuting Datsun CBer, coming into St. Louis from the west. He spots three picture takers (police radar) he has passed and we "lighten up" in the designated areas. Sure enough, there they are, just as he said. We overtake *Little Beaver* in outstate Missouri. We are overtaken by *Rolling Gold*. (That Mazda could really haul on the top end!) We're all smokin' along when we spot what appears to be a "county mounty." His car has two gumballs, no antenna, but he's suitably attired, stroking it along at 55 miles per hour with what seems to be his wife riding shotgun. Everybody wants to pass but no one will make the move. Some 50 miles later as he enters Oklahoma, obviously out of jurisdiction, we edge by, followed by our two compatriots. Almost, anyway. The mountie cuts between *Little Beaver* and *Rolling Gold* and ever so slowly begins to overtake us. Much discussion regarding his jurisdiction, wife, and lack of antennae follows. Finally Bob, Steve, and I all assume the most bored expressions we can muster and blow by him at 71 miles per hour. He had been escorting us in Oklahoma at 70 miles per hour, possibly an out-of-state courtesy. We edge away followed by *Rolling Gold*. Once again *Little Beaver* is cut off at the pass.

All this effort is to no avail because we're soon picked up in Oklahoma by a state trooper, for the next 40 miles. Finally the trooper splits and we get the program back on with Steve motoring.

5:11 P.M.—Near Sayre, Oklahoma, Steve clears a crest in excess of 100. Coming up the other side is a state trooper and his sidekick working a rolling VASCAR. The four-wheeler working our back door, 5 miles to the rear, does not report passing the cop. We discuss ducking off an exit. We continue, and lose nine minutes for a 75-miles per hour ticket, talked down from 100. Steve is in the cruiser as *Rolling Gold* goes by talking to *Little Beaver*. The troopers' CB told it all: "Hey, they got that little silver blue Volvo. Ho Ho Ho—Whoa! Whoa! Whoa!" A quarter-mile up the road and over the crest, a radar car got *Rolling Gold* as they began to pick up the beat. "Eighty miles per hour," they said, as we passed them parked with Smokey. We had lost nine minutes to the police. *Little Beaver* slipped through and was now four minutes ahead of us.

5:41 P.M.—We stop for a red light in Erick, Oklahoma, our first since the Big Apple.

6:06 P.M.—We enter Texas and switch to Channel 19, only to discover we can send but not receive. We decide send with the front unit and receive with our backseat unit. Unfortunately, we also discover that western truckers are a curiously silent lot.

6:26 P.M.—We pass *Rolling Gold* at a gas stop with the hood up. A silent prayer for trouble goes unanswered.

8:10 P.M.—We reach New Mexico. The first inkling that our 40-hour strategy was erroneous came in New Mexico. We were cruising along at 90 when we noticed bright lights gaining at the rear. A few minutes later, the Targa blew by going conservatively 130 miles per hour. A few miles later we saw him parked sedately at a gas station allowing the attendant to service his car. Still later, we were again overtaken at speed, on a very rough section of pavement. We thought he had left New York at 11 P.M., because that was his announced strategy on the Red Ball roof, during the photo session. Therefore, when he passed us in New Mexico, at that speed, it was difficult to imagine that he had indeed made up three hours instead of the actual one hour. In fact, as he motored by the first time, Olds loudly exclaimed: "That's 11 P.M. going by!"

Just before we do the Ash Fork cutoff we change alternators (25 minutes) because we are getting strange dimmings. We had tried a new regulator (2 minutes) to no avail.

Hourihan motors us through the cutoff thoroughly bored for the flat initial miles. Much berating of Olds follows his BS about the cutoff's excitement. Then, he gets to the driver's portion. A moderate amount of interest builds as he expertly negotiates the switchbacks. We see some dark tracks that go straight off and wonder if we are now 18. Down on the desert floor, we pass several deflated jackrabbits and decide we are not alone.

Boredom. We cruise the Los Angeles freeway at 75 miles per hour, over a superroute done by Volvo's West Coast Competition Department. Steve adds a few twists at the end, and we have no problem attaining the Portofino without stopping, save a few lights. The last 10 miles of the trip were made somewhat lighter by a serious gastrointestinal pain Fernald had developed. (No pit stops of a major nature for 40 hours.) Much merriment accompanied each moan of anguish from the rear seat. Steve was given our card to punch at the desk, and he continued directly into a guest's open door, availing himself of the throne. The guest was dumbfounded but fortunately raised no objection. Possibly, he could detect that Steve was not in a position and/or mood to negotiate.

Our mistakes and observations:

1. 55 miles per hour is good only in Ohio, Oklahoma, and (sometimes) California.
2. Donna Fargo has displaced Tammy Wynette as the 18-wheeler sweetheart, probably 'cause Tammy dumped good ol' George Jones.
3. Faron Young is alive and living in Enith, Oklahoma, and driving a '48 Chevy pickup.
4. The cbbstssmts can be seriously approached only in a vehicle capable of 135 miles per hour; 160 would be better.
5. Boredom sets in about Amarillo or Liberal, Kansas, depending on the route you're taking. How about a control or checkpoint of some kind in Tucumcari?
6. Good fun—good times—and we'd like very much to do it again.

Steve Fernald teamed with rally expert Bob Hourihan and 1972 co-winner Fred Olds to finish 10th at 40 hours and 31 minutes.

Jim Atwell
1975

The madness began with my purchase of a 1973 Porsche 911E. My salesman and I, both Porsche nuts, were sitting in a darkened cubicle of the dealership, closed at that time, discussing the latest running of the Cannonball Sea-to-Shining-Sea Memorial Trophy Dash. The infamous Yogi Behr, driving, of all things, a brand-new Cadillac sedan, had won it. Behr was delivering the Caddy to the West Coast for its naïve and unsuspecting owner. A wonderful saga all by itself.

My salesman and friend, Chick Stanton, after discussing the foregoing, decided that we had the ideal vehicle for such an adventure, my new 73 Porsche 911E! And we were right!

In the weeks that followed I conducted an exhaustive map reconnaissance and came up with what I believed to be the best route from the Red Ball Garage at 31st Street and Lexington Avenue in New York City to the Portofino Inn at Redondo Beach, California.

Finally Chick and I stowed our gear in the Porsche and drove to my parent's home on Long Island. Thus we positioned ourselves for a timely departure the next evening on our practice Cannonball.

The very next night we drove to the Red Ball Garage, punched out, and departed promptly at 8 P.M. Across 31st Street westbound to Dyer Avenue, thence into the Lincoln Tunnel. We traversed the tunnel at 100 miles per hour! Fourteen minutes later we exited the New Jersey Turnpike at the Newark airport. We were on our way.

The Porsche had been fitted with a 110-liter fuel tank and a radar detector. We had rehearsed our fuel stops—pull between two rows of pumps, use two hoses, one from each row, pay in cash, and be gone. The first finished got to use the men's room.

We were slow in the East due to traffic and surveillance. The further west we ran, the faster we ran. All went well until we encountered Trooper Peeples, Oklahoma State Police. He was hidden under a bridge in the shadows. Got me on radar at 91 miles per hour. Once ticketed, the only way we could proceed was to pay the $29 fine by personal check. With the check, I surrendered my driver's license, to be returned to me with the receipt when my check cleared the bank. Meanwhile, the ticket provided me authority to drive in Oklahoma for five days! Away we went! Good weather, light traffic, we were running a constant 100-plus miles per hour. Amarillo, Tucumcari, the Ash Fork cutoff, I10 to Blythe and beyond all at high speed with little or no surveillance. The approach to L.A. slowed us a bit; our intense map reconnaissance that included L.A. streets helped us minimize times of approach. We rolled into the Portofino Inn with an elapsed time of 36 hours 6 minutes—12 minutes short of breaking the record of 35:54, held by Yates and Gurney in the Daytona Ferrari!

Our near eclipse of the Gurney/Yates record gave us an entree to the two of them by phone. Dan Gurney demanded an examination of our timing apparatus and let it go at that. Brock said, "Who the hell are you?" And then went on to take our names and promise to invite us to run the next official Cannonball!

My next new Porsche was a 1975 911 Carrera, red with black leather interior. A hot car! Almost immediately after delivery we received a long-awaited, highly coveted invitation to run the '75 Cannonball.

On arrival in New York City we reported to Ziff-Davis Publishing at One Park Avenue for a drivers' meeting. All of us seated at the appointed hour, Brock made a grand entry wearing a hero race driver jacket and big grin! His speech was short and to the point.

There are no rules. First car away 8 P.M. tonight. Punch out, leaving the Red Ball, take any route you choose. Punch in on arrival at the Portofino Inn. Shortest elapsed time is the winner! Questions? Prizes? There are none. Memento? There are none. Dash Plaques? There are none. Tickets? They're yours! The meeting quickly ended and we headed to the Red Ball. All the entries except the Travco Motor Home driven by William "don't call me Bill" Jeannes, parked on the roof. An ugly 1973 Ferrari Dino 246GTS was quickly removed to the street upon discovery of a badly leaking fuel tank. The Dino had been driven from Jacksonville without one headlight and had no radar detector! Preparation? The Dino driver, seeing our Autotronics detector, called Dallas for one and had it delivered in timely fashion by an Eastern Airlines pilot (Dallas-NYC!) It arrived just in time. The headlight was also replaced just in time for the start. Preparation!

An interesting car was the 1973 Porsche fitted with a $10,000 IROC engine, driven by Leo Lynch and Dan Rowzie. Lynch had picked up the Porsche with its newly fitted engine at Stoddard's Porsche in Willoughby, Ohio, that morning and driven it to NYC just in time for the start. Dan Rowzie borrowed a road map from me to use for the trip, having failed to do any kind of a route recon prior to the start. Preparation?

Our Carrera was immaculate, fully serviced and gone over with care from end to end. We had a detailed route book prepared and we were ready to go. We didn't even open the engine compartment until we finished at the Portofino. We had once again rehearsed our pit stops, which were executed as we did in our practice Cannonball. We had also fitted a large 110-liter fuel tank to minimize fuel stops (four en route).

The Travco Motor Home was among the first vehicles away. Sponsored by an Italian Restaurant in Cincinnati, it was crewed by Jeannes and friends and equipped with a rack of deep metal trays filled with tasty pasta dishes. The crew was stylishly dressed in bright red mess jackets and white duck trousers. The Travco, capable of 100 miles per hour, was fast! Rounding a curve early along the route it unloaded trays of ravioli with tomato sauce. The floor became a sea of pasta! We passed the Travco before we made the Harrisburg entrance to the Pennsylvania Turnpike. The white duck trousers ended up with a 2-inch red (sort of!) stripe at the shoe toe!

Traversing New Jersey, Pennsylvania, and West Virginia was slowed by traffic and surveillance. We accelerated in the Midwest and into the

Far West. We congratulated ourselves as we passed several Cannon-ballers slower than we were. The run was really uneventful as we dropped down to I-40. Amarillo, Tucumcari, and Albuquerque fell astern as we cruised at 100 miles per hour. We climbed to 9,000 feet near Williams, Arizona, made 10 miles to Ash Fork and left I-40 for State Route 89, the Ash Fork cutoff down through the Prescott National Forest.

Southbound, we motored at high speed in the darkness. Leaving Prescott we passed an Arizona State Police car parked facing out in the driveway of a home. We backed off and watched the mirror as we continued toward I-10. We soon resumed speed. A fun ride down the Yarnell hill, Congress, Aquila, Wenden, and Salome. Bright lights in the mirror closing very quickly. Trooper? No, our friends Rowzie/Lynch in the Porsche! Flying! Vicksburg and then I-10, Quartzite, Yuma, and California. Short of the line, Lynch/Rowzie stopped for fuel. We passed them as the approach to L.A. and Redondo loomed in our sights. Lynch/Rowzie caught up with us but did not pass. They intended to follow us in and thus beat us. Our map work paid off, but we needed to shake them off our trail. As we approached our left exit, off toward the west and the Portofino, we move to the extreme right lane. They did the same. At the last possible moment, we exited with a high-speed, four-lane left turn into the exit. They missed it and we went on to the Portofino alone. We didn't see them again until they arrived, long after us. Their lack of map recon made their approach difficult and time consuming.

We finished without difficulty in seventh place overall, 38 hours and 56 minutes, at an average speed of 74.5 miles per hour. Not as fast as our practice run of 36 hours and 12 minutes! The Ferrari Dino was the winner, setting a new record of 35 hours and 53 minutes, breaking the existing record of 35:54 by one minute! The Dino would have done better, as we would have, with greater speed in the East. In addition they needed a better plan for the L.A. approach to Redondo. Preparation!

Our Porsche performed flawlessly, reinforcing our thoughts that the Porsche was the ideal vehicle with which to Cannonball coast to coast! We came back to do it again, but that's a whole new story!

Jim Atwell, a retired, much-decorated Army colonel, ran two Cannonballs and headed a team that won the 1986 One Lap of America.

John McGovern
1975

My involvement in the Cannonball began with a trans-Atlantic phone call from Brock in April 1975. "How do you fancy driving in this year's Cannonball? Just get over here a few days beforehand and I'll organize a drive for you." It took no more than a nanosecond to say "Yes."

There used to be a number of long-distance races held worldwide. The arduous Gran Premio Internacional del Norte ran from Buenos Aires in Argentina through Bolivia to finish in Lima, Peru, a simple matter of just over 6,960 miles! In Europe there were two equally famous races, the Mille Miglia, a mere 1,000 miles, and the much more difficult Liege-Rome-Liege at a little over 3,000 miles. All of these races were legends to racing enthusiasts, and now I was invited to run in the Cannonball, which must have been the last remaining public highway, long-distance race left. And with only 18 starters, it had to be very special.

Brock collected me from the Buffalo airport and my first question was how to avoid the Highway Patrols. His answer was the CB radio. The CB was unheard of in Europe, but for the 3,000-mile journey, I found that it worked.

I was teamed with racing instructors Robert O'Brien and Richard Gould in a carefully prepared, but standard, Olds Cutlass. Both were generous and welcoming, but somewhat suspicious of my driving abilities.

All 18 entrants assembled at the Red Ball Garage in New York and in a blaze of nonpublicity drove out of the city heading west. The Cutlass team was quickly overtaken by a rainstorm, which lasted the next four to five hours. During this time I cannot recall seeing any other competitors, as visibility was down to near zero.

I do remember thinking after some 30 hours on the road that the United States was a more daunting prospect than I had imagined. We did not seem to be getting anywhere. But, after 41 hours and 35 minutes, we arrived at the Portofino Inn in Redondo Beach and crossed the finish-line at an average speed of 69.7 miles per hour in 15th place! As the infamous 55-miles per-hour national speed limit had come into focus just before, it gave Robert, Richard, and myself enormous satisfaction to have covered the 3,000 miles safely, without a single incident, at nearly 15 miles per hour faster! The 1975 Cannonball was and remains a vivid memory to me. It encouraged me to drive coast to coast eight times more, including a single-handed five-day journey from Modesto to Baltimore in 1990 in a 1955 Ford Thunderbird.

John McGovern, now retired, was a London-based photojournalist who covered motorsports events around the world. He competed in two Cannonballs—1975 and 1979—and several of his photographs are included in this book.

Bill Warner
1975

Back in the 1970s, those of us in Jacksonville who were into cars would rent the Beach Boulevard Go-Kart track every Thursday night for an evening of fun and games. It was at one of these wheeled and somewhat drunken debaucheries that Brock suggested that some of us participate in the upcoming Cannonball Baker Sea-to-Shining-Sea Memorial Trophy Dash. Tom Nehl and I had had just enough to drink that evening that the proposal sounded tempting. After all, I'd never been to California, and it seemed like a good reason at the time to go. Forget that we had to go New York City first.

I had a three-year-old Porsche 911T with about 75,000 miles on it that we thought would be a good candidate. IMSA racer George Drolsom had just purchased a 2.5 Carrera, and he was replacing the 31-gallon fuel tank with an ATS fuel cell. Adding his tank to my car gave us about 600 miles range. We failed to realize at the time that our bladders were not good for 600 miles. I added a pair of Cibie Oscars for night driving, a Snooper radar detector, and a CB radio. In that my car had the Florida license plate "SHAZAM," we went by the CB handle of "Captain Marvel." (I still own the car and it still has the license plate "SHAZAM.") Getting the car to New York was in itself a problem, as Tom crunched the right front fender just days before we were to depart.

Tom isn't very careful with borrowed material. Many long hours, and pounds of Bondo later, the car was ready to go.

Upon arrival in New York, we discovered that we did not have any special edge on this group of ne'er-do-wells, who were about to embark on the longest and fastest protest of the 55-miles-per-hour-speed limit ever. They all looked ready for the transcontinental challenge.

Down the elevator of the Red Ball Garage, out 31st Street, and we were on the way. Once out on the Jersey Turnpike, elation turned to reality when we realized that we had about 40 hours of high-speed driving ahead of us, with the various highway patrols acting as the trump cards in this contest. We did not see any of our competitors until about 11 P.M. somewhere east of Harrisburg, Pennsylvania, when rally ace John Buffum and his ex-wife, Vicki, caught up with us. We ran nose-to-tail in the rain at somewhere around 100 miles per hour for a number of miles, splitting around an 18-wheeler on a three-lane stretch, with Buffum going around the left and me on the right. We learned then and there that you don't surprise or upset the truckers, as the CBs lit up. We were in identical white 911s, so we were not particularly low profile. Buffum chose to stay on the Pennsylvania Turnpike, while Tom and I chose to take the low road, grabbing I-81 South.

We knew the Illinois and Ohio HPs were looking for the Cannonballers, so Tom and I felt the route south through Knoxville, Nashville, and Little Rock was more prudent. As it turned out, the rain in Ohio kept the cops at the doughnut shops, and going south added about 150 miles (and about 1 1/2 hours) to our route.

Tom neglected to tell me that he had a real problem staying awake while driving at night. This was a rude awakening (no pun intended) for me, as I had been driving since 7 P.M. from New York City, and it was now 2 A.M. somewhere in Virginia. Additionally, Tom, who was a part-time thespian when he wasn't purveying GMC trucks, could not master talking on the CB. His pitiful pleas of "Hi, guys" or "Hello, fellows" on the CB resulted in no responses. It was at that moment that I realized that not only was I stuck with all the night driving, but while riding, I'd have to maintain the wireless repartee with the truckers. It was going to be a long, long trip. I drove the first leg from New York to Knoxville, Tom took over from Knoxville through Little Rock, and I took over from Little Rock to Needles, California. With the sun up, Tom took it from Needles to the Portofino Inn, in Redondo Beach.

Nearly all the routes taken came together in Oklahoma City, and we had a roster of entrants with their CB handles to assist in identifying each other over the air waves while en route. It was on I-40, west of Oklahoma City that the call came through . . . "How 'bout ya, Captain Marvel?"

"You got him," I replied, "Who we got there?"

"Sundance," came the reply.

Checking the roster, I couldn't find the handle "Sundance," to which I answered, "I don't know any Sundance."

"Does Redondo Beach mean anything to you?" the voice crackled.

"10-4," I answered, "What's your 20?" 20 was CB for "Where the hell are you?"

"What's yours?" replied Sundance.

"64-mile marker," said I. "What's yours?"

"We're at the 66," answered Sundance.

By then, Tom and I figured it was a Ford van built to run the Cannonball and sponsored by Heyser's Cycle Shop, Towson, Maryland.

"Geez, Tom, we're behind that van. Let's pick up the pace." So I upped the speed from about 85 miles per hour to about 100.

"We're at the 66," said I.

"We're at the 68," came the reply.

I then upped the speed to about 115, and a couple of minutes later, I stated, "We're at the 68."

Sundance radioed, "We're at the 70."

We then opened up the 911 and were flat out at 130 miles per hour.

"We're at the 70," I broadcasted, "where did you say you were?"

Sundance's answer came back very weak; he was behind us, not in front. That crafty old devil had been telling us that he was 2 miles in front of us, knowing we'd take off in the chase, and he'd just hang on until the gendarmes nabbed us. He had not counted on us pulling away.

As night fell, I struggled to keep the car going, as Tom snored his way through northern Texas, New Mexico, and Arizona. At sunrise, somewhere just east of Needles, California, I started seeing things that weren't there, so Tom woke up and took over for the final leg into the Portofino.

Driving in the Cannonball is one of the highlights of my life. I've given more speeches and eaten more cheap chicken dinners at various car and Rotary clubs as a result of my "Cannonball celebrity" than I could have believed possible. To run a Cannonball event in today's litigious society would be impossible, or at least very risky. It was not the type of event in which a conservative Republican, Air Force Reserve Officer, and businessman with three children and a loving wife would or should participate. But you know something? Like my freshman year at the Citadel, it was a great challenge and experience I'll treasure forever. But would I do it again? Hell, yes. Let's go.

Bill Warner is a Jacksonville, Florida, businessman who is also an excellent motorsports photographer, vintage racer, and the award-winning creator and director of the world-class Amelia Island Concours d'Elegance.

Ron McConkey
1975

What a great surprise. Flash Cadillac and the Continental Kids had completed the 1975 Cannonball Sea-to-Shining-Sea Memorial Trophy Dash unscathed. We had left Ann Arbor with ominous thoughts of flaming crashes into a school bus and forecasts from friends (enemies?) of long nights in jail. But what we found was that 20 cars crossed the United States without a single incident other than the inevitable run-ins with the law. We personally accredit this to the excellence of the interstate highway system and the organizers' careful screening of entrants.

The careful screening started with a letter to the organizers outlining who we were and what our plan of attack was. This was followed by completing an entry form outlining our experience. Ron McConkey was our ace in the hole here, with his SCCA and Sebring experience, Dave Shugars helped with his motorcycle and drag racing time, but Dennis Weglarz's one semester of delivering pizzas at the University of Illinois seemed the weak spot. Even so, after a few phone calls and a letter from Brock Yates, we were entered. Now all we needed was money.

Ron McConkey saved the day here, as his friend, Thor Thorson, was the business manager of Flash Cadillac and the Continental Kids, a Los Angeles rock group. We obtained financing for gasoline from them. Barb and Miller Beurman supplied the CB radio, Gary Benedict financed the super sensitive Autotronic radar detector, and Dave Ludwig of the Ring and Pinion Shop in Mt. Clemens dug around and produced a 2.56-ratio axle. The three of us savaged our race cars and employers for the rest of the necessary pieces. The entry fee came from Roger Ashley's Polaris in Fenton.

Two weeks before the event found us modifying Dave Shugar's baby into a monster. Up until now Dave's 1974 SD-455 Trans Am had never been driven in the rain and had never spent a night outside of a heated garage. Now, the Firebird received all of the donated equipment listed above, plus Q-I lights and a 15-gallon auxiliary fuel cell.

April 23, at 6:45 P.M., all the picture taking was over and the three of us were jammed into the Firebird in front of the Red Ball Garage. At 6:46, we were the fifth car away amid applause and cheers. At 6:46:05, we were stopped by a red light 100 yards from the start. In fact, we hit every light on 31st Street. Finally, Dave drafted a VW into the Lincoln Tunnel and we were on our way.

Our plan, decided during a five-minute summit conference, was to hit I-80 to I-71 to I-70 to St. Louis. From there it was old Route 66, now called I-40 or I-44. Speed was not considered all-important. In our naïveté we felt that a time of 38 hours would be sufficient to win. We decided to cruise at 90 miles per hour, which worked out to 3,000 rpm with the 2.56 rear end. The Super Duty never knew it was running at that speed and delivered 14 to 15 miles per gallon.

7:55 P.M.—Average speed was now 60 miles per hour as we headed into Pennsylvania. Many deer were spotted along the shoulder, and we start having new nightmares. The radar detector saved us at 8:45 by finding a Smokey the truckers had missed in the grass. It began to rain, but the super Uniroyal Radials under the Firebird never noticed. Dave held 90 and the average speed rose to 67. Talk about confidence—in the middle of the rain Dave decided that Robert Redford could portray him in the movie version.

We couldn't believe it, but at 10:15 we passed Yates and Behr in the Challenger. Dave was now wondering if Redford would be sufficient after all.

Ohio was wall-to-wall bears, just as predicted. At 12:20 A.M. (now April 24) we made our first gas stop, just west of Youngstown. Our overconfidence faded as Yates pulled in to gas up, just after we discovered our air shocks had failed. Dennis started driving as we headed back out. We cursed ourselves over the air shocks. They were a last-minute addition installed in a speed shop's parking lot in New Jersey immediately before the event. We figured we would continue with the air shocks deflated and hope for the best.

Yates followed as we cruised through Ohio at 55. Then just after 1 A.M. the clouds opened and the world turned to water. The Challenger fell back as once again the Uniroyals worked their magic. We left Ohio at 3:24 A.M., averaging 70 miles per hour.

Indiana brought the worst luck of the trip. A bump over a bridge allowed the exhaust pipe to bottom out, now that the air shocks were gone, causing an exhaust leak. Then at 4:01 we were stopped to feed the bears. Smokey said that he clocked us at 69 on VASCAR. However, we know that we spotted him and got down to 55 before he could clock us. We feel that the truckers got us. Minutes earlier we had passed a group of 18-wheelers who had flooded Channel 10 with overblown stories about a red race car doing 115. Later at the Portofino Inn, Yates commented that the reason we caught him was that a trucker reported him to the police and that the police responded.

They escaped by parking in the woods for 20 minutes. After 12 minutes we were on the road again and made the mistake of doing 60 for the rest of the state. Yates passed us then, and we never saw him again.

In Illinois we exposed a plain-brown-wrapper bear who invited us to put the hammer down. We were severely reprimanded. Then at 7:18 A.M. we made our second stop in St. Elmo, Illinois. A real gentleman runs a Standard station there. One Jerry Snaps repaired our exhaust leak, lent us his pickup to fetch parts and then helped repair the shocks. We lost 1 hour and 20 minutes, but felt that we would last the distance. Ron took over driving with our average speed a dismal 65.

Missouri passed by unnoticed, except that another irate Smokey threatened us with shotgun justice as the radar detector saved us again.

3:15 P.M.—Halfway through Oklahoma we made our third gas stop, and Dave took over on his second driving shift. Oklahoma City found us making our only route mistake, and we lost another 10 minutes.

In Texas we discovered a mistake in calculating our average speed and elapsed time. (Ron wonders why he brought along two engineers.) To make up time, Dave really put the hammer down, averaging 80 through Texas.

9:14 P.M.—We made the fourth gas stop, just inside New Mexico. Dennis took over driving, as Ron served another round of peanut butter and jelly sandwiches. With a full moon and open roads through New Mexico, the average moved up to 67 miles per hour.

12:46 A.M. (April 25)—We entered Arizona and kept the hammer down. We were startled when we see lights catching us; luckily, it turned out to be another Cannonballer, a Carrera. We follow after he passed us doing 130. That's when Dennis spotted the bear in the median. We don't know why he didn't attempt to chase us, but we are still making novenas on Thanksgiving. At 3:20 A.M. in Winslow, we again stopped for gas. Ron took over driving.

6:53 A.M.—We entered California, approximately 36 hours into the run. Our average speed had laboriously been built back up to 68. Fatigue was becoming evident and Ron was elected to drive the remainder. At 7:07 we bought gas in Needles and decided to try to make the run in under 40 hours. Ron headed across the desert with a beautiful sunrise lighting the way and the Firebird smiling at 110 miles per hour. At 8:30 we saw the Buffums' Carrera losing some green stamps to the bears, and we felt confident again. The Buffums followed us as we neared our trick turn-off in Victorville (which turned out to be slower than the Buffums'). Ron cleverly used an 18-wheeler to hide our exit. California Route 18 has bumps that make a Firebird leave the ground. Ron was staying awake by trying to achieve weight-lessness. At 10:45 we gave up. We were stuck in the freeway traffic and stood still for five minutes. At 11:30 Dennis fell across the Portofino Inn's desk and was awarded a bottle of champagne. Our 40:49 time was good for a 12th-place finish.

McConkey, Shugars, and Weglarz were employed as engineers in the emissions laboratory at GM's Warren, Michigan, proving grounds. Their Firebird is one of the few remaining original Cannonball cars and is in an Illinois collection.

The Last Blast
The 1979 Cannonball, Fastest of them all

IT'S UNLIKELY THAT THE FINAL CANNONBALL would ever have been run, had it not been my friendship with Hal Needham. He is perhaps the bravest man I ever met—and that is saying something, considering the myriad great race drivers that I encountered during my life. Thought by many to be the greatest stunt man of them all, Needham is rivaled only by Yakima Canute and Dar Robinson. Needham rose out of rural Missouri to first wing-walk and wrangle horses in a Hollywood career that led to a long friendship with Burt Reynolds. That friendship led to Needham's first directorship, presiding over the madcap comedy *Smokey and the Bandit* in 1977, starring Reynolds and Jackie Gleason. Two years later he directed Reynolds again in the stunt-man comedy-thriller *Hooper* and was at the height of his powers in the film business. Never satisfied with the status quo, Needham had organized a stunt-man's union called "Stunts Unlimited," launched a NASCAR stock car racing program, and set out to break the land speed record in a rocket car on a stretch of desert outside Tonapah, Nevada. I was assigned by CBS as part of the television crew to cover the attempt—which ended when one of the car's chutes failed at over 400 miles per hour, leaving Needham in the sand dunes over half a mile beyond the course.

I was the first to reach the crash site and discovered him to be as relaxed in the crumpled cockpit as if he'd just finished an Egg McMuffin for breakfast. Needham's no-nonsense good humor and his audacious face-off with life somehow established a firm link between us, based in part on his passion for fast cars and motorsport. It would lead to my cowriting for him the script of *Smokey and the Bandit II,* a pilot for a television series starring Terry Bradshaw and Mel Tillis that was never produced, and of course, the craziest enterprise of them all, *The Cannonball Run,* as well as the last race upon which that ragged picture was loosely based.

It all began at the United States Grand Prix at Watkins Glen in the autumn of 1978. Needham was fascinated with the idea of making a movie based on the book *Stand on It,* a faux autobiography by "Stroker Ace" (in fact written by the late *Sports Illustrated* writer Bob Ottum and Goodyear public relations man Bill Neeley). The rights to the book had been held by Paul Newman, who, after numerous treatments (including one by me) had given up on the project. Needham had come to the Glen to discuss how to proceed with the idea of obtaining the Ottum/Neeley book, and during a few drinks in the bar of the Holiday Inn in Painted Post, New York, I offhandedly mentioned the Cannonball races. Needham was instantly intrigued. "Hell, we'll make a movie about 'em," he said, his gravelly voice turning serious.

"Don't bother," I replied. "They've already done *Gumball Rally* and *Cannonball.*"

"Fuck 'em," he declared. "We'll make a better one."

At that moment the movie was created, although it was instantly agreed that we would have to run another race to develop a story. We chatted at length about the route, the timing, the tactics, and what kind of car to use. It was Needham who decided on the ambulance. Such subterfuge had been discussed casually before, but it was Needham who firmed up the deal, assigning me to obtain the actual vehicle while he would foot the bill for the modifications.

Much had changed for me since the last running of the Cannonball in 1975. My long marriage to my first wife, Sally, had broken up in an acrimonious divorce battle. Resolution was reached only after my marriage to the beautiful and charming Pamela Reynolds (soon to be known throughout the racing community as "Lady Pamela") in February 1978 and our settlement in a four-bedroom townhouse in northwestern Connecticut.

David E. Davis Jr., who had hired me at *Car and Driver* 14 years earlier, took umbrage at my plans to publish the *Cannonball Express* newsletter in July of that year and fired me—by Western Union night letter. That capped an increasingly stormy relationship with him and the magazine. Dave had warned me earlier that he would dismiss me if I ever attempted to run another Cannonball, which now became a toothless threat. We would go again in the spring of 1979. April 1. April Fool's Day seemed a perfect date.

Carrying out Needham's plan for an ambulance, I arranged with old Chrysler pal Moon Mullins, who had also provided the Cotton Owens Challenger, for a full-size Dodge van with a 383-cubic-inch V-

8. It would be converted by ex-GM engineer and master race car fabricator Bill Mitchell of Cheshire, Connecticut. I felt the stealth capabilities embodied in the ambulance livery (to be called the totally bogus *TransCon MediVac*) would be a sufficient performance enhancement, but Hal wanted more. He arranged with drag racing pro Dick Landy to build a 440 wedge engine with a B&M conversion for the three-speed Torqueflite automatic to handle the extra torque. This decision led to the addition of larger ATL fuel cells to compensate for the anticipated extra fuel consumption, a modified Quickor suspension to handle the heavier loads and other exotic changes that added both cost and complexity to the van. But if the scam worked, the ambulance would be a major contender.

The plan was set to start the Cannonball at the Lock Stock & Barrel Restaurant in Darien. It was owned and operated by George Lysle, a great friend and ex-roommate and close friend of the late Peter Revson. Located in the Good Wives Shopping Center, the restaurant was cheek-by-jowl with interstate 95, which in turn led across the George Washington Bridge to the great West. The "Barrel," thanks to George's marketing skills, had become a major hangout for motor racing enthusiasts in the tony southern Connecticut suburbs, and word

The bogus TransCon MediVac team in mufti. (Left to right) Brock Yates, Dr. Lyle Royer, Pamela Yates, Hal Needham, and the Lock Stock & Barrel owner, George Lysle.

quickly passed that the Cannonball was to start there. Too quickly. Mitchell called to report that he had heard that the governor's office in Hartford knew of the race and was not pleased. Then an acquaintance in *The New York Times* sports department called to report that the national desk had gotten wind of the event and planned to cover it. This we did not need. I implored the sports writer to intervene. He begged helplessness, explaining that the national desk paid no attention to the jocks in the sports department. The story would run.

The Dodge van was finished up by Mitchell and it was superb, save for the Landy engine, which featured a giant 850 Holley four-barrel carburetor that refused to operate properly. We also had to paint a tiny counterfeit Michigan registration sticker on the rear license plate.

Our crew would be first class. Needham and I would be joined by my wife, Pamela, who would serve as the patient . . . a senator's wife with a rare lung ailment that precluded flying in a pressurized cabin.

The 454 Dually of "Mad Dog" Dennis Menesini, Charlie Robinson, Ken Smith, and Mark Miller. The truck finished 5th overall, despite a long stop with cops in Arizona. They started the race by crashing through a fence to create a short cut onto interstate 95 ("If you're gonna be a bear, be a grizzly," was the Menesini mantra). The Dually averaged 5.4 miles to the gallon and consumed 590 gallons of high-test to win the "Friends of OPEC" award.

The authentication for this hopeless fabrication would be a doctor named Lyle Royer, a Los Angeles anesthesiologist whom Needham had met at the Smokehouse Restaurant on Sunset Boulevard. Royer arrived in Darien without the vaguest idea of what lay ahead, other than he was about to embark on a rapid cross-country trip back to Los

Hollywood stuntmen Loyal Truesdale and Keith Patchett planned to ride their BMW R90S coast to coast non stop.

Angeles. Hal and I had found a medical supply house to obtain ambulance driver's whites and jackets plus a set of giant emergency lights for the Dodge's roof. A gurney and a few IV bottles helped make the van's interior appear like a legitimate ambulance. Royer's seat would be a Recaro unit mounted to the floor next to the so-called patient.

As Mitchell scrambled to finish the van/ambulance, hordes of entrants, hangers-on, and the local enthusiast crowd began to jam the Barrel. A total of 47 teams were entered, including an ancient 1948 Rolls-Royce Silver Wraith flown in from England, a number of very hot sedans and sports cars and one luminary—George Willig, the human fly who had recently scaled the World Trade Center. He would team up with *Sports Illustrated* writer Sam Moses in a Boss 302 Mustang. Also entered was Gilles Villeneuve's race driver brother, Jacques, in a Porsche 928. Advertising executive and future Sebring 12 Hour winner Jim Mullen entered in a lovely Ferrari SWB 250GT with his wife. Former winner Yogi Behr was in another 928, and Loyal Truesdale and Keith Patchett rode in on a BMW R90S motorcycle that they planned to run *nonstop*.

Yet another scam. The Chevy Suburban of Jim Sensebaugh, Charles Martin, Peter Defty and Tom Gallford carried U.S. Government livery and the official sign: "Satellite Tracking associates—Warning, Stay Clear." They wore safety garb and carried Geiger counters, which struck fear into gas station attendants near the Three Mile Island nuclear plant.

The driver's meeting, such as it was, took place behind the restaurant with me standing on a dumpster. The symbolism of this was not missed by the gathered throng, who heard me spout what was only a few words about the rules: the cars would be driven the entire distance and the car with the lowest elapsed time, point to point, would be the winner. The theme of the meeting boiled down to the elemental rationale for the Cannonball: "*There is only one rule. There are no rules.*"

As the late-night starting time arrived, paranoia seized me. Not only was the Dodge refusing to run right, but word had filtered in that the Connecticut Highway Patrol was setting up a roadblock in the area. The Lock Stock & Barrel and the adjacent parking lot were swarming with people. George Lysle reported that perhaps 3,000 revelers were on hand and that the local police had been called in to control traffic. So much for a secret start. And then there was *The New York Times*.

Suddenly word arrived that the nuclear reactor at Three Mile Island outside Harrisburg, Pennsylvania, was acting up. The neutrons were bubbling and a giant explosion was feared. My friends at the *Times* sports desk called to report that the national desk was giving up on the Cannonball and heading to Pennsylvania. Then a friend who had been sent out to scout the cops on interstate 95 came back to report that all was quiet while word was filtering in that a speed trap had been set up on the Merritt Parkway, miles to the north and off the route. In a matter of moments the Cannonball had been cleared for takeoff.

This was of little comfort, considering that everybody north of Richmond and east of Toledo seemed to know about the Cannonball and had pounded into Darien to witness the start. For obvious reasons we had tried to keep the time and place confidential, but the crowd that milled around the cars and plugged the bar of the Lock Stock & Barrel made the place look more like a five-alarm fire than the commencement of a clandestine sporting event of dubious legality. Engines were revving. A Dixieland band was laboring against the noise and confusion. Every few minutes, a cheer would rise up as one of the competitors rumbled away into the darkness.

The first car to leave was a white Z-28 entered by the Polish Racing Drivers of America, who had been given their traditional "Pole" position. Tom Hickey, a teaching fellow at Harvard and a Boston Marathon veteran, sped off in his powerful 6.9 Mercedes; he and his two partners were conservatively buttoned up in shirts, ties, and tweed sports coats. A lethal-looking, all-black BMW motorcycle revved up and shot into the night carrying a pair of Hollywood stunt men, Loyal Truesdale and

Keith Patchett. Their plan was to have the rider on the back rest while wearing a blonde wig—to work in concert with a "Just Married" sign hung off the tail. Unfortunately, they left the wig in a Bronx saloon. Silently, and with a kind of defiant serenity, the 1948 Rolls-Royce Silver Wraith of Stephen Kendall-Lane of Mayfair, London, slipped into the night. At the wheel was former royal family chauffeur, Edwin Harmston. Seated in the back with Kendall-Lane was his wife, Fiona.

A new Mercury station wagon, driven by their personal mechanic and purchased specifically to serve as support vehicle, fell obediently into their wake. The Kendall-Lanes were doing the Cannonball in style. They had arrived by Concorde, rested for the event in a Waldorf-Astoria suite, and provisioned their journey with delicacies from Fortnum and Mason. The great, bustle-backed Rolls motored off in the general direction of California. (Stephen Kendall-Lane had observed, rather imperiously prior to the start, "I haven't even the foggiest notion of what states we'll be passing through.") The Rolls featured one final touch of regalia—the Union Jack fluttered proudly from a small silver standard mounted on the radiator grille.

Also involved in this mad enterprise was mountaineer extraordinaire George Willig, conqueror of the still-standing World Trade Center and El Capitan. ("I have always looked on the Cannonball as not trying

John McGovern rode shotgun in the 1948 Rolls-Royce Silver Wraith, another English import for the Cannonball.

to beat anyone else, but rather as a challenge to do the best we could under the conditions. The fact that our Boss 302 Mustang had serious brake problems was a nice challenge," said Willig when it was over.) Other entrants included former World Offshore Powerboat titleholder Sandy Satullo; karting champion Terry Baker; Indy driver John Mahler; plus a number of prominent doctors, lawyers, and otherwise proper industrialists, mixed in with the hard-core racers and playboys. In all, a pretty eclectic collection of personalities. Hardly your local hot rod club out for a cross-country pavement rip-up.

While everybody else was starting without incident, our ambulance developed a mysterious carburetor problem in its radically modified engine. It refused to run more than a few feet before bucking and stalling. Needham smoked constantly while Pamela, Doc, and I paced nervously. The mechanics pawed at the engine like a pack of Beagles around a rabbit hole. More of the field ripped away—knifesharp Ferraris and Lotuses; two "drive-aways"; several powerful XJS Jaguars; more Mercedes-Benz sedans; a hairy 1962 Ferrari coupe; a 1936 Ford Panel truck; and a monster, dual-wheel Chevrolet crew cab pickup driven by Dennis Menesini, a wild super-modified driver from

The ancient 1936 Ford panel truck entered by Hemmings Magazine *crew Terry Ehrich, Dave Brownell, and Justus Taylor.*

Sparks, Nevada, who had set a certain tone for the Cannonball by arriving in staid little Darien and barging into the local Howard Johnson's to demand of the desk clerk, "Where's the goddam hookers?"

We watched them go, cursing our bad luck and itching to get on the road before the alarm spread among the police. Faint murmurings had indicated the Connecticut State Police might know what was going on. We had received word from several sources that the vaunted California Highway Patrol was ready and waiting. And of course the storm troopers who man the Ohio State Police, and who had given the Buckeye State a reputation for merciless speed enforcement unequaled in the free world, would always be ready, day or night. Our trump card with the TransCon Medivac ambulance was a surprise. My paranoia was telling me that already the word was flashing from state to state that the Cannonball was under way again and to be especially watchful for a gang of crazies trying to slip through the cordon in a phony ambulance. And one of the drivers would be myself, the perpetrator of this

Suzuki rider George Egloff headed a five person team including female Wendy Epstein to run 30th. They employed a support vehicle that stretched the rules a bit but enabled them to easily beat the Truesdale/Patchett nonstop BMW.

entire affair and surely the most prized highway fugitive of the moment. I began to feel like Clyde Barrow and imagined my bullet-riddled body being hauled from a pile of smoking wreckage.

A friend brought good news. He had made a scouting run down nearby interstate 95—the only effective route away from the Lock Stock & Barrel—and had seen no extra concentrations of cops. "There's one Smokey out there on routine patrol. Otherwise, it's cool," he said. I was comforted for a moment until I recalled that Custer was also told there were no Sioux near Little Big Horn. The Titanic was unsinkable. The Maginot Line could not be breached. I also remembered that the clock was ticking toward midnight. Tomorrow would be the first of April. April Fool's Day.

The big Dodge engine started. Its powerful exhaust note rattled off the nearby walls. It settled into a lumpy, diffident idle. Somebody came up and said, "She's ready. We got her fixed." We scrambled on board. Pamela, in a white pajama top, crawled between the blankets of the stretcher. The Doc sat beside her, checking his medical equipment. Needham sprinted to the time clock near the restaurant's kitchen. I restarted the engine. Things still did not feel right. Needham

The TransCon MediVac is initially delayed by a cranky 850cfm Holley carburetor, but it would be the modified TorqueFlite automatic transmission that caused problems down the road.

hopped aboard. I dropped the ambulance in gear and punched the throttle. We lurched ahead. We left a small cluster of people yelling and waving cocktail glasses in the faint light. Flashbulbs arced in the darkness. Finally we were under way. California, here we come.

We traveled 100 yards. The engine crapped out again. Cursing, we sprinted for help. Our mechanic friends, who seemed to understand the mysteries of four-barrel carburetors better than anyone else, appeared again, decided that the ignition timing had gone wonky and hauled us off to his service station. There, in a frenzy to make the repairs, he torched the padlock off his garage door—having left the keys with a friend—and set to work. More chain smoking by Needham. More pacing and growling by the rest of us.

An hour ticked away before we started again. Under normal circumstances, that hour would have put us 80 miles down the road, with the potential hassles of Connecticut and the real congestion of New York City behind us. The rain had subsided by the time we thundered onto interstate 95, our emergency lights strobing a mad tattoo of color on the low clouds and surrounding traffic. The lights were an amulet for open roads. Slower cars leapt out of our way, even on the perennially jammed-up Cross Bronx Expressway, which funnels all interstate traffic through the perimeter of New York City. We reached the George Washington Bridge in record time and punched the speed up to 100 miles per hour on New Jersey's interstate 80. As is *de rigueur* on the Cannonball, our vehicle was equipped with a CB radio and all manner of maps, calculators, and scouting reports to determine optimum fuel stops, proper routes, and driver's shifts. Some of our competitors had sophisticated police radar scanners on board, while experimental radar jammers were rumored but did not appear. Owing to our cover, we decided against such gadgetry, reasoning that too much time would be wasted reprogramming the scanner, etc., when that time could be more effectively used for acting like legitimate ambulance personnel.

We got our chance on Route 80. "Jesus, they've got us!" I yelled, sighting another set of flashing lights in our mirrors.

"Let's go. Let's put it on these sumbitches," said Needham as he zipped up his orange and white ambulance attendant's jacket. Doc was attaching an IV bottle to a hook on the roof. Pamela was tucked deeply into the covers. By the time I eased the ambulance to the roadside everything seemed ready for our acting debut.

I jumped out. The turbulence and noise of the fleets of passing semis buffeted my body and ears. I walked to the rear of the ambulance. A pair of New Jersey cops were crawling out of their unmarked cruiser. In case you haven't heard, New Jersey likes to think of itself as a very hard-ass state. Its residents exhibit a kind of curt, tough-guy insolence that seems to be embodied in all Garden State police officers. Based on my experience, they are among the surliest churls to wear uniforms in any of the 50 states, and I knew if we could con the pair now confronting us, we would be golden for the rest of the way.

"What's the trouble?" I asked with feigned innocence.

"Whatdaya mean, what's the trouble? You guys were runnin' too fast and flashing your lights all over the place! That's the trouble," countered one of the cops, a beefy youth with a nascent pot belly.

"Well, we're kind of in a hurry," added Needham in his easy Missouri accent.

"So what. You're not supposed to be flashing those lights like that in the fast lane," snapped the other cop.

"You got a patient in there?" asked the young fat boy.

"Yep," I replied.

"And she's pretty sick," added Needham.

"Where you headed?"

"California," said Needham calmly.

"California!" yelped the fat one over the din of the traffic.

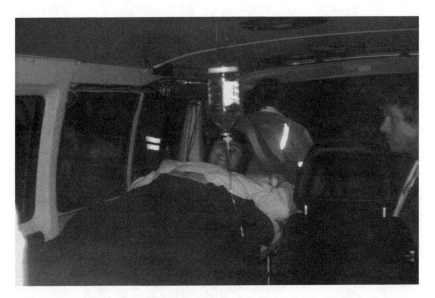

Pamela Yates made an impressive patient during the TransCon MediVac's encounter with the New Jersey Highway Patrol early in the race.

Staggered by this information, the pair both stuttered for a moment before one finally blurted the obvious question.

"Well, why don't you fly her out there?"

I walked past them and flung open the side door. "I guess you better ask the doctor," I said crisply.

It was perfect. The Doc looked up from Pamela, who was lying with her face covered with an oxygen mask. The tube from the IV bottle disappeared beneath the woolen blanket. "What's this all about?" said Royer angrily.

"These guys don't know what's going on," I said patiently, gesturing to the cops.

"This woman is very ill and has to be transported to the UCLA Medical Center in Los Angeles," said Royer, his voice tinged with impatience.

"Why can't you fly her?" persisted the cops.

"She has a rare disease involving tiny lesions on the linings of her lungs. She cannot survive in a pressured airplane."

"But you guys were runnin' pretty fast," groped the chubby one.

"Look, we've got 72 hours to get her on the heart-lung machine. How long are we going to have to hang around here?" Royer asked, his face darkening, his voice turning harder.

Defeated, and slightly baffled, the cops weakly warned, "You guys better take it a little easy," and trudged back to their cruiser.*

Jackpot! We leapt back into our van and guffawed our way to Pennsylvania border. We kicked the speed back up to 100 miles per hour but made more judicious use of the flashing lights. After all, you don't learn how to be an ambulance driver in just one night.

We drove through rain and heavy fog across Pennsylvania, then rattled over a stretch of interstate 70 in West Virginia so bumpy we flung off two hubcaps while leaping the potholes. Ahead lay Ohio, the dreaded MIG Alley for motorists. We would learn later that one of our associates, driving a black Ferrari Dino, would be nailed three times within 5 miles of the state line. Another would be hit with a $900 bond for running 105 miles per hour. But to us in the steel womb of our TransCon Medivac, Ohio resembled the Bonneville Salt Flats. By the time we wailed into Indiana our average speed was rising toward 70 miles per hour, including the hour delay. Our spirits were on the same radical upswing.

The downpour persisted. The dawn was bleak and gray. The inside of the ambulance was beginning to look less like an emergency medical vehicle than a goat's pen. Needham's cigarette butts billowed out

For more on this story see page 272.

of the ashtrays. Empty Pepsi cans, jackets, rumpled maps, sandwich wrappers and a few odd tools littered the floor. But that was hardly the problem. The TransCon Medivac seemed to be losing speed. A subtle slipping in the transmission seemed to limit us to 90 miles per hour. Bright lights flared in our mirrors. A turbo diesel Mercedes-Benz flew past. Offshore powerboat racer Charlie McCarthy. Then came a Porsche 928, running perhaps 140 miles per hour. Its driver was Jacques Villeneuve, brother of Grand Prix driving superstar Gilles Villeneuve (who wanted to run the Cannonball, but a Formula Atlantic obligation intervened). This pair sailed into the distance, leaving nothing but winking taillights in their rooster-tails.

Hal Needham, still in his oil-soaked ambulance driver's uniform, shares tales of the adventure at the Portofino. The same uniforms were used by Burt Reynolds and Dom DeLuise in the movie "Cannonball Run" directed by Needham.

We continued to press ahead, crossing into Illinois at somewhat reduced speed. As we neared Effingham, the engine belched a volley of gunshot backfires and expired. We coasted to the roadside and sat in stunned silence. "Christ, I never heard anything like that before," I said.

"Sounds like the sumbitch blew sky high," said Needham.

"Does this mean we can fly the rest of the way?" asked Royer hopefully.

"I just hope it'll run far enough so I can get to a john," added Pamela.

"Kick it over once. Just see what happens," said Needham. I tentatively twisted the ignition key, and the engine thundered away as if nothing had happened. "What the hell was that all about?" I asked absently as I slipped the Dodge into gear. With the gear lever firmly notched in "Drive" the ambulance sat idling at the roadside. It would not move. "Oh shit, now the transmission's gone south," I moaned.

"We must have run out of fluid," said Needham as he fumbled through a box of spare lubricants. "Let's throw in a few cans and see if it helps."

By the time the field sped into Missouri on April 2, the word was out among High-way Patrols and the big-rig truckers. Police enforcement seriously inhibited the pace of most competitors.

It helped. But the TransCon Medivac was terminally ill. It had ruptured a main transmission seal and from that moment onward our journey would be punctuated with repeated stops to pour gallon upon gallon of transmission fluid, enough sealer to plug a leak in the Goodyear Blimp, and even a few quarts of 40 weight engine oil into the ravenous transmission. Now the mission became not one of outright, intimidating triumph, but of merely limping our crippled ambulance to the finish.

We slipped through Missouri and its heavy traffic with little problem, although at this moment the state police were acting like tom cats in a room full of mice. Cannonball cars were scurrying everywhere. Radar beams were humming, CBs were chattering, red lights were flashing, sirens were moaning in the chilly spring afternoon. Missouri accounted for perhaps 30 arrests in a 12-hour span. One competitor was stuck in the slammer for seven hours. Others were hauled before a dozen judges across the sate. Chaos reigned. Example: A police scanner picked up the following message, "If we catch that black Jaguar we're gonna put it in the crusher and its drivers in jail for life."

Night fell and the smokeys seemed to get thicker in New Mexico and Arizona. More and more truckers, bored and frustrated while lumbering along at 65–70 miles per hour, began to yelp CB alarms about the speeding machinery. Others tried to run various Cannonball cars off the road. We were untroubled by all this, although we could barely run more than 85 miles per hour between the increasingly frequent transmission fill-ups. One pair of Cannonballers in a red 930 Porsche Turbo were stopped by the Arizona Highway Patrol and told politely, "We know what you guys are up to. You are being watched all across the state." Dennis Menesini, the Nevada supermodified driver and his partner, Charlie "Batman" Robinson, had a different encounter with the Arizona authorities. After missing the notorious Ash Fork cutoff (the secret route to California) they ended up in the tiny mountain town of Jerome, where a pack of teenagers in an old Chevelle began following their truck with the high beams boiling in their mirrors. "Switch off the tail lights and spike the brakes," Dennis ordered Batman. "See if they're paying attention." Batman hammered the brakes. The Chevelle veered off the road, barely missing the truck. It roared alongside and a beer bottle splattered against a window. Now nobody heaves anything at Dennis' truck. A chase. Dennis, his compact 220-pound frame vibrating with anger, was swearing revenge when a local police cruiser joined the pursuit. "We're being attacked by those kids in that Chevelle. They threw a beer bottle at our truck," Dennis reported over the CB. "Don't worry. I'll handle it," assured the cop, roaring off in pursuit of the Chevelle.

Dennis and Batman motored along quietly for a few miles before coming across the cruiser and the Chevelle—which had blown its engine in an escape attempt. Stopping, Dennis jumped out and sprinted toward the broken car. It was driven by a large, meaty-faced kid with a big nose. He was sitting there, morosely watching the smoke and steam drift from beneath his Chevelle's hood. His mouth was hanging open. Dennis shoved his business card into the cavity. "If you ever want to try that again, here's my address. Next time I'll pinch your head off and shit in the hole." Dennis and Batman then drove on to finish an incredible fifth, consuming nearly 600 gallons of gasoline along the way.

We barely made the Ash Fork cutoff, which twists its way over a crest of mountain in the Prescott National Forest. The transmission was loaded with our last few cans of fluid halfway up the summit and by some bonus of good fortune we staggered to the top with enough momentum to limp 20 miles to another gas station. The fatigue was

Joan Mullen checks the L.A. Times *story on the Cannonball from the front seat of their 250GT SWB Ferrari, far and away the most valuable car ever to compete in the five races. Mrs. Mullen established an all-time women's record when she endured over 28 hours of driving before a visit to the ladies' room.*

Potent Shugars/Weglarz/McConkey Trans Am at the start, 1975.

Challenger headed west, 1975. Note long CB antenna.

Race to finish: Challenger next to Porsche, 1975. John McGovern

Moon Mullins provided the Dodge van that would become the TransCon MediVac. The van's 383 V8 was swapped for a 440 wedge.

Yates (right) and George Lysle on dumpster at start, 1979. John McGovern

Night run in the Rolls. Eddie Harmston driving, Stephen Kendall-Lane beside him,
1979. John McGovern

Rolls-Royce at speed, 1979. John McGovern

George Willig at the finish, 1979. Michael Hollander

Dennis "Mad Dog" Menesini runs to the finish, 1979. Michael Hollander

1979 winners David Yarborough and Dave Heinz. Michael Hollander

Second-placers Al Alden, Tom Hickey, and Dick Field. Their Mercedes-Benz 6.9 would have won, save for gas receipts, in 1979. John McGovern

Ambulance is shoved around Long Beach GP track, 1979. Michael Hollander

Driving the Bradshaw/Tillis stock car into the motel pool was based on the actual incident involving the legendary southern stock car hero Curtis Turner. He performed a similar stunt with his own Cadillac.

Dom DeLuise as Captain Chaos in the movie. John McGovern

Roger Moore drags on a cigar between shots while Hal Needham (right) and Yates (left) improvise more scenes at the Decatur, Georgia, location.

Hal Needham (left) directs a scene involving Brock Yates' wife, Pamela (center), and production assistant Kathy Shea. Yates stands to the right.

Dean Martin and Sammy Davis Jr., playing priests based roughly on the 1972 trio of Peter Brock/Jack Cowell/Dick Gilmartin, await shooting in Decatur. Martin surprisingly is holding a drink.

starting to burrow into our bodies. Coffee, cigarettes, and candy bars were no longer enough to keep us alert. Our spirits were beginning to roller-coaster through euphoric highs and gnawing, black lows. We were soaked in transmission fluid. We reeked of perspiration. We needed shaves. Each stammer in the engine pounded home the message that we were in the middle of the great Western desert and a breakdown would leave us stranded for hours. Our good humor was drifting away in the onslaught. The incessant blat of the faintly muffled exhaust and the vibration of the stiff suspension were no longer reassuring messages of power and stability, but rather merciless assaults on our physical and emotional energies. For a while, in the lonely first light of dawn, the sense of adventure endemic in the Cannonball seemed to be draining away as steadily as the transmission fluid.

Then the sun came up. A bright California morning was upon us. Our hopes of breaking 36 hours had long since passed, and the goal of making it in less than 40 hours seemed to be slipping away as well. We were losers, but we were determined to finish. Then came Palm

The TransCon MediVac was loaded on to the Kenworth flatbed under the rather baffled gaze of the famed Palm Desert Brontosaurus.

Desert. Suddenly interstate 10 was engulfed in a massive plume of smoke pouring from the TransCon Medivac. The transmission vomited its last. As we sat inert at the roadside a California Highway Patrol car—black, white and malevolent—pulled up. In the traditionally clonelike manner of the CHP, the patrolman missed the salient fact that we were an out-of-state ambulance, carrying what might have been a bogus license plate (it was) and quite obviously not your ordinary travelers. He merely called for a wrecker and accelerated off in search of less-complicated prey. (It is interesting to note that the CHP was almost impotent in the face of the Cannonball onslaught. They made very few arrests, and several cars averaged 90 miles per hour inside the Golden State, including the greater Los Angeles sprawl.)

We coaxed one final gasp of power from the transmission and stuttered 2 more miles to a truck stop. While buying up all the fluid and sealer in the place, a pair of youthful truck drivers appeared. They were running a massive, twin-stack Kenworth sleeper-cab hooked on to an empty flatbed. The brilliant notion swept over us simultaneously. Load

The winners: David Yarborough and David Heinz pose with their winning XJS after crossing the country in an amazing 32 hours and 51 minutes. Sadly, Dave Heinz passed to his reward several years ago. David Yarborough is a successful Lexus dealer in Charleston, South Carolina.

the ambulance on the flatbed and haul it to the Portofino! "Why not?" said the driver, a lean, laconic man from Las Vegas. "We was supposed to pick up a load of Sheet Rock in Riverside, but we're three hours late already. A little more won't hurt." Laboring mightily beneath a massive cement dinosaur someone had built as a sightseeing platform, we managed to hoist the broken ambulance onto the flatbed.

We piled into the Kenworth cab and our canted, superkiller, Q-ship, can't-miss Cannonball winner arrived at the Portofino Inn, tucked in the picturesque Kings Harbor, hard by the Pacific Ocean in Redondo Beach, ignominiously chained to the floor of a truck. Something over 40 hours had ticked away since leaving Darien.

The winners had been lolling around the Portofino for 12 hours by the time we staggered in. David Heinz of Tampa, Florida., and David Yarborough of Charleston, South Carolina, had won the fifth Cannonball in the staggering time of 32 hours and 51 minutes! Theirs was the black Jaguar XJS that had cause all the fury and confusion among the Missouri Highway Patrol. A mere 8 minutes behind them was the

Dan Gurney, left, presents the winner's trophy to Dave Heinz and David Yarborough, marking their record-shattering victory.

Harvard contingent, led by Prof. Thomas Hickey, and its Mercedes-Benz. Both cars averaged nearly 88 miles per hour coast to coast!

We won by losing. Needham came away loaded with stories and impressions for the movie he planned to make about the real Cannonball. Moreover, I suppose my winning the Cannonball would have been like getting the door prize at your own birthday party. As a bonus, the event netted $2,500 for the Gunnar Nilson Cancer Fund. Perhaps most important, we had proved once again that good cars and good drivers can use the interstate system at speeds far beyond the farcical 55-mile per hour speed limit with great safety. (Cannonball cars had now run over 300,000 miles, averaging over 76 miles per hour with only two minor accidents, involving no serious injuries.)

Better yet, the postrace party blitzed on for an entire week.

The Way It Was

(as reported in the May 1979 issue of the Cannonball Express)

On the first weekend of this month, which included April Fool's Day, David Heinz of Tampa, Florida, and David Yarborough of Charleston, South Carolina, drove a black XJS Jaguar from Darien, Connecticut, to Redondo Beach, California, in the rather astounding time of 32 hours and 51 minutes. This feat by a pair of mannerly and otherwise quite sensible British Leyland automobile dealers won the fifth running of the Cannonball Sea-to-Shining-Sea Memorial Dash and established them as the fastest transcontinental drivers in history.

Therein lies a story.

It started on a black, rainy night at the Lock, Stock & Barrel Restaurant in Darien. Forty-six vehicles, ranging from a BMW R90S motorcycle to a 1948 Rolls-Royce, were spread around the parking lot. Perhaps 3,000 people milled through the area, turning the pretenses for a secret start into a bad joke. A band was playing. Kids were running around. The one who observed that this scene was just like the Gumball Rally nearly got slugged. The local Darien police were lurking in the background, promising their blessings, provided no laws were broken. Scouts were observing that no serious concentrations of State Police could be found on nearby interstate 95, although that organization had ironically announced a weekend of massive enforcement on the Merritt Parkway a few miles to the north. Somehow the event had bulged all out of proportion. What had been planned as a starting field of 20 had doubled in size when more and more qualified entrants came out of the woodwork. Thanks to friends in high places and some simple good luck, *The New York Times* had barely missed writing advance stories on the Cannonball, which would have blown the entire affair. As it was, everyone on the East Coast seemed to know what was going on. Word came that a small group was hanging around the Red Ball Garage, the old starting spot in Manhattan. Press people seemed to be everywhere, blazing away with Nikons and scribbling notes. The Barrel was clogged with drinkers and warm Coca-Colas. A substantial number of manufacturer's reps were on hand to unofficially cheer the proceedings. The merry men from Cincinnati Microwave appeared, complete with test equipment, to ensure that their Escorts being used in the event were operating perfectly. (Almost all of the starting field carried these state-of-the-art units.)

We had received repeated intelligence that the vaunted California Highway Patrol was awaiting with a certain perverted eagerness. An anonymous phone call informed us that unnamed Connecticut officials were displeased with the Cannonball and planned undetermined countermeasures. A snowstorm was said to be building in the Rockies. interstate 80 through the western Pennsylvania mountains was riddled with 4-inch-deep potholes and the nuclear accident at the Three Mile Island facility near Harrisburg threatened to cut off the Pennsylvania Turnpike. And there was always the fear of the crazed storm troopers who compose the Ohio State Police.

Into this obstacle course slipped the crazed 46. As the perpetrator of this affair, I felt like old Lord Raglan watching the charge of the Light Brigade. The first away was Bob Kovaleski, Oscar's kid, at the wheel of a white Z-28 carrying the Polish Racing Drivers of America emblem. (By tradition, the PRDA always get the Cannonball's "Pole" position.) Urged on by the good luck kiss of Rae Cameron, the lovely lady whose organizational zeal permitted uncounted multitudes of problems to be solved, and a lusty cheer from the crowd, Kovaleski and company slipped into the rainy night.

Others quickly followed; Hollywood stunt men and general handymen Loyal Truesdale and Keith Patchett buttoned up their leathers, cranked their BMW to life and fled into the darkness. Jim Mullen and his willowy wife, Joan, howled away in their elegantly tatty but wonderfully noisy 1962 Short Wheelbase Berlinetta Ferrari. The Mullens have a number of new Ferraris in their extensive car collection but Jim, a Boston advertising executive, felt it only right and proper that the Cannonball be done in the old SWB.

The 1947 Silver Wraith slipped away quietly with chauffeur Edwin Harmston at the wheel and its elegantly dressed owners, Mr. and Mrs. Stephen Kendall-Lane of Mayfair, London, nibbling at provisions from Fortnum and Mason in the back seat. Mark Pritch, a feisty little man from Long Island who, in company with Bondurant School instructor Bill Cooper, pledged he would break the record of 35 hours and 53 minutes, bustled off in his jet-black Ferrari 308 GT. A silver 6.9 Mercedes-Benz handled by a lean Boston Marathoner and Harvard teaching fellow named Tom Hickey moved out sedately. Hickey and his associates, Al Alden and Dick Field, were immaculately dressed in sport coats and ties, which was perhaps the best cover of all. However, others tried. The California Chevy suburban team led by Jim Sensebaugh appeared in muted gray and white government colors with large "Satellite Tracking Radiation. Stay Clear" signs on its flanks. The team was equipped with Geiger counters and delighted in scanning unwitting gas station attendants across the nation. The trick was particularly effective in the Harrisburg area.

Lou Sellyei and Gary Arentz, a couple of M.D.s from Reno, Nevada, drove off in an XKJ carrying a box containing a pair of pig's eyes. The emergency eye-bank scam. Not bad.

Two teams went the drive-away route, one with a 1977 Chrysler, the other with a 1972 Thunderbird provided by the same New York operation that had supplied a Sedan DeVille in the 1971 run and the winning Coupe DeVille in 1972!

Dennis Menesini, the super-modified driver, had appeared in Darien several days early with his massive 454 Chevy dual-wheel crew-cab and Charlie "Batman" Robinson.

Motor Trend staffer Fred Gregory and *Oui* editor Peter Brennan tried to drive the same Herb Adams Pontiac "Fire-Am" that competed in the Daytona 24 Hours, but a broken suspension and numerous carburetor fires prior to the start, and a terminal oil leak shortly thereafter, left them no choice but to fly to California carrying the car's trunk lid as a souvenir of disaster.

In all, 123 crazies—wastrels, rich men, poor men, beggarmen, and thieves—got under way in the participating vehicles. Among them were notables like Jacques Villeneuve, Gilles' brother (Gilles was an enthusiastic entrant with his old Formula Atlantic car owner John Lane, until his Long Beach GP schedule interfered); Indy car pilot John Mahler; human fly extraordinaire George Willig; *Sports Illustrated* writer Sam Moses; offshore powerboat champions Sandy Satullo and Charlie McCarthy; Karting champ Terry Baker; and my partner, Hal Needham, whose plan to run a bogus ambulance was perhaps the best number ever to be tried in the Cannonball.

Somehow the entire field slipped through Connecticut and New York without notice (the ambulance's flashing lights were magical on the crowded Cross-Bronx Expressway). However, the Mullens' old Ferrari faltered near the George Washington Bridge and they were forced to stagger back to Darien for repairs. Paul Fassler and Bob Ziegel, a pair of bon vivants in a flame-red Porsche 930 Turbo, got lost in New Jersey and blew their chances for victory early in the going.

Most of the field split across rainy, fog-bound interstate 80 and into the jaws of the bright-eyed morning shift of the Ohio State Police.

Mark Pritch crossed the border in the beam of a K-55 and was arrested for a panic-stopped 80 miles per hour. Overcome by the urgency of the moment, he was nailed twice more in the next 5 miles, developing in that brief interval a first-name relationship with the Smokeys, a much-lightened wallet and absolutely no chance of winning the Cannonball. Charlie McCarthy was among a number of casualties in Ohio, but set some sort of dubious mark by leaving a bond of $900 for his speeding citation (he was later fined $90). Others fell to the state police here, giving Ohio the honors, along with Missouri, of accounting for the lion's share of the 50 speeding tickets issued along the way.

An examination of the map will reveal that most of the serious westbound routes race their way through some parts of Missouri. Moreover, the schedule of the Cannonballers caused them to hit the state in broad daylight, when the highway patrol was operating at peak strength. Missouri was the Cannonball's MIG Alley. Several dozen worthies were zapped, including 1972 winner Yogi Behr. Poor Behr was sleeping while his driving partner, Rod Dornsife, outran a patrol car in their 928. They exchanged seats and Behr drove back onto the interstate and into the arms of the enraged law. As the British so politely put it, Yogi was "detained" for five hours while the situation was clarified.

While compiling the exact movement of 40-odd vehicles in a scatological event like the Cannonball is impossible, it seems that Sunday afternoon, April 1, 1979, was a day of high-speed madness on interstate 44 in Missouri. Those competitors who carried police radio scanners in their vehicles reported crazed chatter on the part of the Smokeys as they sped up and down the road in search of squadrons of cars rocketing through their state. The second night shrouded the runners as they sped into Texas and New Mexico. There the old bugaboo of yapping truckers appeared, as it had in 1975. Enraged by the bright quartz-halogen headlights or simple speed, not a few 18-wheel drivers set out to sabotage the Cannonballers, either by squawking warnings on the CB (to be countermeasured in some cases by competitors simply keying their 100-amp linears and blowing them off the air) or blocking the road.

Things got nasty on several occasions, with second-placer Tom Hickey's 6.9 being run onto the shoulder and the third-place Trans Am of Jeff Pierce and Mike Snyder almost becoming the sausage in a monster Mack sandwich in Arizona. Terry Bernius and Tom Cripe reacted to the challenge by announcing to the truckers that they were engaged in a protest against the 55-miles-per-hour speed limit. This elicited support from the truckers, who began calling the tiny Lotus Esprit "the Snowplow" and beckoning it on with blinking turn signals.

Exhaustion led to paranoia. Bob Kovaleski blew his chances for a high finish when he convinced himself that a road block lay ahead in Arizona and doubled back 50 miles to avoid the nonexistent barrier. In the meantime the old Rolls-Royce was rolling serenely ahead, although its windshield wipers (fabricated at the last minute from odd bits) failed, and its drivers were reduced to operating them by hand.

Cannonball veteran Wes Dawn, who has competed in every Dash since 1972, teamed up with Jeff Martini in a new Eldorado and tried, for the second time, to beat the system by running I-80 to Salt Lake City and then cutting south on I-15—surely the long way around. Their journey started badly when they hit an accident scene in Ohio and sat in the jam-up until Dawn and Martini leaped out, grabbed brooms and helped sweep the debris.

In the meantime Hickey, Adam, and Field and their 6.9 Mercedes were becoming the children of destiny on the Cannonball. Operating without an escort, making only rudimentary use of the CB, and waiting for credit card receipts at their gas stops, they were stopped but once by the gendarmes and were maintaining an incredible 85-miles per-hour-plus average speed. At one point in Arizona they smoked by the fourth-place finishers, Mark Whiteside and Stephen Fog and their Trans Am, at perhaps 140 miles per hour. All this in an area swarming with police. While this was going on, the oldest vehicle in the race, a 1936 Ford panel truck, entered by *Hemmings Motor News*, was struggling through a series of minor disasters. After a blitz of electrical troubles early in the going, drivers Terry Erich, Dave Brownell, and Justus Taylor settled into a routine of stopping every 50–60 miles to lubricate a noisy generator bearing. While cruising nicely at 85–90 miles per hour for most of the distance, BMW worthies Truesdale and Patchett rode into a snow squall near Winslow, Arizona, and were forced to hole up in a motel until the weather cleared.

Because of their pace, the first six cars, all of which shattered the old record of 35 hours and 53 minutes, slipped into California in the black hours of Monday morning, when the CHP forces were minimal. However, much of the field arrived after the 5:30–6:30 A.M. shift change, when a whole armada of Chippies, complete with their new Z-28s and old 440 Magnums were supposed to be waiting. But what was happening? Could this be the California Hype Patrol? Were these bears grizzlies or pandas? Cannonball car after car flogged across the border with its crews' eyes probing for black-and-whites, only to find clear horizons in all directions. Sixth-placer Rick Doherty and his Mazda RX-7 were nailed for 90 miles per hour, but little else affected the front-runners in California. Chris Romine and Terry Baker, driving a pristine red Ferrari 308GTS ran the entire distance without being arrested or even warned. What does that do to the theory about cops and their attraction to flashy cars? They averaged 91 miles per hour from the California border to the Portofino—including about 6 miles of urban, stop-and-go traffic.

The finishers straggled into the Portofino for much of Monday. By Tuesday the English *Truck Magazine* entry of Andrew Frankl and John Hitchins—a miniature, Capri V-6 dual-axle cab-over-tractor, had arrived, as had the BMW motorcycle. The other motorcycle, an 850-cc, shaft-drive Suzuki that had finished in a creditable 43 hours and 32 minutes, was ridden, pony-express fashion, by five riders from the Western-Eastern Road Racing Club.

Finally, as the thoroughly zany victory banquet was under way and Chris Pook of the Long Beach GP was accepting a $2,500 donation on behalf of the Cannonball for the Gunnar Nillsen Cancer Fund and old teammate Dan Gurney was presenting the winner's trophy, it was over and an amazing, weeklong celebration was about to commerce.

OFFICIAL RESULTS
1979 Cannonball Sea-To-Shining-Sea
Memorial Trophy Dash

Pos.	Car	Drivers	Time
1.	1978 Jaguar XJS	Dave Heinz/Dave Yarborough	32:51
2.	1978 Mercedes-Benz 6.9	Tom Hickey/Al Alden/ Dick Field	32:59
3.	1979 Trans Am	Jeff Pierce/Michael Snyder	33:42
4.	1979 Trans Am	Mark Whiteside/Stephen Fog	34:07
5.	1979 Chevy 454 Dually	Dennis Menesini/Mark Miller Ken Smith/Charlie Robinson	34:52
6.	1979 Mazda RX7	Richard Doherty/Tad Richardson	35:17
7.	1978 Ferrari 308GTS	Chris Romine/Terry Baker	35:58

Pos.	Car	Drivers	Time
8.	1978 Buick Park Avenue	Joel Rosenblatt/Jim Crittenden	36:00
9.	1978 Mercedes-Benz Turbo Diesel	Charlie McCarthy/Harvey Adelbert/ Jon Dunaj	36:19
10.	1977 Excalibur	David Stevens/Daniel Simkin/ Gerald Allen	36:20
11.	1979 Camaro Z28	Bob Kovaleski/Jim Kirby	36:40
12.	1979 Pontiac	S. Sandy Satullo/S. Sandy Satullo II	36:49
13.	1979 Chevrolet Malibu	E. Pierce Marshall/David Faust/ Kirby Goodman	36:51
14.	1978 Porsche 930 Turbo	Paul Frassler/Robert Ziegel	37:25
15.	Porsche 928	Jacques Villeneuve/John Lane	37:31
16.	1971 Camaro Z28	Tom Leonard/John Mahler	37:46
17.	1973 Chevrolet Blazer	R. David Jones/Scott Visniewski/ Edward Mayo/Willie Williams	38:10
18.	1977 Ferrari 308GT350	Mark Pritch/Bill Cooper	38:52
19.	1976 Jaguar XJS	Dr. Louis Sellyei Jr./Dr. Gary Arentz	39:10
20.	1976 El Camino	Ted Armstrong/Keith Armstrong/ Buzz Rasmussen	39:20
21.	Boss 302 Mustang	Sam Moses/George Willig	39:45
22.	1977 Camaro	Gary Smith/Paul Graham/ John Nichols	39:45
23.	1962 Ferrari SWB	Jim Mullen/Joan Mullen	40:11
24.	1969 Volvo 242GT	Anatoly Arutunoff/Bill Pryor/ Boo Browning	40:33
25.	1977 Chrysler	Doug Mockett/Peter Jessick/ Bill Moore/John Micek	40:53
26.	1972 T-Bird	Bill Lovell/Bill Campbell/ Jim Hunt	41:00
27.	1963 Corvette	Gerald McWhorter/ Donald McWhorter	41:17
28.	1975 Porsche Carrera	Chick Stanton/Jim Atwell	41:27
29.	Porsche 928	Stephen "Yogi" Behr/Rod Dornsife	42:27
30.	1979 Suzuki 850	George Egloff/Wendy Epstein/ Ken Ward/Steve Ward/Dirk James	43:32

Pos.	Car	Drivers	Time
31.	1969 Jensen Interceptor	Gero Hoschek/Andreas Zoeltner/ Ursula Nerger	43:47
32.	1978 Lotus Esprit	Terry Bernius/Tom Cripe	44:13
33.	1974 Chevy Suburban	Jim Sensebaugh/Charles Martin/ Peter Defty/Tom Gafford	45:32
34.	1970 Mercedes-Benz 300 SEL	Alex Senehi/Alain E. Sportiche	46:31
35.	1974 Porsche Carrera	Larry Prentiss/Benjamin Ralston	46:37
36.	1964 Ferrari 330 GT	Tony Quartararo/Jim Peelor/ Stuart Davidson	46:48
37.	1976 Cadillac Eldorado	Bill O'Donnell/Donald Race/ Charles Schmidt	53:00
38.	1965 Shelby Mustang GT350	Rick Kopec/Robert Key	48:53
39.	1948 Rolls-Royce Silver Wraith	John McGovern/Edwin Harmston/ Roger Bell/Fiona Kendall-Lane/ Stephen Kendall-Lane	58:04
40.	1936 Ford Panel Truck	Terry Ehrich/Dave Brownell/ Justus Taylor	61:51
41.	1978 Truck	Andrew Frankl/John Hitchins	65:55
42.	BMW R90S	Loyal Truesdale/Keith Patchett	72:54

Did not officially finish:

1.	TransCon Medivac	Brock Yates/Hal Needham/ Pamela Yates/ Lyle Royer left at 9:36 P.M. towed in at 2:24 P.M.	
2.	1978 Lotus Esprit	John Harrison left 9:04, 3/31 P.M.	
3.	1979 Trans Am	Fred Gregory/Peter Brennan left 1:32 A.M., 4/1	
4.	1971 Fiat 127	Massimo Paggio/Mike Menzel left 1:52 A.M. 4/1	

Cannonball Special Awards 1979

In addition to a variety of trophies and awards to the high finishers, a number of citations were reserved for those whose accomplishments in the Cannonball were notable, if not conventional.

FRIENDS OF THE OPEC AWARD—To Dennis Menesini, for averaging 5.4 miles per gallon and consuming 590 gallons of gas in his Chevy crew-cab.

DIAMOND JIM BRADY MODERATION AWARD—To Stephen Kendall-Lane and his 1948 Rolls-Royce Silver Wraith.

THE BANDIT'S HIGHWAY SAFETY AWARD—To Mark Pritch, for collecting three speeding tickets in a 5-mile stretch of Ohio's Route 80.

CHAMPION BALLOONFOOT AWARD—To Terry Bernius and Tom Cripe, for averaging 28 miles per gallon in their Lotus Esprit.

LAST BUT NOT LOST AWARD—To Andrew Frankl and Tom Hitchins, for a leisurely time of 65 hours and 55 minutes.

THE DIEHARD AWARD—To Fred Gregory and Peter Brennan, for repeated mechanical failures before and during the run, and for arriving at the finish with the trunk lid of their "Fire-Am."

TOW-AWAY AWARD—To Hal Needham, for entering a vehicle that only went 100 yards before its first breakdown.

WORST TIME AWARD—To Shelby GT 350 drivers Rick Kopec and Bob Key, who attempted to pawn themselves off as cops with a borrowed badge and ended up in handcuffs in Ohio.

IN THE TANK AWARD—To Steve "Yogi" Behr, for five hours in the Lebanon, Missouri, slammer, a new Cannonball record.

BALLS OUT AWARD—To Chris Romine and Terry Baker, for averaging 91 miles per hour through California in an all-out effort to break 36 hours, which they did, by 2 minutes.

NIGHT OWL AWARD—To Joan Mullen, who, while codriving with her husband, Jim, in their SWB Ferrari, set a modern-day female record by not going to the john for 28 hours and 10 minutes.

DOCTOR STRANGELOVE AWARD—To BMW riders Loyal Truesdale and Keith Patchett, for all kinds of reasons.

THE ALLISON-YARBOROUGH GOOD SPORTS AWARD—To Dennis Menesini and crew for their near punch-out in Jerome, Arizona.

PIRELLI PARIS-TO-PEKING AWARD—To Tom Hickey, Al Alden, and Dick Field.

David Yarborough
1979

In the fall of 1978 I was attending a National Automobile Dealer's Association meeting in Orlando, Florida, with my fellow Jaguar dealer, Dave Heinz. He told me about the possibility of another Cannonball Dash and asked if I would like to codrive with him. I told him that I had been practicing since the day I got my driver's license for an opportunity like this. I considered it an honor to be his partner.

Unfortunately, since Dave is not here to share his memories, it may seem that I am taking credit for winning the Cannonball. Nothing could be further from the truth. He was a talented, skillful driver and a wonderful person. I really enjoyed my time with him. When you spend that much time with someone—on the ride from South Carolina to Darien, Connecticut, and then racing across the country and back—you get to know each other pretty well. He truly was a great driver and I learned a lot from him during this trip.

One of the most interesting things about the 1979 Cannonball was meeting all of the different characters who were involved in this fifth running. As one might imagine, it takes a combination of craziness, steel nerves, a dash of wild abandon, and a pretty good sense of humor to make a person want to do something like this. So it was an interesting cast and crew we met when we arrived in Darien. Another thing that sticks in my mind is how caught up the locals got in the festivities of the event. There was a big party the night before with lots of locals in attendance. My Southern accent served me particularly well that night!

Dave and I spent several hours the day before the race planning our route. As you know, we chose pretty much the middle route of the country, running through Pennsylvania, Ohio, Indiana, and Missouri, which is where I got my first ticket.

It was raining about 7 A.M., Sunday, in St. Louis, and this very young trooper with a commando haircut—who had obviously just come on the job—was sitting at the top of an on-ramp as we passed underneath. All of a sudden, both radar detectors went off and I hit the brakes as hard as I could. When my eyes hit the speedometer, it had slowed to 100 miles per hour. I started to skid and lose the rear end, so I let off the brakes and hit them again. At this point, the officer cleared his radar gun, not believing the initial reading, and hit us again. The final score: 78 miles per hour, and I was told that at 80 miles per hour, he would have been required to take me to the magistrate. Fortunately, I received a ticket for $39.50, which, by the way, he would not let me pay on the spot. It took 10 minutes to write the ticket and get us out of there. Part of our "ticket" conversation was why I was going so fast. I told him we were headed to California for a week's vacation and there wasn't much traffic at that time of the morning. He dutifully reminded me that it was raining and advised me to slow down. I didn't do a whole lot of arguing. I just took the ticket and got on the way. When I got back in the car, I remember telling Dave, "This guy has just come on duty and we were probably his first catch of the day. By the time noon gets here, it will be the biggest day of his life!"

As I recall, we gassed the car four times on this trip. On our gas stop after St. Louis, we decided to check the oil. In taking off the oil cap, we dropped it by the side of the engine. As you can imagine, it was pretty hot in there and we had a hard time reaching the oil cap. We wasted probably 10 minutes on that gas stop. I do believe fate plays a lot into this. My initial thought was that 10 minutes could have helped us finish 10 minutes earlier and beat the record by that much more. But who is to say that those 10 minutes didn't help us win the race? Who knows what would have happened or could have happened? Maybe the police in Arizona tagged someone else instead of us because of the delay in Missouri.

We left Darien at 8:27 in the evening, according to our plan, in order to arrive before 5:00 A.M. in California, when we had been told the traffic would really begin to pick up. Hoping to avoid that, we planned our start around that time. Of course, Bobby Kovaleski and the Polish Racing Drivers Team was the first car off the line at 7 P.M. We caught them right at the Arizona line. The fact that they left an hour and a half ahead of us made us feel pretty good. As soon as we got a little bit of a lead on them, our radar detector went off. So we hit our brakes and they passed us. We rode along behind them for a little while and then we passed them again. Damn if the radar detector didn't go off again! So we slowed down and they passed us and we rode behind them for a while. We were looking all over for the Smokey. It didn't take too awfully long to figure out what was going on. They had a radar gun! That was something we laughed about later, but at the time, it was not particularly funny!

We were involved in an incident with Kovaleski and some angry truckers. They were riding side by side, trying to slow us down. Bobby pulled out on the shoulder and kicked it. It was a pretty close call for him getting back in before a bridge abutment. But he made it and when he reentered from the shoulder of the road, he threw rocks all over the place and one hit the windshield of a truck. Of course, all the truckers went ballistic with that and told us we better not even think about passing on the right or we would end up in the middle of the desert. Then they began to radio ahead for another truck to stop Kovaleski. Bobby was pretty sharp and had done this before. He had a booster on his CB radio and was able to block their transmission forward by just holding the transmit button. You could hear them from behind but not ahead. We rode along for a few minutes and then a highway patrolman came along and broke up the roadblock.

I have had many people over the years say to me, "Man, that sounds like great fun. Next time you run the Cannonball, I would sure like to drive with you." My standard answer to them is, "If you think you would really like to do that, I'd like for you to pick a weekend and sit in your car in the driveway. Don't drive it anywhere; don't run 120 miles per hour; just go sit in your car for 32 hours and 51 minutes. When you get out, call me and tell me if you think you would still like to run the Cannonball."

I think one of my most depressing moments ever was during this race. We had been running all night and all day through three time zones and we were seeing the sun begin to set in the West. The tumbleweeds were blowing and I looked up and saw a sign that said, Los Angeles, 1,021 miles. I thought to myself, "My God, we've been running as hard as we can run all night and all day and we are still 1,000 miles away." To put it in perspective, this was farther than it was from Charlotte, South Carolina, to Darien, Connecticut, where we started. And it seemed like it took forever to get there. After running so long, you have a tendency to get a little paranoid. You have a couple of encounters with the police and the truckers and you begin to wonder, "How much longer can I get away with this?" interstate 40 in 1979 wasn't anything like we know it today. There were times when we would go through a little town and the chickens would be running back and forth across the highway, otherwise known as Route 66.

We had to keep reminding ourselves that we had to press even harder the further into the race we got, because what you are hoping for is that the other drivers will let up. Dave played a big role in keeping us motivated to push and push harder. During the 13th, 14th, and 15th hour in the race, we averaged 91 miles per hour. Our 32nd hour was 91.5 miles per hour. We made some very good times during the last part of the race. That is when we really pushed it.

Dave was driving when we hit Albuquerque in the late afternoon. We had some music playing. We were rolling through four lanes of traffic and one of the things you fear is that as people are riding along at 55 miles per hour, and you are running 100–110 miles per hour in fairly heavy traffic, someone taps the brakes and sets off a chain reaction. Dave danced in and out of those four lanes like Fred Astaire. We just slipped tight through there without ever slowing down. It was a beautiful piece of driving. It was a really special moment in the race that I will never forget. I would give anything if we had been able to film that.

The only really serious problem we had was on a stretch between Kingman, Arizona, and Needles, California. I happened to be driving at the time. There is quite a drop in altitude and we made it in a short period of time. It was nightfall and we were sailing down the mountain in the Jaguar XJS—like flying an airplane. Most of the trucks were running in low gear, just kind of gliding down the mountain. We averaged 100 miles per hour in that short stretch. We had high intensity headlamps and would come up on one of these guys and wait until the last possible moment to dim our lights. They got a little pissed. When we got to the bottom of the mountain headed into Needles, all traffic had to exit onto a particular ramp with really high curbing. The truckers were waiting for us.

When we got to the ramp, there were four 18-wheelers in front of us and three or four behind us. They had us at a dead standstill and would not move. We got on the CB and said, "Hey fellas, what's going on?" They identified us as the two guys in the black Jaguar and said, "You have been blowing down the mountain and it's not safe, and we're calling the police." So we got off the CB and tried to plot a strategy, which did not include trying to pull over the curb, because there was just no way to do that. As luck would have it, someone in a motor home pulled onto the ramp and got on the CB and said, "What the hell is going on here?"

One of the truckers radioed back and said, "These guys were going too fast, disturbing the truckers, and we're calling the police."

The guy came back on and said, "It sounds like that's none of your business, so let's get this traffic moving."

To which the trucker reported, "You just mind your own business. We'll start moving when we get ready."

At which point the motor home driver said, in a harsher tone, "If you don't get moving, I'm going to shoot your tires out."

With that, the trucks began to move forward and we were able to get outside the curb and go on our way. In the rear-view mirror, we could see the truckers herding this motor home into a service station.

When we got to the other side of town, it was time for a driver change. We pulled over, jumped out and ran around the car, trading places. At about the same time, two police cars went flying by us in the other direction. I'm not sure what happened, but I'm pretty confident that the truckers won the confrontation with the motor home. Anyway, that was certainly the most intense point of the race for us.

You hear all sorts of horror stories about different police forces. I think the California Highway Patrol is one of the most feared. I remember on that last driver's change in Needles, Dave took over and said, "You know, I think we are running pretty strong. What do you say we go all out last leg?" And we did. We averaged 91.5 miles per hour in hour 32. So the famed California Highway Patrol must have been sleeping that night because we cannonballed! It was great fun. When we got to Redondo Beach, and slid through the parking lot to the front door of the Portofino Inn, there was some confusion because they did not expect anyone for another hour. We had to run around a little bit before we could find the time clock to punch our card. We probably could have knocked another couple minutes off our time.

All in all, it was a great experience and a great race. I have had my 15 minutes of fame and enjoyed it thoroughly. Being in the automobile business, winning the Cannonball, and setting the U.S. transcontinental record has been a source of conversation and great entertainment for many a car buff over the last 23 years. I would not trade the experience for anything in the world. Today, my trophy sits in the place of honor on a pedestal in my office—a hard-fought, well-earned place of honor.

David Yarborough is a Lexus dealer in Charleston, South Carolina. David Heinz passed away several years ago.

Hal Needham
1979

I thought I was a crazy son of a bitch until I met Brock Yates. I am shocked that he's made it this far in life. I worry about his pretty brunette wife, Pam. What kind of a story did he lay on her? Whatever it was, it worked.

Pam took on his bravado without skipping a beat. With that lunatic, Brock and another "schizo," (me), driving that ambulance 140 miles an hour from coast to coast, it was enough to test the best of nerves. She never blinked an eye. Hang in there, Pam—you're a jewel. Hanging out in bars until 2 A.M. and working every day had me acclimated. Forty-eight hours without sleep was no problem. I was wondering how the rest of our team was going to stay awake. Then I found the answer.

We came upon a detour at a hundred and a quarter, outdriving our headlights. It was quite a surprise. Did you ever have a van sideways at 125? If not, I'll tell you what it does. It gets everybody's attention. Believe me, no one slept from coast to coast.

The ambulance was a good idea. It got us past the New Jersey Highway Patrol. It worked quite well in Missouri, also. A rodeo crowd was leaving the arena and traffic was backed up for a mile. We turned on our red lights, moved over into the oncoming lane and never missed a beat. The local sheriff directing traffic stopped everyone in all directions and waved us through. We started to believe we were legit. At least we acted like we were.

Brock is the writer and storyteller, so I'll tell to him fill in the blanks. I know we're getting a little long in the tooth for this kind of bullshit . . . but, if he comes up with something like the Cannonball again, count me in. Then I could have two great experiences to talk about in my rocking chair. Remember, when we're old and gray, all we'll have is memories.

Anyone who doesn't know about Hal Needham has never been to the movies.

Fred M. H. Gregory
THE CANNONBALL: 1979

*It takes skill, smarts, and speed
to run in this infamous outlaw race.
We had the speed . . .*

She was tall, beautiful, and more than a little drunk. Soft round parts of her swayed back and forth under a loose white dress. She looked up with her big, unfocused eyes and pleaded: "Please, take me with you . . . I wanna go."

"There's no room," I told her, and then edged my way through the bodies packed at the bar. I couldn't really blame her for wanting to come along. She'd been exposed to the high-voltage madness radiating through the place.

It was nearly midnight in Darien, Connecticut, and most of the crowd at the pubby Lock, Stock & Barrel had been getting bombed for hours, waiting to witness the start of the fifth Cannonball Sea-to-Shining-Sea Memorial Trophy Dash. Watching these killer cars roar off must have worked like an aphrodisiac on the tipsy good-looker. She was hot for 35 hours of red-eyed, raw-nerved, high-revving speed through the great flat middle of the United States. The Cannonball quickens your pulse like sex.

I was trying to fight the adrenaline pounding through my veins: Stay calm, stay sober. So the good-looker took her case to my driving partner, Peter Brennan. "Maybe we could strap her on the hood?" He ventured. "It would screw up the aerodynamics." I said. Our car was a delicately balanced brute, and there was hardly room for the two of us in its jungle-gym interior.

To win the Cannonball, you need a car that can cruise 110, 120, 130, all day and all night for 2,800 miles. And we had the perfect killer for the job, a '79 Pontiac Firebird built by the automotive genius Herb Adams. He had outfitted the car with a 425-horsepower engine, a full roll cage, a 32-gallon fuel tank, and a racing suspension that kept it stuck to the ground like a barnacle. To test the car, Herb ran it in the grueling Daytona 24-hour race. It hung in there for 19 hours, running the high banks of the speedway at over 150 miles per hour. Then it broke down. But it was an impressive showing, especially since what we would call the "Fire-Am" had been driven over interstate highways from Detroit to Daytona and then, after it was fixed, driven back.

Before giving us the car for the Cannonball, Herb put in a new motor, a powerful CB and an Escort Radar detector. And even though he took off the Daytona racing numbers, the Fire-Am still looked like a balls-out racer. Its nose nearly touched the ground, and the sound from its 3-inch straight pipes could be heard into the next dimension. It was one of the fastest street cars in the country—and a match for anything in the Cannonball.

I had picked up the car in Detroit a few days before the race, intending to work out the bugs on the 600-mile run to New York. Brennan, who was managing editor of the now-defunct *Oui* magazine, was flying in from Los Angeles to meet me the day before the Cannonball started.

Heading east on interstate 80 though Pennsylvania, the Fire-Am ran fast and true, gliding at 80 and 90 like a shark through water. I ran it up to 140 a few times, and even in a light rain it hugged the road.

I was cruising effortlessly through the Pocono Mountains at about 80. It was Thursday night; there was plenty of time left before the start of the race. I was thinking good thoughts of ways to kill time in Manhattan. Suddenly, I hit a pothole. The wheel jerked in my hands, the Fire-Am's nose dipped, and the car jumped off the road. I pulled off the throttle and fought to keep the car on the gravel shoulder, but horrible metal-ripping sounds were coming from the front end.

There was a truck stop just ahead. I limped in to check the damage. The right front wheel had broken off and was tucked under the fender at a sickening angle.

It took the whole next day to get the damn thing fixed.

By Saturday morning, I was on the road again. At least, I thought, that's about as bad as things can get. Then the engine caught fire. Flames kicked back against the windshield from the Fire-Am's shaker scoop. I pulled over and smothered the fire with my jacket. It was a bad carburetor, and the car caught fire every 20 miles as I nursed it across New Jersey and charbroiled my jacket in the process.

Time was running short, and Brennan was becoming dangerously nervous in New York. He was pacing the floor, concocting elaborate excuses to account for the vast amount of money that *Oui* was spending on what was slowly turning into a nightmare.

With the help of some hot rodders in Summit, New Jersey, the Fire-Am was fitted with a new carburetor and a couple of strong fire extinguishers. On the short ride to Manhattan, the car purred like a contented tiger. Coming through the Holland Tunnel, its pipes sounded like feedback from an atomic guitar. The bugs were worked out, I thought. It was running fine and we're going to make it.

Then I made a wrong turn and wound up on the East Side of Manhattan instead of the West side. The bombed-out streets of Fun City began to take more out of the Fire-Am than Daytona had. Navigating between potholes and pedestrians, the car simply quit. The engine overheated and went up in a cloud of steam on a particularly nasty corner of the lower East Side that was packed with cruising hookers. I called Brennan from a phone booth, keeping an eye on some pimps who were taking an unusual interest in the Fire-Am's wheels and tires.

When he arrived in a Checker cab with a cooler full of provisions, he was wearing a pair of eyes that definitely did not look normal. "Jesus, fuck," he said, "this car is an animal." Brennan had never seen the car, let alone driven it. "We'll never get this thing out of New York without getting busted."

I was only hoping the car would start. It did, I pushed the throttle, and a sound like sheet metal being torn in half ripped through the neighborhood. Junkies nodding in doorways must have thought the city had been hit by an earthquake. I smiled. Brennan smiled. We were on our way.

We pulled into the Lock, Stock &Barrel in Darien just before midnight. We had missed the Cannonball drivers' meeting and most of the party. But we arrived in time to start the race and that, we felt, was a moral victory.

Brennan unloaded in front of the Barrel to get us checked in while I pulled the Fire-Am around back to the loading bay. The band was taking a breather and a handful of partiers were lounging around. I pumped the throttle twice to clear the new car, and the roar must have broken bottles on the bar. A crowd suddenly converged on the car, the band snapped back into life, and Brennan emerged from the back door with a vodka and tonic and a grin that said, "Hey, man, we might just kick some ass."

Because of our problems, we had been given a late start—1:32 in the morning. As we fiddled with last-minute packing and planning, the crowd continued to mill around the Fire-Am. We were the center of attention, and it felt good. It cranked up our energy and made us forget, for the moment, the Fire-Am's temperamental treachery.

The go-for-broke girl in the white dress pushed her way through the crowd and gave it one more try. "Listen," she said, "I got a couple grams of fantastic speed."

"Forget it," I said. "We've got all we need."

And indeed we did. Brennan's chemical pit crew had supplied us with a combination of ingredients that would have kept an army on the move for a week: Benzedrine for driving, Quaaludes for sleeping. The drugs were artfully mixed in bottles of natural fruit juices and stashed in the cooler with other drinks. The only problem was how to tell all the stuff apart. "Don't worry," said Brennan. "Anything that looks too healthy has drugs in it."

At 1:32 Brennan punched out our time card and made a running dash for the Fire-Am. I gunned it out of the Barrel and headed for the Connecticut Turnpike.

Since the Fire-Am was as conspicuous as an anarchist at a Rotary meeting, we kept the speed down to 55. We wanted to at least get out of Connecticut before we got busted.

Other Cannonballers took the Light Brigade approach and charged into the traffic with sabers drawn.

By the time Brennan and I got into New Jersey we'd bumped the average up to 70, but we were still keeping the car under rein. Our plan was to run straight across interstate 80, going slow through New Jersey, Pennsylvania, Ohio and Indiana, and then race the Fire-Am across the plains at 130 miles per hour to Salt Lake City, hang a left on I-15, and coast through the desert to L.A..

We flew across the Garden State like it wasn't there. There was no point in us wasting time on tricks—one look at the Fire-Am and any cop would know we were up to no good. We just had to count on the car's power and put our faith in the radar detector.

Driving the Fire-Am was demanding. You had to keep your eyes moving all the time: checking the vital signs of the instrument panel, watching the mirrors for cops, looking straight ahead as fast as you could see. There was so little ground clearance, you had to drive around every pimple on the road to avoid ripping off the oil pan.

By the time we crossed the Delaware River into Pennsylvania, my eyes were aching. We pulled over, Brennan took a hit of banana-pineapple-apricot nectar. "I'm sure I put the Benzedrine in this one," he said, "because it sounds so disgusting." And we switched positions.

Brennan was intimidated by the Fire-Am, just as I had been at first. In a youth misspent on professional drag racing and adulthood spent writing about fast cars, I had never seen the Fire-Am's equal. It was an intimidating machine. Being strapped into a racing harness with a five-pound buckle on your belly and a fire extinguisher dangling in your face didn't do anything to lessen the tension.

Brennan strapped himself in, lit a cigarette and pulled out on the highway cautiously. "I'm gonna take it real easy," he said, "real slow."

The sun was just coming up as we cruised through the morning mist that hung low in the Pennsylvania valleys. Brennan was adjusting to the car, concentrating, eyes moving, gearing his mind and body to the machine. "I think I'll bump it up a little," he said. "Look at the speedometer." I told him. We were already going 110 miles per hour. "Shit," he said, easing off the gas, "I thought we were doing 65."

The Fire-Am gave that illusion. It didn't roll or sway even around the worst curve; the engine was hardly working at 100; and the faster it went, the better the car held the road.

Brennan drew up smoothly alongside a speeding 18-wheeler at 80 miles per hour and put his foot to the floor. The Fire-Am gave a low roar and shot away as though the truck were standing still.

We were moving fast and loose. Our average was inching up with every mile. Fuck the game plan of going slow through the East, we decided, we're just going to open this mother up and go for it.

I was just starting to settle back with a smile on my face when Brennan noticed that the oil gauge was jumping up and down erratically. "We're down to 50 pounds," he said, "Now it's 40. Now it's 30." A sour ball was forming in my stomach. Either the engine was about to blow, or we had a bad oil leak. "We've got a problem," I said, "a big problem."

The Fire-Am was pumping a quart of oil onto the road every 10 minutes. The faster we tried to drive, the faster the oil pressure dropped. We limped across western Pennsylvania, stopping every 50 miles. Our average speed was sinking fast. At this rate it would take us two days to reach Redondo Beach.

We pulled off I-80 into Du Bois, Pennsylvania. It was early Sunday morning, and this little town was all closed up tight. The noise from the Fire-Am alone would probably get us busted for disturbing the peace. We finally found an open gas station and paid the guy on duty 20 bucks to let us use the lift. Every kid in town showed up to take a look at the furious Fire-Am. And we had them running all over the country chasing down parts and tools. The leak was caused by the goddamned little screw on the oil pan that had come loose and broken the gasket. On most cars it would have been a snap to fix, but on the Fire-Am it meant taking off the whole racing exhaust system just to get at the problem.

With the help of a little banana-pineapple-apricot nectar, I worked for six or seven hours trying to fix the thing. When we brought the car down and cranked up the engine, oil sprayed out all over, hitting the exhaust pipes and turning into ugly blue smoke. We were carrying 32 gallons of gas, and the fuel lines ran right up next to the hot pipes. "If this thing goes up," Brennan offered, "they won't even find our dental work."

We decided to pack it in.

We found a motel and drove across town with a fire extinguisher in our laps. Trailing a hundred yards of blue smoke, we pulled into a motel parking lot and bailed out. It was all over.

That night Brennan and I consoled ourselves with a half-dozen pitchers of Genesee Ale and came up with a new plan. We wouldn't give up.

The next morning we ripped the trunk lid off the Fire-Am, swallowed the remainder of our drugs and caught a plane to Pittsburgh. From there we flew to Houston and grabbed another flight to Los Angeles. A chauffeur-driven limo picked us up at LAX, and we sped off to the time card—42 hours had elapsed since we left Darien—and I carried the trunk lid. "Where's your car?" yelled the timekeeper. "The fucking thing went up in a ball of flames," we said holding up the oil-smeared sheets of metal with the Fire-Am logo. "This is all that's left."

Despite our trunk-lid ploy, Brennan and I were listed among the DNFs—did not officially finish. The next night, Cannonball awards were handed out at an appropriately bizarre and boozy banquet, and Brennan and I got the Diehard trophy, a rusty pogo stick on a dead battery, for having suffered the most trials and tribulations. We were already plotting for the next Cannonball. The Fire-Am was too delicate a machine. But if we just tooled a 1971 Camaro with a 454 engine, threw in a 50-gallon gas tank and a good set of tools . . . maybe we could beat the record . . . next time.

Fred Gregory is a well-known motorsports journalist and is on the staff of Car and Driver *magazine.*

Boo Browning
TOLY ARUTUNOFF
1979

It is the curse of my generation that we should acquire lusty and long-standing habits that, after becoming ingrained into our daily routines, are suddenly deemed by some ominously acronymed federal or scientific group to be a menace to health, mental hygiene, the economy, and world peace. Because of this I have spent a good deal of effort over the last few years attempting to restructure my behavior to a more socially acceptable mode, trying to stay one jump ahead by guessing which in my dwindling repertoire of personal traditions will be next to fall under the hatchet of omni phobia that symbolizes the new national spirit.

This ongoing task requires great discipline and self-sacrifice, but, being a solid American, I have so far managed to cast sugar, aerosol deodorants, white bread, hair dryers, and electric can openers from my life forever. And I have cut down considerably on cholesterol, saccharine, tobacco, diet soft drinks, heat in winter, and air-conditioning in the summer. But they will have to put me away in some dark, mean cell before I get out of my car, before I stop lusting for the sound of asphalt rushing beneath my wheels.

Which, of course, they may do.

My driving passion was instilled in me by my father, who took quite seriously the responsibilities inherent in operating a vehicle. In the rural southern state where I was raised, driving was more a necessity than a luxury, and one earned one's operator license at 15. To this end, my father began giving me sober, intensive driving lessons when I reached the tender age of 12 (although I can recall steering a massive Buick from the vantage point of his lap in even earlier times.)

The seriousness and concentration with which my father imbued my lessons evoked in me a trancelike state, a kind of nirvana, which in those days he must have mistaken for preoccupation with the task at hand. Watching the scenery melt past me, I could sort out my problems and solidify my future with a serenity uncharacteristic in my pedestrian activities, and while other kids dragged Main Street and cruised the burger joints, I headed for those long stretches of highway where I would drive for hours, seeking peace with myself and the world.

My father came to understand my high-speed spiritual needs, but he could not have predicted the terrible troubles brewing in Iran even as I was earning the sobriquet of "The Datsun Kid." Neither could I, but in 1976, overwhelmed by the National Conscience, I traded my Porsche for a midsize gas-saver whose speedometer spoke only a two-digit language.

My intentions were noble, but by sacrificing my hypermania, I inadvertently lost the concentration from which it had emerged. Within two months, I stood in disbelief as a patrolman wrote out my first speeding ticket; six months later, I was rear-ended by a pickup truck in my first accident; my whiplash had barely subsided when I became the recipient of a permanent Kirk Douglas chin, the result of a spectacular encounter with a school bus, which made the local newspaper.

It took the Cannonball to bring me to my senses. Though labeled a form of protest by the ill informed, the Cannonball Sea-to-Shining-Sea Memorial Trophy Dash has nothing to do with the 55-miles-per-hour speed limit, nor any other speed limit, for that matter. It is a race from East Coast to West Coast, nonstop, and it is named for the late Prince of Autophilia, Cannon Ball Baker, who took to heart the dictum, "See the USA in your Chevrolet," and set out to do just that, setting 36 records in the process.

The idea of the Cannonball was conceived in 1971 by Brock Yates, the most decidedly arduous of Baker's modern-day disciples and at that time the editor of *Car and Driver* magazine. (You may have seen Yates covering a variety of racing events for television, always stationed in the pits where, amid the roar of engines, he delivers his commentary with a strange, upper-torso jiggling motion uncannily reminiscent of those little effigies people used to put on their dashboards.) Yates is an autophile from way back.

Four Cannonball races were run between 1971 and 1975, the participants an unlikely hodgepodge of people who met the only two requirements set down by Yates: that they be car lovers and proven competent drivers. Bringing up the rear of the 18-car field in the 1975 Cannonball was Anatoly Armisevich Arutunoff, a race driver/car dealer/mystic/racetrack entrepreneur/notary public from Tulsa who is known in racing circles as "The Mad Russian."

Even though I had heard it rumored there would be no more Cannonball races, due to the drop in stature of speeding from misdemeanor to mortal crime, I still thought a story on Aruntunoff and his participation in the 1975 rally would be intriguing. So last November, I set off in my beleaguered Nova for Tulsa.

I spent an entire day interviewing Arutunoff. As it appears the racing world does not hand out nicknames recklessly. Arutunoff comes by his eccentricity naturally, the son of an ingenious inventor who, among other odd practices, ensured the punctuality of his employees by furnishing his office with only three chairs, to be divided up for the entire day on a first-come, first-served basis.

Arutunoff is himself the semantic equivalent of Evel Knievel, leaping from topic to topic with a singular disregard for continuity. His thought processes, like mine, seem to become cogent most often when he is behind a steering wheel. So it was that, during a conversation about the benefits of mail-ordering shopping, some lapse in judgment caused Arutunoff to let slip that another Cannonball race was in the offing "—sometime in June," he added nonchalantly.

Perhaps it was the glint in my eye that tipped Arutunoff to the fact that he might have erred in making me privy to this information. "If you'd like," he muttered, "I can give you a call when we gas up in Oklahoma, and maybe you can stand around on the turnpike and get a picture or something."

But I was prepared to badger him till the wee hours of the morning, if necessary. Besides stirring up my journalistic fervor, he had awakened that old fondness for the road which I had traded two years ago for a piece of the National Conscience. In the end, Arutunoff agreed, however reluctantly, to let me come along on the next Cannonball.

I drove home that evening in record time, without even crossing a white line. Moreover, I decided on that trip that as long as there was enough fuel to bathe America's night skies in neon, there would be plenty to keep my soul at peace.

Two weeks to the day after my interview with Arutunoff, I plunked down half my life savings at a local car dealership and, with not so much as a backward glance to the old gas-saver, sped off in my new RX7GS.

The Mad Russian

I saw Arutunoff only a few times over the next few months. Part of the reason for this was his out-of-town racing schedule; part of it was my writing schedule. Also, I had decided not to make a pest of myself or give him the slightest cause to renege on his promise.

When we did meet, Arutunoff's conversation was as nonsequito as ever. In my eagerness to find out more about him, however, I devised a clever method for skirting this problem. By slicing my notes into thin strips in chronological order, I was able to reconstruct a surprisingly cogent, if brief, biography.

Arutunoff is 44 years old (or, as he would have it, 33 Martian years), the youngest of three children born to Russian immigrants. His father, Armais, invented the world's first submergible oil pump at the venerable age of 23, and this invention subsequently brought the family to Bartlesville, the home base of Phillips Petroleum, where Armais established Reda Pump, Inc.

The most traumatic moments of the young Arutunoff's childhood actually came in his first few days of life in the Tulsa hospital where he was born. Colic-ridden and weak, he was given elixir sulfomilifide, a popular drug among pediatricians of the day, and one that promptly made his condition worse.

Arutunoff's mother watched this spectacle quietly for a few days then took matters into her own hands, throwing open a window one sunny morning and threatening to jump if she and her son were not soon released. The doctors relented. Arutunoff lost his symptoms and the racing world gained another maniac.

The Arutunoff family spent winters in Bartlesville, summers in Beverly Hills, California, in a rambling house they later sold to Vincent Price. Having inherited his mother's flair for drama, Arutunoff dabbled occasionally in a halfhearted movie career, but he spent the better part of his childhood "making a vice out of being virtuous until one day I realized I wasn't doing anything."

Predictably, Arutunoff's first spoken word was "car," but it wasn't until the happy days of the Eisenhower administration that he began thinking seriously about a racing career. "My first car was a 1951 Chevy Bel Air," he says nostalgically. "I was a hot rodder in those days—I didn't think European cars were very pretty." He ran his first official lap at Stuttgart, Arkansas, in 1959, and several others after that. But his interest seemed sporadic, interrupted by school, trips to California, and periods of indecision.

Arutunoff earned bachelor degrees in math and philosophy at Tulsa University, where he also made "the longest broad jump of any nonathletic scholarship holder," for whatever that's worth. He remained at TU long enough to get his master's in English, writing his thesis on "The Cruise of the Rolling Junk," one of F. Scott Fitzgerald's more obscure short stories, whose central theme concerns a cross-country automobile trip.

With characteristic randomness, Arutunoff went on to Vanderbilt to study astronomy. He was on his way to earning a Ph.D. in that subject when his mentor, Dr. Seyfert, was killed in a car collision—"one of those five-mile-an-hour jobs." This turn of events caused him to do some serious soul-searching about his future, the upshot of which was his decision to make the quantum leap from astronomy to a full-fledged racing career.

So Arutunoff moved back to Tulsa, where he opened two car dealerships. With the help of his partner, Joe Marina, he was able to quickly establish himself as a respected racer, despite his penchant for zany, outdated vehicles.

The two spent years looking for land suitable for building a race track, and decided on a site near the town of Hallett, where the project was completed in 1976. Hallett Raceway is reputed to be one of the most impressive, difficult, and well-appointed motor raceways in the Southwest, and it is managed by Marina's wife, Marty.

"It was just my way of putting something back into the sport," explains Arutunoff. His further plans include surrounding the track with flowers and sculptures, an unprecedented (and here to fore unheard of) idea in racing sports.

Arutunoff's preference for racing runs to endurance rallies. "It feels so good when you stop," he explained. His typical season, however, consists of a variety of events. He attends such prestige races as Sebring, the 24 Hours at Daytona, the Road Race of Champions, and the Carrera Del Alamo; he also participates in races with names like Jim Bowie, Polar Prix, Jubilation T. Cornpone, and Cannonball.

When he is not racing, Arutunoff can be found in his cluttered office at Automobiles International, munching vitamins and leafing through his hundreds of mail-order catalogs, or perhaps puffing furiously on a disgustingly scatological corona while he dashes off scathing letters to the local newspapers, decrying the national speed limit. Sometimes he can be spied with Joe and Marty Marina, rehashing his most recent race over dinner in a Tulsa eatery.

In fact, that's where I found him on March 25, one day after I had received a call from him informing me that the Cannonball was only a week away. In my diligence to avoid pressing my luck, I had overlooked the possibility that Arutunoff might be intentionally vague about the date of the race. His call left me in a state of shock.

Fresh from his recent foray at Sebring, where he had crashed due to the loss of two tires, he had sounded cheerful but hurried over the phone.

"Hi, Boo, Toly here. Just wanted to let you know that the meeting's at noon on March 31st. You need to be in Darien, Connecticut, at a place called the Lock Stock & Barrel." (All this said in one breath.)

"Oh, Toly. Hello. Now what's this? A meeting place? You mean . . . "

"That's right. The Cannonball. You did want to go start to finish, didn't you? I mean we could pick you up in Oklahoma if you prefer that."

"No. Oh no. You mean, this is it?"

"That's right."

"Oh, I thought it was in June. How come I thought it was in June, Toly?"

"I have no idea, dear. See you Saturday in Darien. Ta-ta."

I wanted to be outraged about this, but my excitement got in the way. So I left my work-in-progress scattered about my office, babbled incoherently at my editor on the way out the door and left for Tulsa to track down Arutunoff for more details. By the time I pinned him down at an Italian Restaurant, I was pretty well over my shock, but I couldn't resist an opening jab.

"How was Sebring?" I beamed at him.

"It's in Florida. Very nice weather," he countered without missing a beat.

And so it went, a little rough around the edges at first, due to our mutual suspicions—mine, that he might try to skip Darien without me, and his, that I might turn out to be a general pain in the neck. Joe Marina seemed to sense all the weirdness in the air, and made some lighthearted stabs at conversation. It was all presided over by the ever-serene Marty, whose fate it is to endure this kind of thing on a daily basis, and her presence had a mellowing effect on us all.

By the time we finished our linguini, we were all laughing and chattering like old cronies, and we topped off the evening by filing over to Arutunoff's toy-store of a house for some really awful champagne. I say toy-store because it is literally packed with all manner of mail-order mishmash: gadgets, books, trinkets of every kind; it turns out that Arutunoff's office at AI is only the tip of the iceberg.

Toward the end of my third glass of champagne, I spotted an interesting T-shirt on a rag doll in the corner of the room. Before I could even read it, Arutunoff had thrust it upon me. "Take it. Keep it," he insisted. "You might want to wear it on the Cannonball." Touched by his generosity, I finished the last of the terrible champagne, thanked him and promised to see him in Darien a week later. The next morning, I looked at the T-shirt again, and this is what it said: "Fear crowded me in the cockpit. I could almost feel the jagged metal tearing into me, imagine the flaming petrol searing my cringing flesh."

Such is the wit of the Mad Russian.

The Lock Stock and Barrel

I arrived at the Lock Stock and Barrel at 10 minutes before noon on Saturday, March 31. Located at one end of a shopping center in suburban Darien, it is a restaurant belonging to George Lysle, decorated in a strange olio of relics from the vigorous, but otherwise unrelated sports of racing, hunting, cow punching, and drinking. Photographs of stock cars are hung about the dining rooms, and on a wall near the bar rests a heart-stopping blowup of Mario Andretti in his younger days, taken moments after a victory at the track.

I was early, of course. The restaurant was closed to the non-Cannonball public for the day, and although Arutunoff had instructed me to be there no later than noon, only Lysle, Brock Yates, and his entourage were present. I sat down at their table under a banner, which read, "Have you hugged your car today?"

Yates was in the middle of a discussion of starting times with his wife, Pamela, race coordinator Rae Cameron, and Hal Needham, who was the stunt driver for *Smokey and the Bandit, Gator,* and a host of other crash-and-burn movies. My suspicions that he might be part of Yates' own Cannonball team were later confirmed.

"Each Cannonball participant will be given a badge identifying him as such," Yates was explaining, "and as each car leaves, the teams will have to surrender the badges in order to be counted as valid participants. Now, there are some press people coming in from New York, and they'll be given the badges with the red dots. There'll be someone from CBS, UPI, *Newsweek* and *Look,* that I know of."

"That's right," broke in Lysle. "Those with press badges will be given unlimited access to the restaurant throughout the day, drinks on the house. But the drivers will have to buy their own drinks. We don't want the public thinking a bunch of drunks are driving the Cannonball. We're here to make friends, not enemies." Nods all around.

Pamela reported that she had checked the New York papers, and that they were clean, meaning nothing had been reported that would tip off the highway patrol just yet, although we knew that Connecticut troopers were already waiting on the interstate just 2 miles away.

Presently, the place began to fill up with eager Cannonballers, and the air became charged with excitement and a kind of restlessness. Each time an entrant pulled into the parking lot, large groups of us were pulled as in a current to the window to see what new, outrageous vehicle was joining the field. This went on for some time, and still Arutunoff had not arrived.

One burly fellow plopped down next to me, put his feet on the table and commenced to psychologically harass another entrant sitting across from us. He looked dog tired, as if he had just finished a cross-country race, and I didn't see him move from that spot the entire time I was in Darien.

The guy across from us proved to be easy prey. "I broke down and bought a Trans Am for this one," he said with a glow of pride, but Slouch just snorted derisively.

"Hope you've got an extra transmission, then," was his reply. "Taking plenty of food along?"

"Yeah, I'm having some sandwiches made up this afternoon."

"Sandwiches, huh?" Slouch made a serious face. "Don't you know that about Kansas, you're gonna want some sugar? You're gonna crave sweets so bad you'll hafta stop at a Stuckey's just to get some."

Our friend shifted defensively in his chair. "Not me. I don't eat that junk. I'm not taking nothing but nutritious food, like roast beef, peanut butter, stuff like that."

"Well, now," said Slouch, moving in for the kill, "you know if you eat, you're gonna have to stop more often. Me, I'll just go straight through. I don't need to eat and I don't need to sleep. They don't call me Superman for nothing. But tell you what: I'll have a Snickers waiting for you at Redondo."

And so on. All over the restaurant I could hear this kind of ego-jousting, mixed in with a little scheming and last-minute planning.

Yates' two lawyers arrived with a stack of release forms to be signed by all the participants and the drone of conversations stopped for a minute. They looked somewhat out of place in their vested suits, smiling nervously and exuding an air of mild disapproval. I saw one of them wince when a driver yelled out, "Hey, it's the Corleone brothers."

Arutunoff finally arrived, just in time for Yates' speech. He had driven our car to New York via Nashville, where he had picked up Bill Pryor, his codriver.

Pryor had also joined Arutunoff in the 1975 Cannonball race. He owns an advertising agency in Nashville, and he has gained some notoriety in those parts by being a general mischief-maker. (Pryor's most recent coup came last November, when he sent Tennessee's well-to-do engraved invitations to a bridal shower, to be held at the governor's mansion. Then-Governor Blanton was not amused.) Short and semi-bald, with incredibly thick spectacles that make his eyes seem to bulge out, he was dressed this day in blue jeans and a green and yellow striped T-shirt. He looked for all the world like a cross between Woody Allen and a killer bee, and I took an instant liking to him.

Arutunoff was in fine spirits himself. The three of us trooped out to the rear of the restaurant, which is taken up by Bianco & Gilman's Bicycle Garage. There most of the Cannonball participants had gathered around a panel truck, on top of which stood Brock Yates, armed with instructions and the lineup. To my dismay, Yates delivered his speech without so much as a hint of a jiggle.

Our own vehicle, a 1979 Volvo 242GT, was a last-minute replacement for Arutunoff's first preference, his father's 1967 Cadillac limousine, which he had decided was too clunky and uncomfortable. Arutunoff figured right off we could beat both the Silver Wraith and a 1971 Fiat 127.

Each team was given a priority number, by which it could choose any starting time not already taken between the hours of 7 P.M. and 2 A.M. We were sixth in line and Arutunoff and Pryor agreed to pick the earliest possible start time.

Yates refused to disclose any information about the vehicle his team was taking, which turned out to be an ambulance with "TransCon Medi-Vac" emblazoned on its sides. Instead, he turned the discussion to the topic of good behavior, warning us that the California Highway Patrol was already lying in wait for us, according to an anonymous phone call he had recently received.

"I also want to warn you that interstate 80 is very, very bumpy, and that all you guys going through Harrisburg had better wear a lead-lined jock. (This was the first of many references to the Three Mile Island disaster.) Remember, if there is anything we're trying to prove here, it's that the American interstate system can be driven at high speeds without threat to anybody's safety, and it's theoretically possible to do it without breaking the law." This brought guffaws and applause from the crowd.

We returned to the restaurant to sign our release forms and choose our starting time, which was 7:08. After passing inspection by the Corleone brothers, we went out to the parking lot to pack up the Volvo.

It was a warm spring day, and the parking lot was heavily trafficked by cruising natives of Darien, some aware of what was going on and others only curious about all the vehicles.

"What's going on in there, anyway?" one man asked Pryor suspiciously.

"Oh, it's some kind of sporting event," he replied.

"Sporting event, huh? I bet," snorted the Darienite, but he was grinning broadly.

We had plenty of time to kill, and Pryor and I, having gone all day without food, were having visions of steak and seafood and even Big Macs. But Arutunoff had got hung up at the car, searching for vitamins and screwing an Andorra license tag onto the Volvo.

"Isn't he wonderful?" muttered Pryor in his syrupy Tennessee drawl, jerking his head toward Arutunoff. "He's just like some old lady. Can't keep his mind on anything for more than a minute."

I allowed that I had noticed this tendency in our leader, and Pryor and I decided to fight our way into the buffet line back at the Lock Stock & Barrel.

Two lady friends of Arutunoff and Pryor came to see us off, both Vanderbilt alumnae now living in New York. Susan, a financial analyst for CBS who hated her work, handed Arutunoff a mysterious box, which he put in the trunk, despite Pryor's pleas to check out its contents. Gail was a staffer for *Vogue* magazine, a career with which she seemed wholly unimpressed. "It's not real journalism," she confided.

It had been no small trick for our well-wishers to slip past the guards without an identification badge. Each driver had paid an entry fee of $750, and almost everyone was carrying large sums of cash in small bills to pay speeding tickets, toll fees and other miscellaneous cost. "If someone got wind of all the cash in here and decided to stick us up," Lysle had mused, "he'd walk out of this place a millionaire."

We all went outside for a picture-taking session and gathered around Arutunoff, who was sitting in the Volvo, studying his atlas and checking his radar detector. He pulled out our uniforms—long-sleeved T-shirts with fronts made to look like tuxedos—and instructed us to put them on. This I gladly did, for rain clouds had boiled up above the Darien skies, making the evening breeze chilly.

Our appointed starting time drew near. The first car would leave at 7 P.M., and the Volvo, third in the lineup, was due to leave eight minutes later. Arutunoff was cool and unhurried, but Pryor and I looked at each other with unabashed excitement as the realization came over us that we were not just here to party the night away at the Lock Stock and Barrel.

A huge crowd had gathered around the garage, perhaps as many as 2,500 curiosity seekers. It seemed everybody in Darien, at least, was aware of this subterranean affair. A light rain began to fall.

The first car pulled out of the garage, to thunderous cheers, and I went to take my place in the Volvo's back seat, next to the huge box of food Pryor had prepared. Seven minutes to go.

Arutunoff and Pryor went to turn in our three badges. They had left the motor running, which caused me to be even more restless as the minutes dragged on. Presently, Rae Cameron came to lean through the window and check the odometer, which she would do again when we reached our destination at the Portofino Inn in Redondo Beach, "Sixty-four seventy," she recited, then, "Good luck. See you at the Portofino."

The second car, the ridiculous Silver Wraith with its host of chauffeurs and its store of provisions from elegant Fortnum and Mason, made a regal exit, and I began to sweat. Where was Arutunoff? Where was Pryor? Would we not even make our starting time?

Just when the suspense became unbearable and I was poised to leap out into the rainy blackness to find them, they came jaunting up to the car. We waited for the signal for what seemed like yet another eon, and finally our time came. We drove ever so demurely out of sight of the Darien peace officers and I watched the excited faces of the crowd recede.

Three blocks away, we made a wrong turn and Arutunoff become momentarily distraught. But he quickly righted his mistake, and by the time we reached the first tollbooth, we had already passed the Rolls.

I settled back for what I knew would be the most exciting hours I had ever spent. The night, as Kerouac might have said, was on.

I was right, of course, about those high-speed hours being some of the most thrilling I have spent. They were also splashed with intervals of worry, boredom, conversations deep and shallow, inspirational highs and lows of extreme fatigue, all soaked through with humor. If it seems on paper as though I represent our little Volvo as some sort of microcosm, some tiny compendium of life itself streaking across America, that's only because it was.

Now, a lot of people who know about the Cannonball think it's a crazy idea, and that the people who take part in it are also crazy. This sentiment stems in part from a rash of B movies that capitalized on the gist of the whole thing, that being a coast-to-coast, high-speed, unsponsored, and basically illegal race, movies such as *Cannonball*, *The Gumball Rally*, *Two-Lane Black-top*, *Vanishing Point*, and the utterly tasteless *Death Race 2000*. They are all that most people have in the way of reference to the real thing.

I don't mind the participants, including myself, being labeled as crazy, for in truth, we were probably some of the most eccentric people ever gathered in one place. But I wonder about the validity of the term as applied to the race itself.

For instance, here is what was going on in the rest of the world as we pelted out of Darien that rainy night:

On the home front, the entire supply of drinking water in Tuttle, Oklahoma, had been mysteriously polluted; a giant bubble had formed in the Three Mile Island nuclear core that threatened to obliterate a large portion of Pennsylvania; the airports of America were teeming with stranded travelers, the result of an airline strike, and the Teamsters were also striking selectively. As for the world at large, 18 nations had agreed to impose an economic boycott against Israel, and the Tanzanians were being viciously driven back by angry Libyans, among other frightening developments.

What I am trying to say is that "crazy" is a relative term. To anyone who was not living in Tuttle or Harrisburg, or who wasn't trying to get himself or his products somewhere else that day, the Cannonball might have seemed irresponsible, wildly dangerous, Flip City. But I don't think it would have been given a second thought by, say, the Tanzanians.

The other distressing accusations most frequently hurled at the Cannonball is that it is un-American, which I am compelled to categorically refute. What could be more American than making a mad dash westward from the Atlantic, which is what Americans seem to have been doing since the first pilgrim landed at Plymouth Rock? The very principle of the Cannonball is fraught with historical and symbolic significance.

As for the "waste of fuel" argument, allow me to point out that the 47 Cannonball vehicles did not consume enough fuel to even approach the cost in energy of flying one team to one city to play an all-American game of football.

And so the little Volvo and its relatively sane American occupants hurtled across the fog-shrouded Poconos and down through Harrisburg, where we blended in with hundreds of other cars whose drivers seemed to have little regard for the speed limit as they made their exit from the beleaguered town. We saw the sun rise behind us in rainy, green Ohio, saw it set in a brilliant performance among billowy clouds (angel droppings, Arutunoff called them) on the flat panhandle roads of Oklahoma, and watched it climb up again alongside us as we made our way through the Rockies.

A complete account of our trip would be tiresome to write, and perhaps also to read. What follows, therefore, are highlights of what transpired between the Mad Russian, the killer bee, and yours truly as we made our way to the Portofino Inn.

We took turns sleeping in the back and making sandwiches from Pryor's huge box of goodies, although Arutunoff ate little food and had almost no sleep the entire time. Our stops for fuel were something like real racing pit stops, except performed by the closest thing to the Keystone Kops.

Breakneck speed for the Volvo proved to be only 110 miles per hour, and that was on a good downhill slope. Pryor and I whined that Arutunoff was too conservative and, sensing a conspiracy in the air, he slept with one eye open whenever Pryor took the wheel.

Each time we were passed by a car we recognized as a Cannonball vehicle, we were inspired to new heights, and whoever was driving would press the pedal to the floor with renewed enthusiasm. Often we would talk to these competitors on our CB, and they would make good-natured promises to have our drinks waiting at the Portofino, or tell us some tidbit about the fate of other Cannonballers they had heard along the way.

Somewhere in Kansas, we were latched onto a couple in a black Trans Am bearing Texas plates. After following us for some time, they pulled into the same gas station where we were making one of our pit stops and tried to pump Arutunoff for information about where we were headed.

Arutunoff was polite but reserved, thinking that by refusing to divulge our destination, they would go away. But they followed us all the way through Kansas and into the Oklahoma flatlands, where we breathed a sigh of relief upon seeing them pull into a Hooker, Oklahoma, chicken stand. Pryor and I were so astounded when we saw them gaining on us in New Mexico that we both shouted, "It's them!" waking Arutunoff.

"Who?" yelled Arutunoff, thinking surely it was the local arm of the law.

"The Trans Am," we told him.

"Oh, be still, my beating heart," he moaned. "It's going to be hard to explain this when they show up right behind us at the Portofino." But we lost our fast-moving friends somewhere around Albuquerque.

It was in Albuquerque that I became disenchanted with Pryor's lovingly prepared box of provisions. For one thing, it was bad enough sharing the back seat with it, and for another, Arutunoff had taunted us all across Kansas, Oklahoma, and Texas with his incessant talk of chili dogs. "Oh, the softness of the buns," he would say, "the tenderness of the beans." And so on until Pryor and I were fairly wild-eyed with junk-food withdrawal.

What I needed was not sugar, as Slouch had predicted, but a healing dose of BHT, some tri-Butyl toluene and maybe even some sodium caseinate. My body was crying out for chemicals, and I spotted some in an Albuquerque gas station. It was a veritable gold mine in carcinogens, one of those push-button machines with 25 selections, all loaded with artificial flavor and/or colors.

A quick glance through the station glass told me I had enough time to throw in some quarters, but not enough to make a conscious selection, since Arutunoff and Pryor were still hopping madly about the pump. I did that and headed back to the car bearing an armload of preservatives.

Arutunoff had to inspect my cache, of course, and I must admit there was room for disappointment.

"My 11 unfavorites," he sneered, but opened a bag of Cheezits anyway. That left me with the imitation barbecue corn nuts and the fried pork rinds, which, in my struggle to open them, flew all over the car, eliciting a string of blasphemy from Arutunoff. Nevertheless, we managed to scarf it all down in less than 20 minutes.

"When we get to the Portofino Inn," Arutunoff mused between bites, "I'm going to ask them what kind of bread they have that's waterproof, then I'm going to stand in the shower eating it as long as I like." This remark set us to thinking about how dirty we were.

We were only stopped once, in Arizona. Apparently we had blown the doors off one trucker too many, and he had reported us, but we were coasting into another pit stop, and all he could do was stall us a little for time.

We pulled into the Portofino at 8:40 A.M., April 2, to Pryor's gleeful shouts of: "There's the shining sea!" We had made the finish line in 40 hours and 33 minutes, hardly a record, but more respectable than several of the other fast movers. (The Volvo finished 24th.)

We got out proudly amid cheers, indifferent to the fact that our hair (Pryor's and mine, anyway) was greasy, our clothes rumpled, and the road grime an inch thick on our skin. I noticed that Slouch was sprawled on the hotel steps, just as if someone had picked him up at the Lock Stock & Barrel and dropped him down here, ever so gently so as not to disturb his repose. The only difference in his appearance was a two-day growth of beard.

The stories went on and on, into the night and the next day, even into the next week. The participants celebrated, recovered, and celebrated some more, and at the end of the week filed out to see the Long Beach Grand Prix. The last Cannonballer finally straggled out of the Portofino two weeks after the race was run, carrying a lightweight overnight bag and enough memories to last a lifetime. "Nobody wanted to leave," Rae Cameron told me later. "Nobody wanted to admit that it was finally over."

But then, the Cannonball is never really over, the same way that it is never really lost. Just last week, I flipped on the tube in a fit of boredom and what I saw was George Willig, shivering and grunting his way up craggy Devil's Tower.

"Some people would call this kind of activity crazy," the commentator was saying, and I had to laugh out loud. I knew old George must have been feeling pretty damn serene.

Boo Browning's charming recollection was originally published in Oklahoma Monthly, *which is no longer in business.*

Cannonball-John McGovern
1979

The 1979 Cannonball would prove to be a very different event from all previous runs, with a much larger entry list, a greater variety of vehicles, and huge organizational problems. It would prove to be the last Sea-to-Shining-Sea competition.

After the 1975 event Brock had asked me if I could put together a British entry for the next Cannonball, and four years later when the 1979 run was announced I began to investigate this possibility. One morning in early April I was driving into London with the car radio tuned to a BBC chat program. One of the people interviewed was Fiona Kendall, a friend's girlfriend. Fiona was now Fiona Kendall-Lane—She had married a man who ran a chauffeur/limo service. At her suggestion he had made this a very selective service, with champagne and flowers in their Rolls-Royce cars.

On an impulse I called and told Fiona and her husband Stephen about the last Cannonball. They bought the idea of entering a Rolls-Royce and we set about organizing a team.

The Kendall-Lanes put a 1948 Rolls Silver Wraith into the capable hands of John Homes, who prepared it for the trip across the States. Our main concern was the Lucas electrical system.

Eddie Harmston, the Kendall-Lanes personal chauffeur, my wife Molly, and I flew over and met up with the K-Ls, who had come by Concorde. The old RR entry received massive media coverage, which was the main and only reason for the K-L's interest.

Luckily for the team, John Homes had anticipated massive electrical hitches and visited a parts shop and had stocked up on AC Delco pieces. Within 600 miles of the start we had used all the spare Lucas parts, but AC Delco saw us through to L.A. without any further trouble. The 3,000 miles were covered at a speed of 63 miles per hour and we finished in the penultimate position: second to last.

Stephen's behavior quickly became boring and, with Toly Aruntunoff, Molly and I left the Portofino Inn and drove back east. Two weeks later, in London, I wasn't really surprised by Stephen reneging on his contract with me. Within a few months his business collapsed, and Fiona was gone. It was some months later, with no great surprise, I saw his name listed in as a "front man" in a TV show dealing with the paranormal, aliens, UFO sightings, and haunted houses. Stephen presented the 30-minute show seated at a piano positioned in the knee-deep surf off the beach in Brighton! It lasted for two or three weeks, then was canned. Stephen vanished. Fiona resumed her acting career, but like the rest of us, remembers the unique last running of the Cannonball Sea-to-Shining-Sea Memorial Trophy Dash. I feel privileged to have been involved in the last two runs of this crazy event!

John McGovern, a well-known English motorsports photographer, competed in two Cannonballs, 1975 and 1979.

David Brownell
1979

On Saturday evening, March 31, 1979, the *Hemmings Motor News* 1936 Ford panel truck left Darien, Connecticut, on what was hoped to be a nonstop marathon to Redondo Beach, California, as one of the 46 entrants in the fifth running of the Cannonball Baker Sea-to-Shining-Sea Memorial Trophy Dash. The Dash served, in Yates' own words, no morally defensible purpose whatsoever. It was intended to prove that fast, well-handling automobiles in the hands of competent drivers can roar across the nation at speeds considerably above the double nickel without bringing harm to drivers, passengers, innocent bystanders, or wandering hitchhikers.

At the 11th hour the Ford had been outfitted with a 28-gallon auxiliary fuel cell, storage room for about 200 pounds of spare parts, a bunk, nets for stowing gear, and various other devices for comfort or survival. We carried a CB radio, which was used for all of 10 minutes during the journey. We did not carry a radar detector or any other Smokey-seeking device. The Ford had had a fresh 1947 59AB flathead installed, its transmission rebuilt, front end overhauled, new tires mounted, wiring replaced, brakes converted to hydraulics, and seat belts bolted in place. There were about 300 miles on the engine when it began the Dash.

Three loons deluded themselves into thinking they could go up against the likes of Ferraris, Porsches, Jaguars, and Jensens: myself, Terry Ehrich, publisher of *Hemmings Motor News* and *Special Interest Autos*, and Justus Taylor, freelance TV cameraman and former factory rider for BMW motorcycles in U.S. competition.

Brock Yates was concerned. As he stood up on top of a trash dumpster on an unseasonably warm March afternoon in Connecticut addressing the Cannonball drivers and crew, he was aware that there had been more leaks about the event than you'd find in a porous inner tube. The Cannonball could, said Yates, turn into "the automotive version of the Bay of Pigs." But the entrants were undeterred and eager for the P.M. starting hour. We were scheduled to leave at 8:12.

Rain had begun early in the evening, and the scene behind the Lock, Stock & Barrel restaurant in Darien took on a surrealistic quality. The darkness was punctured by the beams of brilliant quartz headlamps and the roar of departing cars, along with the shadows of about 500 spectators and well-wishers who had found out about the event. Our Ford rolled up to the start line at 8:05, Taylor at the wheel, Ehrich riding shotgun, and Brownell stretched out on the bunk. In our eagerness to get on with it we left one minute early.

The Ford is hardly a low-slung vehicle to begin with. When you fill it with three people, boxes of spare parts, tools, tires, a big auxiliary fuel tank, and sundry other gear, its center of gravity hovers somewhere near the top of the window frames. The weight bias was decidedly toward the rear. These factors and the slick roads combined to give the truck a Wimpy-like gait as it bustled down the pike, swaying gently to and fro and occasionally going into a quick sideslip just to keep us alert.

With 42 miles behind us, the headlights blew, which meant that the taillights were out too, and the only thing preventing a rampaging semi from rolling right over us was a pair of tidy little red reflectors. We switched to our two driving lights and thundered along into Pennsylvania.

"No brakes! No brakes! We've lost the fucking brakes!" This revelation awakened me quickly, and through the windshield a perilous scene loomed before us. We were descending a long hill near Scranton at about 65 miles per hour. A few hundred yards ahead an Oldsmobile was sprawled across two lanes. A trailer truck was stopped in the breakdown lane and some benighted dim bulb had parked his car in the passing lane. People were wandering aimlessly around the cars and we were about to involuntarily join this mess. There was only one escape—the wet median—and Taylor took it, heroically wrestling the swaying, slipping Ford around the obstructions.

Using the handbrake, we left I-80 at the next exit and found an open gas station where we broke out tools and began work on the brakes and lights.

The right rear brake line had been punctured by a seat belt mounting bolt. Fortunately, we had brought along some extra fuel line and fittings, which converted nicely into a new brake line. Brakes bled, left headlight and taillights working, we hopped back on I-80 at 12:04 A.M., April Fool's Day.

Two minutes later we stopped for repairs again. The ammeter was showing a steady discharge. We changed generators and were back on the road in 40 minutes.

At 2:45 A.M. we replaced a loose and frayed fan belt. At 3:24 A.M. we replaced that fan belt after discovering that we had looped it around the wrong bottom pulley. A seam in the upper radiator tank had sprung a leak. Our only can of stop-leak was used to try and plug it.

We had just passed through Akron, Ohio, on a Sunday morning averaging exactly 60 miles per hour for the past three hours. In the rear-view mirror I spotted an old car gaining on us. It was another Cannonball entry: a 1948 Rolls-Royce Silver Wraith from England, chauffeur driven, filled with elegantly dressed passengers, and followed by a tender car carrying luggage and spares. Will we beat them to California? More to the point, will either of us make it to California?

Electrical problems raised their ugly heads again outside Akron. We cleaned the generator commutator, replaced the voltage regulator, and tightened the fan belts. This helped bring voltage up from zero to five volts. Near Columbus we replaced the fan belt again. The one we had been using was a cheap piece of rubbish from South Africa that proved to have all the quality and durability of a rubber band. Thirty-eight miles into Indiana we went through the fan belt routine again.

We'd been running in rain most of the day and the *Red Eye Express'* windshield and vent had been leaking copiously. We'd been dealing with this by plastering gaffer tape around the areas and it seemed to do a decent job, but we had to remove it before it damaged the paint.

At 6:50 P.M. EST on Sunday, we crossed the Mississippi and entered St. Louis, where we missed a turn and took a devious route to I-40. Taylor was driving as if the demons of hell were after him, the Ford was responding well to the treatment, and there was a shared feeling that we just might make it.

The 24-hour mark was passed somewhere in central Missouri. Despite all the breakdowns, we'd logged an average speed of 45.79 miles per hour for the first day. This did not put us in contention for breaking the Cannonball record.

Rain and fog plagued us through Missouri. We passed by Joplin at midnight and entered Oklahoma at 12:18 EST. A few minutes later the right hand wiper blade arm flew off with a bang, but the rain had just about stopped so we rolled along without it.

There was another truck entered in this mad debacle, and we passed it at a truck stop in Oklahoma. It was a one-off British Ford with a turbocharged Capri engine, chrome stacks, dual rear wheels, and looked all the world like a half-scale Kenworth. Developed by the British magazine *Truck* and Ford of England, it probably attracted an inordinate share of attention from drivers of the big rigs.

A few minutes later, we passed an Oklahoma Highway Patrol car. Taylor came tearing up behind him at 70 miles per hour, but had slowed to 55 by the time we passed him. No harm done as he did a flip-flop and headed east. Our headlights picked up an ominous sign that warned "Do Not Drive Into Smoke." No satisfactory explanation of this cryptic hazard was ever revealed.

It had stopped raining, but the wind was whipping itself up, pushing the *Red Eye Express* around like a toy sailboat while the drivers made constant steering corrections. It also raised hell with our average speed, as we passed the theoretical halfway point of the Dash at 2:44 A.M. EST. We'd been on the road for 30 hours and 33 minutes, had driven 1,450 miles, and our average speed to this point was 47.40 miles per hour.

Daybreak, Monday April 2. We crossed into Texas in clear and chilly weather, roaring along with no apparent problems at about 65 miles per hour. A few moments later we passed a salvage yard peppered with a good number of special interest cars on the south side of I-40 in Shamrock, Texas. 8:11 A.M. marked 36 hours on the road. We'd covered 1,742 miles at an average speed of 53.89 miles per hour. For the past 12 hours we'd averaged 62 miles per hour. Stretches of I-40 are in quite poor repair and it's the first interstate I've ever been on that goes through a town where you have to deal with a stoplight and bounce along a cobblestone main street.

Just as we were feeling smug about the Ford's sterling performance, disaster struck at Groom, Texas. We lost the ignition system right in front of Hap's Texaco. Hap was in the station, which hadn't yet opened, and he was wise enough not to get involved in our machinations. Just as we were about to set to work, another Cannonball entrant roared by: perhaps the bravest, craziest entry in the field distinguished by some very strange vehicles including a bogus ambulance, the afore-mentioned Rolls, the British Ford truck, and an Excalibur. But these two guys, Truesdale and Patchett, were crossing the country nonstop on a BMW motorcycle!

The ignition problem delayed us for two hours in Groom. Thanks to Taylor's testing equipment and general wizardry around electronics we isolated the problems quickly, but changing distributor and coil on a flathead Ford is no fun even under the best of circumstances. On top of that, the generator's rear bearing was making protests, so that was changed.

Outside Amarillo, Texas, was the strangest sight we encountered during the Dash. There, sticking out of the plains, were the rear sections of 10 Cadillacs from 1949 to 1959. Standing like a weird, modern Stone-henge, this Cadillac ranch was conceived by a San Francisco design collective called Ant Farm for Stanley Marsh, a wealthy Amarillo resident who seems to have had it constructed just for the fun of it.

The repairs at Groom invested the Ford with new life as it averaged 66 miles per hour over a measured mile outside Amarillo. A few miles farther down I-40 in Adrian, Texas, we spotted a fascinating looking salvage yard brimming with special interest cars, and at 11:53 A.M. EST, we crossed the Texas panhandle and entered New Mexico.

Thirty-five minutes later trouble struck. Just outside Tucumcari, New Mexico, we stopped to let some construction trucks cross the road. And we stalled and didn't start again. The points had gone out of adjustment and we lost 23 minutes divining the fact and correcting the problem. All the natives were friendly and helpful except for the flag person. She watched our performance in stone-faced silence and, as we restarted and rolled past her, she gave us the kind of look you might apply to some hopelessly retarded gang of inmates out for a day's excursion in the country.

New Mexico was bristling with highway patrol, confirming rumors that it's one tough state on speeders. As the *Red Eye Express* climbed to higher elevations, our problem wasn't speed but the lack of it. We removed the air cleaner for a better mixture and this helped a bit. But we had hell's own time switching over from our auxiliary fuel supply to the regular tank near Cline's Corners, New Mexico. While grappling with this, we saw a '55 Dodge Royal Lancer hardtop heading east and a '53 Dodge Coronet two-door sedan going west. Old *Red Eye* finally started and Taylor blamed the problem on a weak spark.

After some quick calculations, our estimated time of arrival at Redondo Beach was reckoned at 7 A.M. PT on Tuesday. This boldly assumed no further major repairs and a running average of 50 miles per hour for the remaining 900 miles separating us from the ocean.

Climbing higher and higher, there were signs warning of dangerous crosswinds and, to emphasize the point, some even had windsocks! Great. Here we are in a vehicle that starts doing disco steps when kissed by the gentlest zephyr and has all the aerodynamics of a billboard. The signs didn't exaggerate. Outside Albuquerque we got racked by a vicious crosswind that sent the truck skittering across two lanes of the highway, nearly out of control. From there on until Arizona it was flat-out traveling. When we weren't being buffeted by crosswinds, we had to deal with headwinds, which held *Red Eye* to a top speed of 50, even at full throttle. Constant sawing of the steering wheel took a physical toll on the driver, and this leg of the Dash has to earn the honors as the most arduous and frustrating.

Crossing into Arizona at 7:30 EST Monday evening, 47 hours and 18 minutes from Darien, we had gone 2,228 miles at an average speed of 47.1 miles per hour. The winds and further breakdowns had taken their toll.

As if the crosswinds, headwinds, rain, and fog weren't enough, we now had snow to contend with. Not a howling blizzard, but enough to start coating the road. The combination of slick roads and the instability of the *Red Eye's* road deportment gave us pause. If things got nasty, would we be forced to stop out of sense of basic self-preservation?

We finally ran out of the storm, but a new concern emerged.

The rear bearing on the generator was making noises and smelling a bit funny. At Holbrook, Arizona, we traded a copy of "Hemmings" for a vial of 90W oil to lube the bearing. Maybe, just maybe, an hourly application of oil would make the bearing last another 650 miles.

Descending into California, the crosswinds visited us again. The Ford went into its usual demented meanderings and Ehrich wrestled constantly with the wheel. One particularly wild gust blew a pickup truck into a ditch, but he was being attended to by several other motorists, so we decided to press on.

We entered California at 4:03 A.M. EST. Our confidence grew by the minute. Over the black expanse of desert to Barstow, more crosswinds deviled us, but the wind was mostly at our back now, and we were hustling along smartly.

The sun was just rising over the San Bernardino mountains when we lubed the generator for the last time, switched our gas to the main tank, and plunged into the hurly-burly of Los Angeles freeway traffic. Even at 5:30 A.M. PT, traffic was already raging along in a 60-miles-per-hour, bumper-to-bumper pack. One false turn was soon corrected and at 10:02 EST or 7:02 Pacific Time on April 3, The *Red Eye Express*, the oldest machine ever to enter the Cannonball, now held a second distinction.

It became the oldest machine ever to complete the Cannonball Baker Sea-to-Shining-Sea Memorial Trophy Dash.

David Brownell is a prominent figure in the world of vintage and exotic collector cars. Sadly, his co-driver, Terry Ehrich, passed away early in 2002.

Jim Mullen
THE CANNONBALL

Nighttime in Oklahoma was made for high-speed motoring: cool horsepower-producing temperatures; glassy smooth highways; few urban communities, none of which metamorphosed into speed-traps inviting tourists to fund local high school athletics; and, best of all, almost no law enforcement patrols to delay one's rapid progress west. Well, almost none.

A rack of quietly threatening gumballs atop the Chevy just ahead of us ensured that our stealth racer maintained its serene 75-mile-per-hour pace across this wide-open part of our (then) double nickel country. Admittedly 75 is not unreasonable by any lawful citizen's standard, but glacial compared to the 85-to-120 speeds we had been clocking since leaving Connecticut a day earlier. We eased toward Texas, hour after torturous hour. The patrol car's occupants experiencing the satisfaction of unchallenged control while we experienced the penetrating frustration of watching a good finish vanish into the ether.

"We need a pigeon," said Joan, my right seat coconspirator, hoping for a sacrificial speeder to provoke Oklahoma's diligent officers into carrying out the protective duties for which their constituents hired them. As if by enchantment, a pinpoint of light appeared in my rearview mirror. Slowly at first, then with increasing energy, the twin beams filled our back window, seemingly pulled forward by our urgent impatience, ignorant of the sworn duties of our pilot fish.

"Damn, they're slowing, too," I muttered, easing the SWB closer to the squad car to block the pigeon's view. All we needed was one lethal double pass and we would be free to resume lawlessness. On cue, after a brief hesitation, the headlights swung confidently outward and an orange-and-white flash swept past both our car and the Oklahoma gendarmerie. Perfect!

Well, not exactly.

"Oh no," Joan and I groaned as the passer blasted off into the Oklahoma night, "Our pigeon is a frigging *ambulance!*" It was not the last time we were to encounter that resolute chariot of mercy. In seething serenity, we glided on until we reached the Texas border and our suffocating police escort let loose their leash.

For me, Cannonball dreams began many years earlier, reading the *Car and Driver* odyssey of *Moon Trash I* and, later, the cross-country dash of the Gurney-Yates Ferrari Daytona. It dazzled my imagination to think that any reasonable person (I was then the CEO of a rapidly growing advertising agency) would suspend all judgment and cross America at hoosegow-guaranteeing speeds. Ridiculous, absolutely—but for someone with a fatal predilection for the word "yes," completely irresistible.

Originally, I attempted to seduce serious racer friends to join me, but both Bob Akin and Skip Barber were much too sober citizens to indulge in this level of irresponsibility. Then, I realized that the perfect codriver/coconspirator was my domestic mate, the tall, cool, competitive and swift-driving Joan. She agreed, on three conditions: 1) We would stop the car whenever she chose to enjoy a cigarette; 2) She could drive at whatever speed she deemed comfortable; and, 3) I would not subject her to the indignity of blowing the horn, no matter how dedicated an antidestination league member the car slowing our progress might be. It was a deal!

From our stable of curious cars, we chose a valiant old stallion—our 1962 Ferrari Short Wheelbase Berlinetta, even then a bit of a classic. Our SWB was a scarred veteran, underloved over many years and many miles. Dented, bubbling with rust at the rockers, paint tarnished to the color of old gray pewter, it was cosmetically scrofulous but, nonetheless, mechanically strong. Years later, Jay Dow, my friend and race car preparer, pronounced it: "The only million-dollar car in the world you have to have a tetanus shot to work on." We equipped it with the usual Cannonball weapons: fuel bladder in the trunk, CB on the dash, foodstuff in a paper bag and . . . well, now that I think of it, that was pretty much it. The vitally important Escort radar detector didn't become part of our kit until we met Cincinnati Microwave president Jim Jaeger and vice president Paul Allen at the gathering place where the event was to begin.

On April 1, 1979, behind George Lysle's Lock, Stock & Barrel restaurant, the last and greatest Cannonball's dubious tone became apparent, when Brock chose to deliver his prestart declamations from atop a fetid dumpster, followed by entrant Dennis Menescini's startling method of commencing the event. Eschewing the nearby highway entrance ramp, Dennis gunned his truck directly up the 30-degree grass embankment, immediately entering the churning Connecticut freeway. Clearly, we had fallen among a group of individuals with somewhat peculiar judgment!

Time card punched by the official Cannonball clock, we left the parking lot and, one might retrospectively argue, our personal sanity.

Twenty minutes down the road, disaster struck. Slowly, in spite of all throttle-foot urging, the SWB ground to a dead halt. Apparently, something in the braking system locked up, most likely the master cylinder. This led to despair, telephone calls for a ramp truck to haul us back to the start, and a summons to Jay in Massachusetts to trailer down our Dino. Our bubble burst, our hopes dashed, our dream curtailed, we became seriously depressed.

Followed by a miracle!

Upon being unloaded, the SWB's brakes appeared to have returned to perfect normalcy. In a (typically Cannonball) lapse of even a scintilla of judgment, Joan and I begged Brock to restart our time clock (the bastard refused) and set off again without a nanosecond of hesitation. Following my suspect theory that it was best to drive around the law-sensitive states of Ohio and Missouri, we angled well south before turning right toward California. I mean, what's an extra 300 miles in a 3,000-mile race? And it worked. Avoid traffic incursions we did, but for one incident in rural Tennessee.

Warned by the Escort detector, I was able to haul the speed down from over 100-plus to something near 70 before the patrolman's radar gun focused us in its sights. Still, there was no denying a significant violation of the sacred 55.

After inspecting our papers and eyeballing the detritus piled up on the SWB's jump seats, the arresting officer queried, "Are you aware that every policeman in Tennessee is looking for you?"

"We're *very* sorry, officer" said Joan. "Would a homemade chocolate chip cookie make things right?" Flicking his head in both directions in classic movie style parody, the policeman grabbed the cookie from her hand. "OK, you two, I know what you're up to. Now just get out of here and drive safely!" We were certain that obeying one of his two recommendations was completely reasonable.

The miles passed with swift and amazing grace. We had no fixed plan; driver fatigue was cause for driver relief. We talked and catnapped. Joan drove brilliantly, sometimes partaking of the occasional roadside smoke (inducing 10 wretchedly long minutes of silent spousal writhing). Speeds of 80 to 120 miles per hour were routine, in and out of traffic, with neither dangerous driving nor applications of the forbidden horn.

After midnight on the aforementioned Oklahoma plains, awhile before we encountered our personal pace car, we stopped for gas at a lonely service station a few hundred yards off the highway. Our usual fueling routine was to park between the parallel sets of pumps, jump out of the car and each grab a hose, Joan filling the main tank from one side, me the trunk bladder from the other. Then, we'd drop the hoses where we stood and stuff a sufficient number of $10 bills into the attendant's hand to cover the costs. This time, however, the old Ferrari was thirsty for a couple of quarts of motor oil. Although always a lover of the English language, I never before had understood what the expression "Oklahoma Sooner" meant until, as I began to pour the motor oil, the concept became poignantly real. Oklahoma's muscular prairie wind grabbed the stream of oil and flung it horizontally, directly onto the windshield.

"You there, get some water and soap!" I screamed at the lone attendant, who was already alarmed by our bizarre refueling dance. Frantically, Joan and I scrubbed as our terrified helper raced back and forth from his little room carrying windshield cleaner and armloads of paper towels. When the glass was reasonably clear, I turned to hand our conscripted assistant a wad of cash.

"Oh, uh, no—it's OK!" he said, backing away, visions of Bonnie and Clyde lighting up his saucer eyes. I actually had to catch him to press the money into his reluctant grasp.

There were many other memorable moments before we arrived at the finish line: passing through Wichita, the bellybutton of the United States, realizing that we were on track to equal the previous Cannonball record; experiencing a purple dawn in the magically perfumed American desert; Joan finally acknowledging the urge in her bladder at an Arizona fuel stop (and asserting that, had she not tanked up on coffee and juice before leaving, she could gone pee-free for the full transcontinental voyage); my 13-hour stint over the construction-ripped mountain roads; her superb slicing through California's Monday morning commuter traffic, utilizing whatever was paved plus some surfaces that were not; thundering into the Portofino parking lot, all 12 of the SWB's cylinders still snorting proudly; feeling the outlaw sensation of being free, and not giving a damn.

Somewhere in this book, a chart will advise you that our Cannonball took over 45 hours, thereby exposing the lie I've told a thousand times. Yates' niggling charts aside, our actual *running* time was 36 hours, 14 minutes—not too bad for a couple of amateurs in an old crock of a car. But, however you choose to view the record book, I can demonstrate categorically that Joan and I were parked, showered, and working on our second tray of drinks when a certain orange and white ambulance arrived, humiliatingly strapped to the back of a puffing ramp truck. Kiss my time card, Brock!

Time has moseyed along, with both Joan and the SWB moving on as well, under what can be gently described as "associated circumstances." The contexts of my life, as well as the mores of the United States, have also evolved. Today, from the perspective of a couple of wretchedly long decades of societal prudence, the Cannonball has to be viewed as a little reckless, a lot outrageous, and something I could never contemplate doing again in a million years. But, to confess the truth, I still think of those 36 hours and 14 minutes, plus the days of partying that followed, as the most fun I ever had with my clothes on.

I did it, and I'm glad!

Jim Mullen is a prominent Boston advertising executive, cowinner of the Sebring 12 Hours, former ocean sailboat racer, and a respected competitor in international vintage car competition.

Pamela Yates
1979

You want me to do what? After mastering the fine art of pretending to be riveted to my man's dreams and aspirations, as of course, any woman worth her salt would claim, I realized I had just outfoxed myself. The man of my dreams happened to be a car guy. Compounding that reality, he and I always agreed that the best thing we could think of was to be trapped in a car together heading down the road on a new adventure. Really dumb and sappy, but us.

Now hold on to this next thought: Remember the old expression be careful what you wish for or you may get it. I was about to become living testimony.

Brock Yates and Hal Needham are by any standards a magnetic pair. Here I was playing the good old wife role while my fate was being decided by two slightly aging teenagers. Granted, I loved and trusted both of them. If I were to be marooned on a desert island, they would be the two people I would want with me. That said, their new scam was a stretch even for them. Another Cannonball. Was I hearing correctly? I could tell by Brock's body language that he wasn't sure if it was just another barroom fantasy. Hal was all excited and pitching it, as only Hal can. He was so good that before I knew it, Brock began to think it was the greatest idea since salted nuts. I on the other hand was pale with dread.

Through the din of the bar, all I could catch was the random word, ambulance, doctor, senator's wife. Then, as if on cue, with turned heads and manipulative smiles, Hal and Brock closed in for the kill. I was to be a senator's wife in the ambulance. There was only one problem: trying to explain why the ambulance was taking a patient from Darien, Connecticut, to Los Angeles for medical treatment.

The two geniuses agreed it was only a slight complication. It couldn't miss, the biggest, best scam since PT Barnum arrived on the scene! Who would stop an ambulance?

The last and best Cannonball remains a series of snapshots and sound bites that play over and over again. The sight of poor Lyle Royer following Hal's wake as they got off the plane in Hartford, Connecticut. Dr. Royer looked like the Colgate Palmolive kid on his way to a bank robbery. He didn't have a clue what he was entering into.

The memories run together. Diana Ross appearing with her current squeeze. The fear of being discovered by the state police and *The New York Times*. The astonishing crowd of 3,000 people at this supposed underground event. The realization that neither my husband nor Hal would stop or give one whit if I had to go to the bathroom, once their competitive juices kicked in. My last-minute search for a porta potty to accompany me in the ambulance. The terrors of headlines splashed across the front page of my local paper saying mother of two arrested for impersonating a patient. The forged license tag with arrest written all over it.

Time and distance alter many things. My memories, like those of all the wonderful free spirits who rode with us, share a unique and special secret. Somewhere deep down in our collective souls we smile and say, "We did it!"

Pam Yates, known in motorsports as "Lady Pamela," is the wife of Brock Yates and a successful businesswoman and former professional singer.

Loyal Truesdale
1979

Speeding ticket in Missouri. We had two radar detectors pointed front and back and when we were pulled over, Keith asked the cop which system he was using to catch us. The cop said, "Hell, boys, you passed me doing 100, I wasn't using radar."

Electric suits quit working in the Texas Panhandle about 5 A.M. We got off the interstate for coffee and to warm up. I asked the waitress where the "poor side of town" was. Keith wondered what was up as we headed that way. We rode down a barely paved road and saw what I was looking for—a sign in a yard saying "appliances, TVs, electrical stuff fixed." I maneuvered through the broken washing machines and debris on the driveway to the house and started banging on the door. A kindly old black gentleman opened the door and saw the Michelin Man and me, still wearing our helmets, waving the end of the cord we used to plug our suits into the bike battery. I explained our problem and he invited us in. He made coffee as Keith and I began cutting duct tape and peeling off layers of clothes to get at our jackets. Coffee in one hand, we went downstairs to the "fix-it" shop, and the oldtimer started troubleshooting, looking for the break in the wire.

A half-hour later the electric suits were working again. We offered him $20, but he wouldn't take it. He laughed and said that he'd done some "dumb stuff" back when he was young but "you boys take the cake." He watched in amazement as we went through the ritual of "layer on, duct tape, next layer, more tape." We looked back as we turned on the road, and he was standing on the porch shaking his head.

Torching Tanks and Truck Stops

Our stops became a routine. Around 150 miles or three hours, we'd exit at the biggest Gas and Food sign.

We'd try to get as close as possible to a pump so we could reach it without getting off the bike. We got pretty good at the trick of the guy on the back getting off without tipping the bike over. (With all the clothes we were wearing our crotch was between our waist and knees.) Patchett would stand up on the pegs, then put one foot on the saddlebag, then on the seat and jump clear of the bike, run to the cashier, leave $20 and head for the coffee shop.

After topping off, I'd try to reinsert the hose (or just drop it) and aim at the warm lights waiting inside. Then it was my turn to get off the bike without dropping it. I'd stop at the cashier, pick up the change, and meet Patchett in the restaurant where he'd have a cup of hot coffee waiting.

I would then start looking around at the new world into which I had just popped. Bright lights, people moving at a snail's pace where time was standing still and we were still moving at 100 miles per hour. Our conversations were limited to grunts, punctuated and directed by "hits to the body" sign language. Truckers and waitresses had seen everything, but we were something else. Shunned at first, but when I asked one of them if "Burt" had been in yet as we were racing him to the West Coast, our coffee cups were never empty again. They'd scribble their name and address on a napkin or something and we promised to have Burt send them an "autographed" picture. (After the race I gave them all to Hal and every waitress from Darien to L.A. got an 8x10 glossy of Burt Reynolds in the *Cannonball Run* movie.)

Loyal Truesdale is the organizer of a revival the famed Mexican Road Race, the "Carrera Panamericana" and a legend in Southern California motorsport circles.

Doug Mockett
1979

A 1977 Chrysler LeBaron beat the other drive-away entrants in the 1979 Cannonball Baker Sea-to-Shining-Sea Memorial Trophy Dash to take top honors in this informal subcategory of the unusual event.

The Chrysler, to be delivered to an unsuspecting owner near Los Angeles, was a drive-away car. The driver receives free transportation in return for delivering the vehicle to the owner within a certain time period. It made the nonstop trip in 40 hours and 53 minutes, just 7 minutes faster than the second-place drive-away, a Thunderbird, ironically also from the same drive-away firm in the East. Both arrived six days earlier than expected.

The margin of difference in this epic subplot boiled down to fuel stops; the superior Chrysler made only 15 stops, while the gas-guzzling T-bird had to make 29. The trip was largely uneventful, according to team manager Peter Jessick.

"We just drove along sanely and kept alert," Jessick said. "With our very sophisticated on-board electronics systems we were continually alert to our airwaves environment. In fact, we had everything so much under control we spent much of the trip photographing the United States as we motored along.

"We were lucky in that we avoided mechanical problems; we kept our sense of humor high, even after passing fellow entrants; and we went through some pretty severe weather, including pea-soup fog near Harrisburg, Pennsylvania, heavy rain in Missouri, and icy roads near Flagstaff, Arizona.

"We made a plan and stuck with it," Jessick continued, "Our only error was about three hours into the event, when we missed the turnoff for the Pennsylvania Turnpike in Harrisburg. That cost us about 10 minutes. We also had refueling problems early in the mornings in Washington, Pennsylvania, and Kingman, Arizona, but those delays cost us no more than 20 minutes total. All in all, we are pleased with our first attempt at the Cannonball."

In addition to major sponsorship from Nikon cameras, other participating sponsors included an anonymous tennis racket manufacturer, SBE electronics, makers of the Brute CB, Whistler radar detectors, and J.I.L., makers of programmable radio scanners.

"Now we know what to do and how to do it," Jessick concluded. "We're throwing down the gauntlet right now. We'll be back for the next Cannonball and this time we're going to win it outright."

Doug Mockett, a successful California businessman, is a prominent competitor with Vintage Formula One cars in the United States and Europe.

Pierce Marshall
1979

From the beginning in 1971, I was captivated by participating in the Cannonball, a long, mobile party for motorsports enthusiasts. By 1979, Brock had run four Cannonballs, each increasing my resolve to participate. I intended to place well.

For a modest first effort, a new plain-looking, pale blue Malibu four-door sedan was chosen with the 9C1 Police Patrol Package, a 350 Z-28 engine, and a CB radio. Obtaining that car was an adventure, as Chevrolet had specifically restricted the sale of Z-28-equipped Malibus to law enforcement units only. Old friend Vince Piggins at Chevrolet helped to get it built at the 11th hour and delivered in the dark of night. Hurriedly, we added a fuel cell and longer range headlights.

My codrivers were two young, married SCCA drivers I had never met before, Dave Faust and Kirby Goodman. We stayed on the interstates and ran quickly, carefully and invisibly. Each of my codrivers was cited once. Other than clipping a bird in the desert, we never came close to threatening a soul. We drove in rain, made a wrong turn, and were stuck in traffic jams. Even so, we placed 13th out of 47, finishing in 36 hours, 51 minutes. The event was a unique experience. Over two decades later, the laughs and the memories are still fresh. I was fortunate to be involved.

Pierce Marshall is a successful businessman living in Dallas, Texas. His ex-mother-in-law is the notorious Anna Nicole Smith.

Kirby Goodman
1979

The Cannonball serves two purposes. The first is to prove that good drivers in good cars can travel at speeds in excess of 55 without wreaking havoc on themselves and others. In the past five times the Cannonball has been run, 200 entrants have traveled 350,000 miles at a total average of 76 miles per hour and no innocent bystanders have been hurt. The second purpose that the Cannonball serves is to become Brock Yates' litmus paper for society. He claims that the good guys love it and the bad guys hate it. It all depends on who you listen to. Maybe that is why Smokeys always wear dark-colored hats.

Dave Faust, Pierce Marshall, and I met our fair share of the good, the bad, and the ugly during the Cannonball. The good were the pro-Cannonball people, the bad were the anti-Cannonball people, and the ugly were the truckers, who generally proved to be on the mental level of spoiled four-year-old children.

Pierce Marshall has always wanted to run the Cannonball, being a racer at heart (Shelby Driving School 1962). He called the SCCA number in the phone book looking for rally drivers and continued calling the suggested names until he got Dave, who then called me. The idea was a complete surprise to me. I have always wanted to run the Cannonball, but thought I would never have the chance.

Our car was a Chevrolet Malibu with the 9C1 Police Package. Pierce took delivery of the 1979 vintage Malibu two weeks before the Cannonball and we spent the next weeks preparing it. An 8-inch spook, driving lights, a CB, a radar detector, and 40 gallons of fuel capacity were the basics.

We left the alternate starting point, the Lock, Stock & Barrel Bar in Darien, Connecticut, on April 1—a date that seems appropriate. We made good progress until the radar detector came on and, in the excitement of the moment, Dave drove past the exit we wanted to take. We came to a likely looking route and turned, only to be met by a car whose driver indicated rather explicitly that we were going the wrong way down a one-way street. The U-turn was made and everything seemed better until we saw that the driver of the other car was an off-duty police officer who was now standing in the middle of the road motioning us to stop. I'll bet that guy never steps out in front of a car with Montana plates again!

Dave got stopped in Pennsylvania (paced at 70 miles per hour) and I got it in Ohio. I didn't think my ticket for 70 was too bad considering that I was going 110 when the patrol car came over the hill. I think it was in Ohio that the Ferrari driver got to know the patrol on a first name basis. "Okay, Mark, pull it over." Three tickets in 5 miles. Our low profile in the Malibu got us to St. Louis with no problems, whereupon we had three traffic jams that apparently nobody else had to deal with. A detour, a bus stopped in the fast lane, and two overturned trucks doomed our average.

We covered Missouri with no problem. In Tulsa we passed the Shelby GT 350 entry, whose driver had spent quite some time with the police back east. From Tulsa we maintained our Team Innocuous low profile. Driving quickly, we picked up our average from 76 to 82, which isn't easy when you have already covered 1,500 miles. In Arizona we came upon the Thunderbird manned by one Air Canada representative and two *Stock Car Racing* magazine representatives. They followed us across the Arizona border, where we parted company. We arrived at the Portofino Inn in Redondo Beach, California, an hour ahead of the T-bird. (So don't ever try to outrun a patrol with your Thunderbird.)

Averaging a speed equal to the old record (80-plus), we expected to finish well at the top, but on arrival we were disappointed to find that the winner had already been named, with an average of just above 90 miles per hour. The beach party Monday night with B.B.Q. and girls from *Oui* and the awards banquet Tuesday night with great food and fun awards improved our spirits.

The cars were great, the race was great, and the people were the greatest. We ran with the big boys and beat more than beat us and, given the chance, I am sure we would do it all again.

Goodman, Marshall, and Faust finished in 13th place.

Rick Kopec
1979

Permit me to take this opportunity to provide you with some of the flotsam and jetsam from my participation in the 1979 Cannonball event. As it turns out, this was one of the high points in my tepid life. It ranks somewhere between collecting my second Purple Heart in Vietnam when our firebase was nearly overrun by a couple of NVA battalions and totaling a brand-new 1968 Torino before I was able to make the first payment. I share the following with you because I believe in two things: One is Andy Warhol's prediction that everyone will be famous for 15 minutes, and the other is that the meek will inherit the shit.

I have been an avid *Car and Driver* reader since a "car-guy" uncle gave me a subscription for Christmas when I was 12 years old. I read each issue cover to cover and followed the very first Cannonball like probably every other *Car and Driver* reader, thinking I had the perfect car, knew the perfect route, and stood just as good a chance to win as anyone else. In fact, in 1972 I came very close to entering. I had a 1966 GT350 that I had purchased while I was in Vietnam in 1969 (it was waiting for me when I got home, and I still have it today). I had been married for all of two years and my naïve wife was willing to accompany me. The only rub was that I was in college and just could not afford to take the time off.

Each time I read about the plans for the next running in the pages of *Car and Driver,* the timing never seemed to be right. I was an early subscriber to the *Cannonball Express.* (I have every issue, somewhere, so that qualifies me as some kind of sicko.) When the December 5, 1978, issue arrived, I had a feeling that this might be the last time the Cannonball would be run, and if I didn't enter then I would be kicking myself for the rest of my life. To add to the challenge, a movie script was envisioned and entries would be judged based on how photogenic their nutball car would be.

I was up to my ears in Shelbys by that time, being one of the founders of the Shelby American Automobile Club and, naturally, I had no trouble envisioning a white and blue striped GT350 being in the resulting movie. The trouble was that my car was sitting in a garage without an engine. So I began calling everyone I knew with a GT350 (no small number) and asked them two questions. "Would you like to run the next Cannonball with me?" To a person they replied, "Yes!" The second question was, "Can we take your car?" Most of the responses contained some form of "Fuck you," but I eventually hit on one kindred soul in the club who had wanted to become a Cannonball participant since he read about that first trip in 1971. We were a perfect match.

Bob Key was a psychologist in Southern California who owned a 1965 GT350. He was willing to drive his car east and turn it around and haul ass back. It seemed too good to be true. I was teaching in an "alternative high school for school-alienated youths," and was able to wrangle two weeks off (I explained to the principal it was the automotive equivalent of going to the Olympics). We began feverishly making plans.

When Key arrived at my home in Norwalk, Connecticut, the first thing I discovered was that his car needed a lot of work before we left on the trip. It had 176,000 miles on it and was on the loose end. Over the next few days we installed new brakes, new tires, a 3:00 rear end, a 32-gallon fuel tank, a new crankshaft dampener, and gave the engine a complete tune-up and valve adjustment. We also wired in two Escort radar detectors and a CB radio.

When the Saturday of the start rolled around, we were still tweaking the car, amid a steady stream of well-wishers who stopped by (because you cannot compete in something like this without bragging about what you are going to do). We were up at 7 A.M. putting the finishing touches on Key's car. The drivers' meeting was at 2 P.M. at the Lock, Stock & Barrel, some 15 minutes away.

At the drivers' meeting, we were instructed to pick the starting time of our choice between 7 P.M. and 2 A.M. We chose 9:24 P.M. for two reasons that seemed logical to us at the time. First, it would give us some time to go back home and get some sleep before we left. Second, it was six minutes ahead of the starting time of Steve Behr, a previous Cannonball winner. We figured Behr would pass us quickly and we would be able to tag along after him through the rat's maze of highways that flow through New York City and northern New Jersey.

Looking back now, it's hard to believe that we could have been so naïve. We went back home after the drivers' meeting and tried to sleep. That proved to be impossible. My wife fixed a large Mexican dinner (in hindsight we would have been smarter to have the exact culinary opposite—enemas). By 6:30 P.M. we realized we would get no sleep, so we headed off to the Lock, Stock & Barrel to watch the cars ahead of us leave.

This had been billed as a "secret" event with no publicity, and that probably explained why there were more than 2,000 people there to watch the cars leave. It was nothing short of a mob scene. In a misting rain, our time came up and because I was from the area, I took the first stint behind the wheel. On full adrenaline boost, I tore out of the parking lot and up onto I-95. We crossed the George Washington Bridge some 20 minutes later (which I still consider an impossibility—on a Saturday night in the rain—but I was there, so I have to believe it).

About one-half hour into New Jersey, cruising at a steady 120 miles per hour, we passed an on-ramp containing a New Jersey state trooper. He caught up with us after a bit and pulled us over. Now came the moment of truth. In doing my research I had posed this hypothetical problem to several of my friends: You are stopped for speeding in another state. What can you do or say that will get you back on your way in the least amount of time? One friend was a police officer, and he said he never had a problem in situations like that because when he opened his wallet to get his license out he made sure the officer saw his badge. A professional courtesy was always extended. The wheel began turning . . .

He offered to lend me his off-duty badge and tutored me on how not to entrap myself. When the officer asked me if I was "on the job" or "on the force" I should say "I'm on vacation." Side-stepping the question seemed so simple. He continued to lecture me about the seriousness of impersonating a police officer, but my eyes glazed over as I held the chrome badge in my fingers. It was the equivalent of the Monopoly "Get Out of Jail Free" card.

So the New Jersey trooper was walking toward the silent Shelby with his flashlight aimed at me. In a monotone he asked for my license and registration, I opened my wallet and made a show of letting him see the badge. The beam of the flashlight makes it sparkle. I can't believe how easy this is turning out to be. "Are you a police officer?" he asked. It was going just like my pal said it would.

"I'm on vacation." I said, looking him straight in the eye. According to the script, the next thing he will say is, "Well, take it easy, and have a nice vacation." And we will drive away.

"Could I see your I.D. card, please?"

I.D. card? My pal never said anything about an I.D. card. In the snap of a finger things were turning to shit. "I, uh, I didn't bring it with me." In hindsight, this pretty much was an admission that I wasn't who I was trying to make him think I was. But I had nowhere else to go with this. In less than 30 seconds I was off the map. He took my license and walked back to his patrol car. He was there a long time. A very long time.

He returned and said, "You're not a police officer, are you?"

"I, uh, never said I was," I offered weakly. I considered whipping the badge out of the passenger's window into the weeds. "Step out of the car, please." He motioned me around to the rear of the car and ordered me to "assume the position." My forehead was pressed on the car's trunk and he was handcuffing my hands behind my back. Cars were whizzing by and I happened to see Steve Behr cruise sedately past in his Porsche 928. Another cruiser rolled up and a grizzled sergeant got out. They put me in the back of the first cruiser, pushing my head down so it doesn't hit the top of the door frame. Just the way they do in the movies. Only this was no movie.

Both officers now had my pal, the psychologist, out of the car. He was looking for the registration in the glove box and they asked him to step away from the car. I'm really not paying much attention at this point. I was stunned that the whole thing could have gone so very wrong so very quickly. And those handcuffs were really pinching my wrists.

Both troopers were searching the Shelby. They inspected my trunk, the interior and the glove box. They came up with a large brown bottle of assorted pills. The psychologist was also a vitamin freak and he had a two-week supply of every vitamin and herb you've ever heard of. Of course, taking drugs out of their original containers is against some law and a comment was made that, "these will have to go to the lab . . . " Things were getting worse.

The ride to headquarters was a quiet one. Key followed the cruiser in the Shelby. All traces of bravado, adrenaline and testosterone had disappeared. Inside the police headquarters I was led to a tiny booking room and told to have a seat on a bench. With my hands still cuffed behind my back I was forced to sit on the front edges of the seat. Occasionally a trooper walked by me without making a comment. If they were trying to make me feel like some kind of criminal, it was working. Suddenly I looked up and an older sergeant was standing in front of me. He was the first one who seemed interested in hearing my story. "What the hell were you trying to do, anyway?"

I started spilling my guts. "Have you ever heard of the Cannonball? The East Coast to West Coast race?" I asked. He said he had. Not only that, but he worked traffic duty when the movie *Gumball Rally* was being filmed in New Jersey. "Well," I continued, "The Cannonball is for real and it's going on right now. And we're in it." My explanation came tumbling out. I got the feeling that if I stopped he might lose interest and walk away, leaving me in even deeper trouble. If that were possible. But he listened attentively. He explained that impersonating a police officer is a felony. This is real trouble. Most people who do this, he explained, do it because they want to carry a gun, and they think it gives them some kind of right to do that. This, as it turns out, was what the two officers were searching the Shelby for.

I knew a fellow Shelby owner in New Jersey who was a State Police officer. I thought the sergeant was starting to warm up to me a little so I asked him if mentioning my friend's name might help me in this situation. He said "maybe" but was noncommittal. I drop the name and he remained skeptical, but offers to call him and see if he knows me. He comes back in a few minutes and said "he wasn't home." My heart sanks. Lower. "But his wife was, and she knew you." He removed the handcuffs just like in the movies, and I was rubbing my wrists.

They kept the badge and let me go with a speeding ticket (80 in a 55) for which I thanked them profusely. We scooted out on the parking lot and we were on our way. We'd lost three hours that we soon discovered could not be made up. Like a whipped puppy, I took the passenger seat. We began commiserating: "It could have been worse . . . " "We got off easy . . . " "What I should have said was . . . "

We crossed into Pennsylvania and stopped for gas. It's a lightning pit stop, as our motivation began to return. I take over the wheel and get back into the flow of traffic, and then out ahead of it. Within five minutes I am again stopped, this time by a Pennsylvania state trooper. Badgeless this time, I silently accepted the 73 in a 55. The trooper asked if we were in that Cannonball race. The word is out, and these guys are having a contest to see who can bag the most participants.

We continued west, trying to hold the speedometer needle on 90. We were listening to the CB (which gave more of a headache than any usable information), trying to monitor both front and rear radar detectors and as the day broke, using binoculars to see ahead and behind us. But the stiffly sprung Shelby made any image through binoculars look out of focus. We managed to stay on our route (the same one Yates and Gurney drove in 1971 when they won in a Ferrari Daytona).

For the most part the trip became uneventful. In Ohio, we were spotted by a State Police car going in the opposite direction. We saw the brake lights come on as it darts for a median turn-around. We instantly pulled off to the side of the road, scrambled out of the car and opened the hood. He rolled to a stop behind us, lights flashing, and as he got out I smiled and said, "Oh, we're okay officer. Nothing serious here." He got back in the car and drove off, doing a 180 at the next median cross-over. Now that's the way it's supposed to work. At least, in our daydreams.

In Missouri we wasted about 15 minutes hiding in an underpass from a pursuing Missouri highway patrolman. We later saw a Jensen-Healey—another Cannonballer—driving over an overpass as he evaded another highway patrol cruiser. By the time we had started the event we had already been awake for 14 hours. What were we thinking? Not even at the halfway point and we were already switching off every 2 hours. Or less.

Oklahoma and Texas were downright boring. Occasionally, we would see another Cannonball entrant. They were easy to spot, because they were the only cars that would rocket past us as we rolled along at a sedate 90 miles per hour. Constant calculations, at this point, revealed that the only chance we had of winning was if every other car in the event suffered some sort of catastrophic mechanical failure or if they were apprehended by the law enforcement authorities and forced to spend the night in the lock-up as we slipped through the blockade.

As we crossed into New Mexico, we had been awake for 42 hours straight. The GT350's seats did not recline and the next-to-nothing exhaust system that was so endearing when we cruised around town on Saturday nights had become a continuous mind-numbing racket that caused the driver to sleep while, at the same time, kept the passenger awake.

Soon we were changing drivers every hour. About four hours east of Albuquerque, at about 2 in the morning, I took the wheel. Not using the hand brake on my own GT350, it never occurred to me to check it before I took off. About a half an hour later I noticed, in the rear-view mirror, small glowing particles floating in the car's wake. Key was asleep and he had told me he thought the fiberglass packing in the muffler was blowing out, so I accepted that this was what it is. Heading up a long hill, there were two big rigs ahead of us, running side by side. I pulled into the left lane and came up behind it, I was running about 95 miles per hour so I gently squeezed the brake, but instead the pedal went to the floor. I downshifted and the trucks crested the hill and the one in front of me moved into the right-hand lane. I upshifted and kept running. The road was straight and mostly flat, and free of other traffic. We had plenty of time to decide what we were going to do.

We had a plan. We coasted to stop in a rest area where there was a phone and I called a fellow club member in Albuquerque. At 4 A.M. the word "Cannonball" injected early into the conversation was like magic. He would meet us at a truck stop he gave us directions to with a box of brake parts. We arrived early and decided to have breakfast in a pancake house. Our first sit-down meal. Key was driving and as he wheeled the GT350 into the parking lot he remembered that he had no brakes. He furiously downshifted and as the car was heading for a plate glass window jammed it into reverse. It stalled less than a foot short of the window. Two state policemen were sitting at a table directly in front of the car, watching us. We tried to exit the car with an air of nonchalance: "Yeah, this is the way we always come to a stop with this car."

Rather than wait for them to find us, I walked over to innocently ask directions to the truck stop. "It's right down the road. Have them check your brakes," he said.

My new best friend met us at the truck stop. We put the car up on a lift and I quickly diagnosed the problem: melted rubber seals in the rear cylinders. We broke out a pair of cylinders and I quickly replaced them. We bled the brakes and were again on our way. We had wasted about an hour and a half. It was gone and we could never make it. After coming so far, that was a disheartening thought.

We took the famed Ash Fork cutoff, through some of the most beautiful country we'd yet seen (because about half of the Cannonball running has been at night). California was so close we could smell the salt air. Once we crossed the state line we caught our second wind. No longer exhausted, we were now hyper alert. Key was at the wheel—this was his home state. He sliced through traffic and we didn't need to open the map. Each mile brought us closer to Redondo Beach and the Portofino Inn.

Finally we were there. The car stopped, but I felt as if we were still in this state of perpetual motion. My wife had been waiting patiently in the hotel lobby for longer than I cared to ask. Every time a car pulled in she had asked if they had seen the Shelby. The only one who had was Steve Behr. When he said the guy with the red beard was being handcuffed in New Jersey, her heart sank.

Our time? 48 hours, 53 minutes. Not the slowest time but the sixth from the bottom—and only about 16 hours behind the winner. We had hoped to break 40 hours at least, but we had to admit the Cannonball was a lot harder than it looks. At the dinner that night we were awarded the "Worst Time" trophy. It's likely this had been envisioned as going to the car that was the last to arrive, but because of our stint in the New Jersey State Police's lock-up, it was given to us. I'll occupy a small footnote in the history of the event as the only entrant ever to plea-bargain a felony down to a speeding ticket in the commission of a Cannonball.

Rick Kopec is the founder, leader, and prime mover of the Shelby American Club and the preeminent historian of the marque. He lives near his favorite race track, Lime Rock Park.

Dr. Lou Sellyei
1979

We knew of the exploits of the Yates-Gurney blue Daytona, the Polish Guys with all the fuel drums, and the many other very funny episodes that took place on the Cannonball. The movie *Gumball Rally* made the event seem mysterious, semi-illicit, and off the edge enough that a rational car person had to do it. Fortunately, a similar thinking friend named Dr. Gary Arentz just happened to have a brand-new dark green Jaguar XJS. Perfect, I thought. We made some minor adjustments like taking the fuel cell from our M8F Can Am Mclaren (the same car a real racer named Revson drove to a championship something or other). The fuel cell filled up the trunk nicely. We had it plumbed into the Jaguar gas tank so the gauge constantly worked—in theory.

We thought it would be an excellent idea to obtain some eye bank paraphernalia, which we filled with pig eyes. The scam: It was not a good idea for the eyes to be carried at high altitude, so it was necessary to rush them along the surface. According to our plan the only eyes that were available were in New York and the patient needed them in California.

The Prince of Darkness struck as we headed from Reno to Connecticut. This first electrical repair was required 25 miles east of Reno, which made us somewhat suspicious about the wisdom of using a Jaguar. We actually used up all the electrical spare parts on the way to

Connecticut, but otherwise the car ran fine.

The truckers were not our friends. They reported all our activity to the local highway patrol. We therefore removed all the emblems from the back of the car.

Thinking that the real Cannonball would be similar to the mysterious *Gumball* race, we were totally flummoxed to find that there was a dinner and that the departure time was widely known. Upon entering the Lock, Stock & Barrel restaurant, we were shocked when the first person we saw informed us that they thought the idea about the pig eyes was terrific. How to have your cover blown.

We opted for a midnight starting time because we felt there would be less traffic leaving from New York City at that time. It was raining quite heavily. We had no problems until we hit a bridge on the Pennsylvania Turnpike. Now, we didn't actually *hit* the bridge, but there such a discrepancy between the road surface and the bridge paving that there was a gigantic bang that resulted in a front tire blowout. After changing the tire we had severe vibration at 110 miles per hour, which of course limited our top speed at that point.

Everything was going along in a capital fashion until we arrived in Albuquerque. At that point two things happened. Gary decided that bathroom stops were unnecessary, so he was urinating into a bottle. In one lousy attempt to throw it out the window he spilled it all over himself. Fortunately, he wasn't driving but it made the rest of the trip rather unpleasant and odiferous.

We also discovered that upon switching the fuel tank the bladder in the trunk appeared to be empty. At first we thought we didn't fill it. The next time we switched, it was again empty. We decided that there must be a problem with the fuel pump so we spent an hour and a half underneath a streetlight in Albuquerque at 1:30 in the morning repairing a fuel pump that turned out to have been working fine.

We finally realized that we had pumped two bladders of gasoline onto the road. We could not use it any further after that.

We proceeded to the Portofino Inn at Redondo Beach and arrived in a rather beat-up condition. Neither one of us had really slept, even though we were working at two-hour intervals of driving. Our wives, who were already at the Portofino Inn, thought we looked like two bubonic plague victims who had recently been thrown out of a hospice. They did appreciate the fact that driving nonstop from coast to coast makes a person quite horny. All in all it was a purgatorial experience, but one that we wanted to do again. Unfortunately, that was the last Cannonball.

Dr. Louis Sellyei is a prominent Reno, Nevada, opthalmologist and a well-known vintage racer in his Ferrari TR250 Testa Rossa. He is also a major presence in the Reno Automotive Museum and international classic car circles. Dr. Gary Arentz is also an active vintage competitor with an ex-Mario Andretti Lotus 79 Grand Prix car.

CHAPTER
SIX

The Legend Established

THE IMMEDIATE RESULT OF THE 1979 CANNONBALL was the movie, which, in my personal life, produced mixed results. Funded by the Hong Kong production company Golden Harvest, which had gained power and prominence in the industry by making a series of Bruce Lee kung fu epics, and distributed by 20th Century Fox, *Cannonball Run* started out as a potential winner. AL Ruddy, the Oscar-winning producer of *The Godfather*, had engaged Steve McQueen to star in the first iteration of *Cannonball Run*. My screenplay, about which I am still proud, was an adventure-comedy far removed from what finally reached the screen.

But sadly, McQueen was stricken with the stomach cancer that finally killed him, and he was forced to withdraw from the project. With McQueen out, the project went into what in the picture business is called "turnaround," until a new star could be found. Initially Burt Reynolds was not a candidate. Holding the Number One box office title, Reynolds claimed he was heading for more lofty dramatic efforts than more nutball car chases. I had worked with him during a rewrite of the script on *Smokey and the Bandit II* and believed that he was out as a McQueen replacement. Somehow he had become convinced that he was the new Cary Grant—a king of drawing room comedy and light drama—and would never again reduce himself to the levels of farce displayed in the two *Smokey* pictures, or even in the well-reviewed *Hooper*, the story of a struggling stunt man. Hal Needham, who had directed those pictures, remained Reynolds' close friend. He even occupied a carriage house apartment on the superstar's Bel Air estate, but it was believed that not even he could persuade Reynolds to sign on.

Then Reynolds' career took a strange turn. He starred in a jewel-robbery story with British actress Leslie Ann Downes called *Rough Cut*. It was a failure at the box office. He then did a serious picture with Jill Clayburgh called *Starting Over* that he believed was Academy Award material. It failed to be nominated while his rival star, Robert Redford, won a best director Oscar for the drama *Ordinary People*. Reynolds, who was never on the A-list of Hollywood royalty, was furious about this lack of recognition by the Brahman establishment and, in a sudden turnaround, signed on to do *Cannonball.* He would be paid $5 million for the picture, at the time a record payday in the industry.

At first the news electrified me. The picture now had the biggest name in the business as its star. He was a good guy personally with a great sense of humor and possessed little of the overpowering ego that cursed so many major entertainers. Better yet, he professed to like fast cars, and optimism that he would simply adapt to the McQueen script was initially high. Then came the first few meetings at his Bel Air home (where I discovered that he was wearing elevator cowboy boots, which seemed curious for a tall former college athlete). Reynolds didn't care a hoot that the races had been actually run and that a "real life" component would energize the story. He wanted a pure farce and owing to his power and strength in the business, no one—Ruddy, Needham, Golden Harvest representative Andre Morgan, or obviously myself as the low-totem screenwriter—was in a position to argue.

Reynolds demanded roles for his friend Dom DeLuise. A role for him as the demented "Captain Chaos" was injected into the script. A pair of priests, based on the actual 1972 trip of Peter Brock, Jack Cowell, and Dick Gilmartin had been written into the script and the first choices for the roles were Jim Garner and Don Rickles. Garner turned down the part when he discovered that his scenes were too limited. Rickles declined, stating that he wouldn't play second banana to DeLuise who, he claimed, couldn't match him as a Las Vegas attraction.

The roles were filled by Dean Martin, who spent most of the shoot in a good-natured alcoholic stupor and Sammy Davis, Jr., who hadn't worked in years and was eager for any part, regardless of size.

The first choice for the female lead was Loni Anderson, who was making major waves as the blonde bimbo in the hit television comedy *WKRP Cincinnati.* But despite never having had a starring role in a motion picture, she demanded $500,000 for the part—big bucks in those days—and was rejected. Reynolds was reported to be dallying with Farrah Fawcett at the time and suggested the blonde ex-Charlie's Angel, who at the time was in the midst of a career drought. "Hell," hooted Al Ruddy at the news she might be available, "She oughta pay *us* to be in the picture."

Fawcett was signed for modest dollars and the casting began in earnest. It became apparent that this would be ensemble comedy much like the successful *It's a Mad, Mad, Mad World*. Frantic rewriting of the script began to accommodate a mass of stars, large and small, who began to appear on the set in Decatur, Georgia. Needham had become good friends with the people running the Georgia film development agency and, based on his enthusiasm for stock car racing and the southern lifestyle in general, shooting would take place there and on location in Las Vegas and the Portofino Inn in Redondo Beach. How a town in rural Georgia and Las Vegas would substitute for Darien, Connecticut, and the vast sweep of the American heartland puzzled me, but I had no choice but to watch the production unfold. Or more, correctly, unravel.

Day by day, all manner of people showed up for cameo roles. Terry Bradshaw, Mel Tillis, Jamie Farr, Valerie Perrine, Roger Moore, even Bianca Jagger, etc., etc. rolled onto the set as the script was shredded to accommodate them. The memories of McQueen and the real Cannonball adventure faded into distant memory. The shooting schedule was modest, to say the least. Reynolds appeared for about three weeks, did his scenes, collected his money and was gone. Needham, a garrulous and delightful man, was heard to crack, "Fuck the dialogue, let's wreck

(Left to right): Yates, Terry Bradshaw and producer Al Ruddy laugh it up between takes. Mel Tillis and Bradshaw shot a TV pilot written by Yates and directed by Needham based on their Cannonball roles. Titled "The Stockers," it was about an itinerant car driver and his mechanic touring the nation. It was never sold.

some cars." He tended to wrap shooting by late afternoon and set up shop at the hotel bar. Daily rushes were baffling. There seemed to be no footage. One-take scenes were common. There were no rehearsals. One stunt scene involving the Polish Racing Drivers van jumping a train clearly showed the ramp, which was a no-no in a production of such alleged cost and magnitude. In the end less than 200,000 feet of the film was exposed for the entire picture, which was little more than some advertising agencies shot for 60-second television commercials.

As an example of the ad hoc shooting structure, it was decided that we ought to have a scene in which the rules of the race were laid out to the competitors. I was selected to give the talk. Within hours I was standing in front of the entire cast, including Reynolds, Fawcett, and Roger Moore. Stiff with fear, I ran through my little speech once and heard Needham say, "Cut." It was over. One take. That is the scene that appears in the movie, which was typical of the level of drama injected into the production.

I could see the entire production descending into a loosely shot, dim-bulb low comedy and could do nothing to control it. Motion pictures, good and bad, gain a life of their own during production and once

Roger Moore relaxes with Pamela Yates.

a course is set, even the best directors and producers can't make real corrections. *Cannonball Run* was headed for critical ruin, but possible box-office success, whether I liked it or not.

Then true disaster hit. The production company had rented a dry lake outside Las Vegas where Needham had shot the final big-rig scene in *Smokey and the Bandit II* for some road stunts on an adjacent highway. One involved a routine run-through by doubles of Roger Moore and actress Susan Hamilton in a replica of the Aston Martin DBII employed in several of the James Bond features. In a send-up of the Bond adventures, the Aston's cockpit was to fill up with the smoke, blinding Moore, who played an addled Bond wannabe. The ensuing maneuver, plotted by Needham and his team of expert stunt men, involved the Aston weaving through oncoming traffic. An aspiring stunt woman named Heidi Von Beltz, a former ski racer and fiancée of the picture's stunt coordinator and Needham pal Bobby Bass, doubled for Hamilton. Von Beltz, a rangy, vivacious athletic type, was seeking seat-time in stunt routines in order to qualify for a full stunt-man's union card and took the assignment from her boyfriend, knowing it would be simple and safe. It wasn't. In a zig when the oncoming cars should have zagged, the Aston-Martin was involved in a head-on crash that gravely injured Von Beltz. She was helicoptered off to a nearby emergency hospital, and it was quickly determined that the young lady would be paralyzed from the waist down. This accident would cause endless lawsuits and elevate Von Beltz to prominence as an advocate for the handicapped. Needham would suffer heavy financial damage as the legalities in the case dragged on through the years.

The picture was completed on schedule with final shooting at the Portofino Inn and postproduction went quickly. Looping (the synchronized voiceover of scenes already shot) was highlighted by Dean Martin's appearance, totally blasted during several early morning sessions. The editing process was handicapped by the sheer lack of film. Every usable inch was spliced into the final cut, plus some that clearly didn't belong.

My wife, Pamela, and I saw a prerelease screening in Los Angeles and were devastated. What I had hoped would set the score right with the picture—dooming the *Gumball Rally* and the first *Cannonball* to the trash heap—was in fact a mess. Reynolds aped and mugged his way through his scenes while over-the-top performances by the likes of Jack Elam, Jamie Farr, and DeLuise were often funny, but bore no relationship to the original script. Because of my friendship and respect for Needham, I muted my reservations and hoped that the general public would enjoy the film, while remaining totally ignorant of the fact that the film was based on reality.

It opened big and stayed big. The critics flayed it, as expected, with TV critics Siskel and Ebert nominating it as one of the 10 worst feature films of all time. But the bucks rolled in, making it the second-largest grossing movie of 1981 (behind Bill Murray's *Stripes*) and producing millions in aftermarket games, toys, a 7–11 soft drink promotion and a paperback book. While the project was a wonderful source of revenue for me and was to be elevated into a late-night cult film, the whole enterprise left a certain hollow feeling in me as I continued to puzzle over how much better a film might have resulted from my original script and McQueen's participation. But as they say, "Hooray for Hollywood."

It was prior to the production of *Cannonball Run* that talk emerged of doing another race. It initially seemed like a good idea, considering the promotional tie-in with the release of the movie.

Early in 1980 I made a trip to Sarasota, Florida, on assignment from *Playboy* and during a break visited the home of Terry Bernius, a successful local contractor who had run a modified Lotus Esprit in the 1979 race. He was a pleasant fellow, with wide-racing enthusiasms, and he eagerly escorted me to his garage where a lethal-looking all-black Lamborghini Countach sulked in a corner. "That's what I'll use to win the next Cannonball," said Bernius.

I looked at the car, recalling the 170-mile-per-hour rush Gurney and I had made across interstate 10 a decade earlier. It was one thing for a world-class driver like Dan to run a car at that velocity; it was another thing entirely to let a rank amateur loose on the public highways with a wild machine like that. I immediately thought, "No you're not. Because I've run the last Cannonball."

That was the end. Never again, although I received a letter from the Sports Car Club of America offering to *sanction* another Cannonball as a long-distance rally. The notion of such a sanction today would cause universal seizures among the SCCA Board of Directors and surely the immediate cancellation of all their competition insurance. But such a letter is an indication of how radically the legal atmosphere has changed in the United States over the last 20 years.

Ironically, the Bernius Lamborghini did participate in the Cannonball, at least in an oblique fashion. He sold the car to the Coppertone sun lotion people, who in turn loaned it to Needham for use in the movie. It is the black machine that opens the picture driven by Adri-anne Barbeau and starlet Tara Buckman, who was included in the scene mainly because she was Needham's girlfriend of the hour.

I admit to being momentarily intrigued with a revival when word was received that no less an eminence than Dr. Hunter S. Thompson wanted to organize another Cannonball. But his plan to run from Big Sur to Key West smacked of Thompson-style madness which, on paper would make for great reading, but only grief for the organizer. But that hardly meant that others wouldn't snitch my idea and run knock-off events. Imitation is the sincerest form of flattery. I might have been pleased to see the Cannonball carried on under another name. I was not. The event had become personal to me, and I resented others pla-giarizing an idea that I had created and nurtured. Petty of me, perhaps, but I chose to ignore other copycat races and to this day cannot even remember the names, their drivers, or their results. One I believe was called the "U.S. Express" and may have run from New York to San Fran-cisco, but otherwise my memory bank is empty. A group of Germans ran two European Cannonballs from somewhere in Scandinavia to the south of France, but I recall that they encountered a shit-storm of trou-ble from the European authorities and never ran again. So too for our Australian friend, Jeff Dinmeade, who tried two Cannonballs across the outback, Sydney to Perth, but had the wrath of the Australian gov-ernment descend upon him. The runs were canceled before Dinmeade headed to the slammer.

Years later an Australian Cannonball was organized as a high-speed rally, but ended when a pair of Japanese drivers lost control of their Ferrari F40 at a checkpoint stop and managed to kill themselves and several course workers. While unrelated to the original races, the Cannonball name was badly damaged in the ensuing publicity.

Since then the Cannonball trademark and intellectual property surrounding the event have been enveloped in an ironclad legal struc-ture and unauthorized use of the name or concept is attempted at one's peril. In 2001 a series of *Survivor*-style shows that aired on the USA Network were produced under license after a spate of last-hour legal wrangling prior to the air date.

The productions of *Cannonball Run II* and *Speed Zone* did not involve me, although the litigations surrounding the sequel produced financial settlements that have no relevance here. Suffice it to say that Cannonball has become part of the worldwide legend, with instant recognition across the globe.

It was hardly the result I expected when Smith, Jim Williams, and my son Brock launched out of the Red Ball Garage on that murky night in 1971. Thirty years later the mad legend continues to grow and for that I remain part grateful and part baffled.

In 1984 I organized the first Cannonball One Lap of America, which began as a ragged tour around the nation (Go to Boston, turn left; go to Seattle, turn left, go to San Diego, turn left, and go to Miami, turn left). Receipts from the four airport parking lots in the above cities would serve as proof that the route had been adhered to and the winners would be the team that ran the 9,000-mile route in the shortest distance. It was an insane idea, poorly conceived and organized, and to this day no one is quite sure who won, although a team from New Hampshire was given the victory. The event shattered, thanks to a Mille Miglia-type ramp that was installed in the parking lot of the Lock Stock & Barrel restaurant. A group of female Jell-O wrestlers performed on the ramp prior to the launch of the first car, a bad idea because the ramp became so slippery from the gelatinous goo that the cars could not ascend the incline.

Worse yet, various police agencies along the route concluded that this was another Cannonball and landed on the competitors (who also thought it was another Cannonball) with an unrelenting fury. The next few One Laps were run as long-distance time-speed-distance rallies featuring endless disputes from the rally pecksniffs over route instructions, rules, and policies. Adding to the fun in 1985 were Ralph Nader and his forces, who tried to stop One Lap. His ally, the egregious Joan Claybrook, even testified in front of a Congressional committee that the object of the event was to circumnavigate the nation averaging 80 miles an hour.

After five years of trying to formalize the rally-style rules and after realizing that I didn't want to compete in my own event because it had descended into such a mud-bog of rules and technicalities, I revamped the event to a simple format: fast car wins. A series of high-speed time trials on a network of race tracks around the route, with no rally-style trivialities would be implemented. It would be a "run-what-you-brung" event, with all types of cars and light trucks eligible. The competitive laps would be timed electronically and winners and losers determined with the simple click of a stop watch. The distances were reduced to about 5,000 miles over a week of competition with daily events at some of the nation's greatest road courses, drag strips, and ovals.

In the late 1990s old friend and fellow motorsports enthusiast Martin Swig and I ran a few events called the "Cannonball Classic" from coast to coast. But they were leisurely tours for vintage cars and bore no relationship to either the original races or to the One Lap of America.

It was hardly the old Cannonball, but better suited to the realities of the American highway environment of today. The Cannonball of yore lives in spirit, but only as a memory of when the world was different and perhaps just a bit crazier.

I wish you'd been there.

Afterthoughts

PERIODIC FANTASIES ARISE about running another Cannonball. After all, the interstate system could theoretically accommodate a nonstop, 30-hour run from coast to coast. Forty hours is currently easy to accomplish with a pair of reasonably healthy and competitive drivers. In 1999 my son, Brock Jr., and I made the run easily in a Chrysler 300M in just over 38 hours despite a nasty snowstorm in the New Mexico mountains. But 30 hours? Forget it. Police detection; Instant-on K and Ka band, Laser, photo-radar, etc. have advanced light years beyond the primitive x-band and VASCAR employed 20 years ago. Moreover, the litigation environment has been elevated to absurd levels. People go to court over the slightest grievance and collect. Imagine the penalties that would land on an individual participating in an illegal cross-country race should an accident occur. Anyone even thinking about organizing such an event and thereby exposing oneself to insane levels of litigation ought to be committed. The time for Cannonball-style races is over. Kaput. A distant memory. As the Mafia would say—even as they are doomed to irrelevancy by changing times—"fuggetaboudit."

Not only have the law enforcement levels and the tort penalties risen to astronomic levels since 1979, but the interstates across the nation have become insanely crowded, even in the vast reaches of the Great West. Moreover, so-called shortcuts like the Ash Fork cutoff have become clogged with traffic. Prescott, Arizona, a Podunk crossroads 20 years ago, is now a burgeoning retirement community. If anyone is insane enough to try another Cannonball, massive changes in strategy will be necessary. Range between stops would have to be increased to 800–900 miles, meaning only two fuel stops would be made. Stealth would be the key. Jailbait like zoomy sports cars would give way to perhaps a tatty, low-profile pickup with a camper cap like the one driven so successfully to second place by Jack McCoy's team in 1975. Laser and radar jammers remain unproven, forcing fast drivers to depend on either a Valentine One or Escort 8500 radar detector, a raggedly unpredictable CB radio network, disciplined running in the 80–90 mile per hour range and sheer luck to make the run successfully.

As for the lost Chord of the Cannonball, 30 hours between New York and Los Angeles, the odds are astronomical. Figuring the route at

2,900 miles, this would require an average speed of 96.6 mph, which, considering the masses of traffic, improved enforcement technology and the general glut of population spread across the nation, 30 hours borders on the impossible. Example: when the Heinz-Yarborough record was set, metro Los Angeles ended well west of Riverside. Today it reaches all the way to Indio and soon will touch the Colorado River border with Arizona. L.A. traffic jams on interstate 10 and 15 can happen anytime, day or night. But in 1979 the highways were essentially vacant until the suburbs were reached.

Moreover, the Cannonballs were run in the spring (April) and in the autumn (November) when vacation traffic was at a minimum. That is no longer the case. Retirees now drift along the western highways all months of the year. There is no relief from truck and camper traffic on any major interstate. Hard to believe, but I-40 in Arizona and New Mexico can be as crowded as the Pennsylvania Turnpike. This is the level of congestion facing a coast-to-coast record-seeker today. A 36-hour trip averaging 80.5 miles per hour is within the realm of possibility, but chopping off an extra 6 hours would border on the miraculous.

So what is left of the Cannonball besides a few old-timers regaling their peers and their grandchildren about the great adventure? A few photographs, some old magazine and newspaper clippings, and a handful of automobiles are all that remains. The Gurney-Yates Ferrari Daytona that won in 1971 currently resides in the collection of vintage car collector, racer, and PacWest CART car owner Bruce McCaw of Bellingham, Washington. The most famous Daytona in the world, it is flawlessly restored in its 1971, Kirk F. White Sunoco livery, and is a regular star at auto shows and concours. Jack May still owns his Ferrari Dino 246GT that won the 1975 race, and it remains in his Gainesville, Florida, collection. Pierce Marshall retains his LT-1 Chevy Malibu that competed in 1979 and I, your humble author, still own the completely restored—and regularly driven—Cotton Owens Dodge Challenger that ran second in 1972 and third in 1973 and also competed in One Lap of America. Steve Loudin, an Illinois businessman, owns the 455 Firebird Trans Am that Weglarz, Shugars, and McConkey drove to 12th place in the 1975, but sadly most of the cars that competed have gone to the Big Crusher in the Sky. Hal Needham donated the TransCon Medivac ambulance that was featured in the 1979 race and the subsequent movie to a charity in North Carolina. The ambulance was later used as a real emergency vehicle during Needham's assault on the land spec record in his Budweiser rocket car, and was clocked at 132 miles per hour on the Bonneville Salt Flats. It has disappeared and may one day arise from a barn or tobacco field in the rural South. Other competitors may exist, but they have either been returned to stock and sold as normal cars with their heritage ignored or forgotten.

A note on the New Jersey police officers who stopped the *Transcon Medivac* in the 1979 running of the Cannonball

Over 20 years later the cops revealed their version of stopping the Yates-Needham ambulance. During a June 2002 telecast of "Car Crazy" on the Speed Channel, host Barry Maguiar requested that if either of the New Jersey policemen who stopped the ambulance in 1979 were viewing the show, they should contact him at the headquarters of Maguiar's Wax in Irvine, California.

Shortly thereafter Marc Fenech, recently retired Deputy of the Bergen County Police Department, responded with a conference call between himself, Barry Maguiar, Hal Needham and Brock Yates. He recalled how he and partner Jack Schmidig spotted the ambulance running 95 miles per hour while the officers were on patrol looking for drug and gun runners. "When it went past every exit near a hospital we got suspicious and stopped it," recalled Fenech, who is a car enthusiast and collector with two Vipers. When Schmidig saw the movie, he called Fenech and mused, "Marc, we've been had." The two officers have laughed about the incident for years, sharing the story many times, proving that even cops have a sense of humor.

Appendix
The Cannonball Competitors

Any barroom discussion about motorsports might produce a reference—or even a direct claim—that someone actually competed in the
five original, authentic Cannonball Sea-to-Shining-Sea Memorial
Trophy Dash races. Unless their names are included on the following
list they are either lying or seriously deluded.

Herewith is the official Cannonball entry list, as compiled by un-
official event historian Jim Hunt of Montreal, who ran the 1979 Cannonball and who helped organize several ensuing celebrations relat-
ed to the races.

Last Name	First Name	Finish Time	Automobile	Year
Adamowicz	Tony	36:47:00	Chevrolet Van	1971
Adelbert	Harvey	36:19:00	Mercedes-Benz 300D	1979
Alden	Al	32:59:00	Mercedes-Benz 450SEL	1979
Allen	Gerald	36:20:00	Excalibur	1979
Ammerman	Craig	45:36:00	Travco Motor Home	1975
Armstrong	Keith	39:20:00	Chevrolet El Camino	1979
Armstrong	Ted	39:20:00	Chevrolet El Camino	1979
Aruntunoff	Anatoly	49:32:00	Bristol 410	1975
		40:33:00	Volvo 242GT	1979
Atwell	Jim	38:56:00	Porsche Carrera	1975
		42:28:00	Porsche Carrera	1979
Baker	Clyde	41:15:00	American Hornet	1972
Baker	Terry	35:58:00	Ferrari 308GTS	1979
Behr	Steve	39:03:00	Dodge Van	1971
		37:26	Cadillac Coupe de Ville	1972
		38:03	Dodge Challenger	1975
		42:27	Porsche 928	1979
Bell	Roger	58:04:00	Rolls-Royce Silver Wraith	1979
Bernius	Terry	44:13:00	Lotus Esprit	1979

Last Name	First Name	Finish Time	Automobile	Year
Blue	Doug	49:04:00	Chevrolet Monte Carlo	1972
Brennan	Peter	DNF	Pontiac Firebird Trans Am	1979
Brock	Pete	37:33:00	Mercedes-Benz 280SEL	1972
Broderick	Bill	57:25:00	Travco Motor Home	1971
		44:42:00	Travco Motor Home	1972
		45:36:00	Travco Motor Home	1975
Brown	Bob	37:26:00	Dodge Challenger	1972
Brownell	Dave	61:51:00	Ford Panel Truck	1979
Browning	Boo	40:33:00	Volvo 242GT	1979
Bruerton	Ed	37:48:00	American AMX	1971
		39:42:00	American AMX	1972
Bruerton	Tom	37:48:00	American AMX	1971
		39:42:00	American AMX	1972
Buffum	John	40:19:00	Porsche Carrera	1975
Buffum	Vicki	40:19:00	Porsche Carrera	1975
Cady	Jack	43:02:00	Ford Van	1972
Campbell	Bill	41:00:00	Ford Thunderbird	1979
Canfield	Bill	37:16:00	Cadillac Coupe deVille	1972
Cannata	Richard	44:23:00	Studebaker	1975
Carey	Bob	57:25:00	Travco Motor Home	1971
Carlson	Tim	40:37:00	Ford Van	1975
Catalano	Christine	35:17:00	Mazda RX7	1979
Chapin	Kim	39:03:00	Dodge van	1971
Chapman	Charles	40:11:00	Chrysler	1972
Cline	Rick	35:53:00	Ferrari Dino 246GTS	1975
Cooper	Bill	38:52:00	Ferrari 308GT 350	1979
Corrizzoni	Tom	49:04:00	Chevrolet Monte Carlo	1972
Coumo		DNF	Studebaker	1972
Cowell	Jack	37:33:00	Mercedes-Benz 280SEL	1972
Crabbe	Paul	45:39:00	Opel Rallye	1972
Cripe	Tom	44:13:00	Lotus Esprit	1979
Crittenden	Jim	36:00:00	Buick Park Avenue	1979
Dainko	Rainec	40:55:00	Chevrolet Van	1972
Davidson	Stuart	46:48:00	Ferrari 330GT	1979
Dawn	Wes	DNF	MGB GT	1971
		39:35:00	Chevrolet Vega	1972
		38:16:00	Mercedes-Benz 450SL	1975
		36:49:00	Cadillac Eldorado	1979
De Van	Fred	39:29:00	Mazda RX2	1972
Defty	Peter	45:32:00	Chevrolet Suburban	1979
Denner	Tom	41:06:00	Chevrolet Vega	1972
Dennison	Scott	40:55:00	Chevrolet Van	1972

Last Name	First Name	Finish Time	Automobile	Year
Doherty	Richard	35:17:00	Mazda RX7	1979
Dornsife	Rod	42:27:00	Porsche 928	1979
Dunaj	Jon	36:19:00	Mercedes-Benz 300D	1979
Durst	Steve	DNF	Chevrolet Vega	1972
Egloff	George	43:32:00	Suzuki 850 Motorcycle	1979
Ehrich	Terry	61:51:00	Ford Panel Truck	1979
Epstein	Wendy	43:32:00	Suzuki 850 Motorcycle	1979
Erickson	Morris	46:17:00	Opel Rallye	1972
Fassler	Paul	37:25:00	Porsche 930	1979
Faust	David	36:51:00	Chevrolet Malibu	1979
Feiner	Fred	DNF	Studebaker	1972
		44:23:00	Studebaker	1975
Fergusson	Alice	42:08:00	Citroen DS19	1972
Fergusson	Joe	42:08:00	Citroen DS19	1972
Fernald	Steve	40:31:00	Volvo 164E	1975
Field	Dick	32:59:00	Mercedes-Benz 450SEL	1979
Fischer	Paul	41:01:00	Ford Torino	1972
		40:53:00	Ford Torino	1975
Fog	Steven	34:07:00	Pontiac Firebird Trans Am	1979
Frankl	Andrew	65:55:00	Ford Mini-Truck	1979
Frasson	Joe	44:42:00	Travco Motor Home	1972
Fuchs	John	41:15:00	American Hornet	1972
Gafford	Tom	45:32:00	Chevrolet Suburban	1979
Gallagher		DNF	Honda 600	1972
Garbarini	Steve	48:25:00	Datsun 240Z	1972
Garcione	William	48:25:00	Datsun 240Z	1972
Gilmartin	Richard	37:33:00	Mercedes-Benz 280SEL	1972
Goodman	Kirby	36:51:00	Chevrolet Malibu	1979
Gould	Richard	41:35:00	Oldsmobile Cutlass	1975
Graham	Paul	37:45:00	Chevrolet Camaro	1979
Gregory	Fred	DNF	Pontiac Firebird Trans Am	1979
Gurney	Dan	35:54:00	Ferrari Daytona	1971
Hammil		DNF	Porsche 911	1972
Harmston	Edwin	58:04:00	Rolls-Royce Silver Wraith	1979
Harris	Richard	DNF	Studebaker	1972
		44:23:00	Studebaker	1975
Harrison	John	DNF	Lotus Esprit	1979
Heinz	Dave	32:51:00	Jaguar XJS	1979
Henry	Bill	41:06:00	Chevrolet Vega	1972
Herisko	Ron	36:56:00	Cadillac Sedan deVille	1971
Hickey	Tom	32:59:00	Mercedes-Benz 450SEL	1979
Hitchins	John	65:55:00	Ford Mini-Truck	1979

Last Name	First Name	Finish Time	Automobile	Year
Honegger	Pierre	39:22:00	Mazda RX4	1975
Hopkins	Danny	38:02:00	De Tomaso Pantera	1972
Hopkins	Hoppy	38:02:00	De Tomaso Pantera	1972
Hoschek	Gero	43:47:00	Jensen Interceptor	1979
Houge	Larry	46:17:00	Opel Rallye	1972
Hourihan	Bob	40:31:00	Volvo 164E	1975
Howlett	Jack	38:45:00	Buick Electra	1975
Hunt	Jim	41:00:00	Ford Thunderbird	1979
James	Dirk	43:32:00	Suzuki 850 Motorcycle	1979
Jeanes	William	45:36:00	Travco Motor Home	1975
Jellison	Rich	57:19:00	Chevrolet Corvette	1972
Jenkins	Richard	38:37:00	Alfa-Romeo Guilia	1972
Jessen	John	57:19:00	Chevrolet Corvette	1972
Jessick	Peter	40:53:00	Chrysler	1979
Johnson		DNF	Austin Healey	1972
Johnson	Gary	37:50:00	Chevrolet Pickup	1975
Jones	David	38:10:00	Chevrolet Blazer	1979
Kendall-Lane	Fiona	58:04:00	Rolls-Royce Silver Wraith	1979
Kendall-Lane	Stephen	58:04:00	Rolls-Royce Silver Wraith	1979
Kenny		DNF	Chevrolet Camaro Z28	1972
Kepler	Fred	DNF	Chevrolet Camaro Z28	1972
Key	Robert	48:53:00	Shelby Mustang GT350	1979
Kirby	Jim	36:40:00	Chevrolet Van	1971
Kopec	Rich	48:53:00	Shelby Mustang GT 350	1979
Kovaleski	Oscar	36:47:00	Chevrolet Van	1971
Kovaleski	Bob	36:40:00	Chevrolet Camaro Z28	1979
Kozlowski	Tom	39:22:00	Mazda RX4	1975
Lane	John	37:31:00	Porsche 928	1979
Leib	Dick	44:54:00	Pontiac	1972
Leonard	Tom	37:46:00	Chevrolet Camaro Z28	1979
Lincoln	Sam	49:04:00	Chevrolet Monte Carlo	1972
Lloyd	David	36:00:00	Buick Park Avenue	1979
Locke	Pete	40:11:00	Chrysler	1972
Lovell	Bill	41:00:00	Ford Thunderbird	1979
Lynch	Leo	DNF	Porsche 911	1972
		38:39:00	Porsche 911 RST	1975
Mahler	John	37:46:00	Chevrolet Camaro Z28	1979
Marbut	Tom	37:45:00	Dodge Van	1971
Marget	Pete	41:41:00	Datsun 510	1972
Marshall	Pierce	36:51:00	Chevrolet Malibu	1979
Martin	Charles	46:32:00	Chevrolet Suburban	1979
Martin	Chauncey	43:02:00	Ford Van	1972

Last Name	First Name	Finish Time	Automobile	Year
Martini	Jeff	39:22:00	Mazda RX4	1975
		36:49:00	Cadillac Eldorado	1979
May	Jack	35:53:00	Ferrari Dino 246GTS	1975
Mayo	Edward	38:10:00	Chevrolet Blazer	1979
McCarthy	Edward	36:19:00	Mercedes-Benz 300D	1979
McConkey	Ron	40:43:00	Pontiac Firebird Trans Am	1975
McCoy	Jack	37:50:00	Chevrolet Pickup	1975
McCoy	Peggy	37:50:00	Chevrolet Pickup	1975
McFaul		DNF	Porsche 911	1972
McGovern	John	41:35:00	Oldsmobile Cutlass	1975
		58:04:00	Rolls-Royce Silver Wraith	1979
McGrail	Tom	44:42:00	Travco Motor Home	1972
		45:36:00	Travco Motor Home	1975
McMeekan	George	44:54:00	Pontiac	1972
McPherson		DNF	Austin Healey	1972
McWhorter	Donald	41:17:00	Chevrolet Corvette	1979
McWhorter	Gerald	41:17:00	Chevrolet Corvette	1979
Menesini	Dennis	34:52:00	Chevrolet Pickup	1979
Menke	Vern	40:53:00	Ford Torino	1975
Menzel	Mike	DNF	Fiat 127	1979
Micek	John	40:53:00	Chrysler	1979
Miller	James	43:45:00	Bradley	1972
Miller	Mark	34:52:00	Chevrolet Pickup	1979
Miller	Robin	39:35:00	Chevrolet Vega	1972
Mims	Donna Mae	DNF	Cadillac Limousine	1972
Mockett	Doug	40:53:00	Chrysler	1979
Moody	Dave	41:01:00	Ford Torino	1972
Moore	Bill	40:53:00	Chrysler	1979
Morin	Holly	39:03:00	Dodge Van	1971
Morton	Tom	41:01:00	Ford Torino	1972
		40:53:00	Ford Torino	1975
Moses	Sam	39:29:00	Ford Mustang Boss 302	1979
Mullen	Jim	40:11:00	Ferrari SWB	1979
Mullen	Joan	40:11:00	Ferrari SWB	1979
Needham	Hal	DNF	Dodge Van	1979
Nehl	Tom	41:32:00	Porsche 911	1975
Nerger	Ursala	43:47:00	Jensen Interceptor	1979
Nichols	John	39:45:00	Chevrolet Camaro	1979
Nickel	Gil	38:16:00	Mercedes-Benz 450SL	1975
Niemcek	Brad	36:47:00	Chevrolet Van	1971
		DNF	Chevrolet Vega	1972
		40:37:00	Ford Van	1975

Last Name	First Name	Finish Time	Automobile	Year
Niemcek	Peggy	DNF	Cadillac Limousine	1972
Nunn	Spike	41:41:00	Datsun 510	1972
O'Brien	Robert	41:35:00	Oldsmobile Cutlass	1975
O'Donnell	Bill	53:00:00	Cadillac Eldorado	1979
Olds	Fred	37:16:00	Cadillac Coupe deVille	1972
		40:31:00	Volvo 164E	1975
Opert	Larry	36:56:00	Cadillac Coupe deVille	1971
Paggio	Massimo	DNF	Fiat 127	1979
Parker	Pal	57:25:00	Travco Motor Home	1972
		44:42:00	Travco Motor Home	1972
		45:36:00	Travco Motor Home	1975
Pash	Phil	57:25:00	Travco Motor Home	1971
Patchett	Keith	72:54:00	BMWR90S Motorcycle	1979
Pearson	Jack	38:45:00	Buick Electra	1975
Peelor	Jim	46:48:00	Ferrari 330GT	1979
Perlow	Bob	DNF	MGB GT	1971
Pfeifer	S.	47:28:00	Ford Pinto	1972
Pierce	Jeff	33:42:00	Pontiac Firebird Trans Am	1979
Pitt	Jesse	40:11:00	Chrysler	1972
Poston	Becky	37:45:00	Dodge Van	1971
Prentiss	Larry	46:37:00	Porsche Carrera	1979
Pritch	Mark	38:52:00	Ferrari 308GT 350	1979
Pritzker	Nate	36:56:00	Cadillac Sedan deVille	1971
Pryor	Bill	49:32:00	Bristol 410	1975
		40:33:00	Volvo 242GT	1979
Quartararo	Tony	46:48:00	Ferrari 330GT	1979
Race	Donald	53:00:00	Cadillac Eldorado	1979
Ralston	Benjamin	46:37:00	Porsche Carrera	1979
Ramsey	John	43:28:00	Ford Torino	1972
Rasmussen	Buzz	39:20:00	Chevrolet El Camino	1979
Regan	Ken	40:37:00	Ford Van	1972
Richardson	Tad	35:17:00	Mazda RX7	1979
Riggs	Clyde	36:49:00	Cadillac Eldorado	1979
Robison	Charlie	34:52:00	Chevrolet Pickup	1979
Roder	Dick	40:55:00	Chevrolet Van	1972
Romine	Chris	35:58:00	Ferrari 308GTS	1979
Rosenblatt	Joel	36:00:00	Buick Park Avenue	1979
Rost	Bob	38:37:00	Alfa-Romeo Guilia	1972
Rowzie	Dan	38:39:00	Porsche 911 RSR	1975
Royer	Lyle	DNF	Dodge Van	1979
Satullo	Sandy	38:45:00	Buick Electra	1975
		36:49:00	Pontiac	1979

Last Name	First Name	Finish Time	Automobile	Year
Satullo	Stuart	36:49:00	Pontiac	1979
Satullo II	Sandy	38:45:00	Buick Electra	1975
		36:49:00	Pontiac	1979
Scarlato	Jerry	45:36:00	Travco Motor Home	1975
Schmidt	Charles	53:00:00	Cadillac Eldorado	1979
Scott		DNF	Porsche 911	1972
Scribner	Doug	49:04:00	Chevrolet Monte Carlo	1972
Sellyei	Louis	39:10:00	Jaguar XJS	1979
Sensebaugh	Jim	45:32:00	Chevrolet Suburban	1979
Senehi	Alex	46:31:00	Mercedes-Benz 300SEL	1979
Shugars	Dave	40:43:00	Pontiac Firebird Trans Am	1975
Sibio	Albert Jr.	36:40:00	Chevrolet Camaro Z28	1979
Simkin	Daniel	12:20	Excalibur	1979
Smith	Gary	39:45:00	Chevrolet Camaro	1979
Smith	Ken	34:52:00	Chevrolet Pickup	1979
Smith	Steve	40:51:00	Dodge Sportsman Van	1971
Snyder	Michael	33:42:00	Pontiac Firebird trans Am	1979
Solski	Paul	39:29:00	Mazda RX2	1972
Sportiche	Alain	46:31:00	Mercedes-Benz 300SEL	1979
Spreadbury	Bill	47:28:00	Ford Pinto	1972
Stanner	Bud	37:26:00	Dodge Challenger	1972
Stanton	Chick	38:56:00	Porsche Carrera	1975
		42:28:00	Porsche Carrera	1979
Stephenson		DNF	Honda 600	1972
Stevens	David	36:20:00	Excalibur	1979
Stropus	Judy	DNF	Cadillac Limousine	1972
Taatjes	Bob	43:45:00	Bradley GT	1972
Talbert	R.A.	44:54:00	Pontiac	1972
Taylor	Justus	61:51:00	Ford Panel Truck	1979
Thibeau	John	45:39:00	Opel Rallye	1972
Trefethen	Jon	43:28:00	Ford Torino	1972
Truesdale	Loyal	72:54:00	BMWR90S Motorcycle	1979
Turkovich	Bob	40:37:00	Ford Van	1975
Unkefer	Duane	43:02:00	Ford Van	1972
Villeneuve	Jacques	37:31:00	Porsche 928	1979
Visniewski	Scott	38:10:00	Chevrolet Blazer	1979
Walle	Ray	39:22:00	Mazda RX4	1975
Ward	Ken	43:32:00	Suzuki 850 Motorcycle	1979
Ward	Steve	43:32:00	Suzuki 850 Motorcycle	1979
Warner	Bill	41:32:00	Porsche 911	1975
Waters	Randy	37:45:00	Dodge Van	1971

Last Name	First Name	Finish Time	Automobile	Year
Weglarz	Dennis	40:43:00	Pontiac Firebird Trans Am	1975
Whiteside	Mark	34:07:00	Pontiac Firebird Trans Am	1975
Williams	Jim	40:51:00	Dodge Sportsman Van	1971
Williams	Willie	38:10:00	Chevrolet Blazer	1979
Willig	George	39:29:00	Ford Mustang Boss 302	1979
Yarborough	Dave	32:51:00	Jaguar XJS	1979
Yates	Brock	40:51:00	Dodge Sportsman Van	1971
		35:54:00	Ferrari Daytona	1971
		37:26:00	Dodge Challenger	1972
		38:03:00	Dodge Challenger	1975
		DNF	Dodge Van	1979
Yates	Brock Jr.	40:51:00	Dodge Sportsman Van	1971
Yates	Pamela	DNF	Dodge Van	1979
Ziegel	Robert	37:25:00	Porsche 930	1979
Zoeltner	Andreas	43:47:00	Jensen Interceptor	1979

Index